NAZI GERMANY 1933–1945

NAZI GERMANY
1933–1945

Faith and Annihilation

JOST DÜLFFER
Professor of History, University of Cologne

Translated from the German by
Dean Scott McMurry

A member of the Hodder Headline Group
LONDON • NEW YORK • SYDNEY • AUCKLAND

First published in Great Britain in 1996 by
Arnold, a member of the Hodder Headline Group
338 Euston Road, London NW1 3BH
175 Fifth Avenue, New York, NY 10010

Reprinted 1996

Distributed exclusively in the USA by
St Martin's Press Inc.,
175 Fifth Avenue,
New York, NY 10010

© 1992 W. Kohlhammer Verlag GmbH Stuttgart-Berlin-Köln
Originally published as *Deutsche Geschichte 1933–1945: Führerglaube und
Vernichtungskrieg*
English translation © 1996 Arnold

British Library Cataloguing in Publication Data
A catalogue entry for this book is available from the British Library

Library of Congress Cataloging-in-Publication Data
Dülfer. Jost. 1943–
[Deustche Geschichte 1933–1945. English]
Nazi Germany 1933–1945 : faith and annihilation / Jost Dülffer : translated
from the German by Dean S. McMurry.
p.   cm.
Includes bibliographical references and index.
ISBN 0–340–65265–9. — ISBN 0–340–61393–9 (pbk.)
1. Germany—Politics and government—1933–1945. 2. Hitler, Adolf.
1889–1945. 3. National socialism—Germany. 4. Holocaust, Jewish
(1939–1945) 5. War crimes. 6. World War, 1939–1945—Atrocities.
I. Title.
DD256.5.D8213   1995
943.086—dc20   95–31743

ISBN 0 340 61393 9 (Pb)
ISBN 0 340 65265 9 (Hb)

Composition in 10/12 Sabon by York House Typographic Ltd, London
Printed and bound in Great Britain by J W Arrowsmith Ltd, Bristol

Contents

Preface

German history under the National Socialist regime has been my major interest for a long time. It is an interest which began with the rather unpolitical atmosphere of my parents' house. They tried to explain to me what had happened during those years but could not provide satisfactory answers. This was not surprising, at a time when teachers such as Ludwig Gerstenkorn at the Stormarn School in Ahrensburg, which I attended in the late 1950s, were discussing in class the simultaneity of war and mass murder, of the Hitler Youth and normal life. During my university studies, lectures by many professors on the National Socialist period made a deep impression on me: in Hamburg, Fritz Fischer, and in Freiburg, Hans Günter Zmarzlik, Gottfried Schramm and, finally, Andreas Hillgruber. I am especially indebted to Professor Hillgruber, with whom I had the opportunity to work closely from 1968 until his premature death in 1989, and from whom I was able to learn over 20 years, while studying German history in general and National Socialist Germany in particular. In the meantime, as well as participating in the usual cordial discussions (and occasional arguments) among historians, I have also had increasing opportunity to learn by teaching. More precisely, I was able to develop my own ideas slowly, and test them by presenting them to my students especially, during the course of two semesters, in a graduate seminar on the German occupation in the Second World War at the University of Cologne from 1988 to 1990.

My old friends Annegrete and Bernd Martin read the manuscript of this book critically and helpfully. Ms Waltraud König typed it with her usual care. Meike Dülffer, Ruth Hohlbein, Ms Margarethe Naurath, and Guido Thiemeyer were of great help in typing and correcting the manuscript.

Finally, I should like to thank the many people, whether named here or not, who have given me their practical help and support: in many cases theirs has been a stimulating and lifelong friendship and influence.

Jost Dülffer
Cologne

Abbreviations

ADGB	*(Allgemeiner Deutscher Gewerkschaftsbund)* German National Trade Union Federation
APA	*(Außenpolitisches Amt der NSDAP)* Foreign Policy Office of the NSDAP
BDM	*(Bund Deutscher Mädel)* Union of German Girls
BVP	*(Bayerische Volkspartei)* Bavarian People's Party
DAF	*(Deutsche Arbeitsfront)* German Labour Front
DDP	*(Deutsche Demokratische Partei)* German Democratic Party
DIHT	*(Deutscher Industrie- und Handelstag)* Union of German Industry and Commerce
DNVP	*(Deutsch-Nationale Volkspartei)* German National People's Party
DVP	*(Deutsche Volkspartei)* German People's Party
GBA	*(Generalbevollmächtigter für den Arbeitseinsatz)* General Plenipotentiary for Labour
GG	*(Generalgouvernement)* Government General
HJ	*(Hitlerjugend)* Hitler Youth
HSSPF	*(Höherer SS- und Polizeiführer)* Higher SS and Police Leader
KdF	*(Kraft durch Freude)* Strength through Joy
KPD	*(Kommunistische Partei Deutschlands)* German Communist Party
NSB	*(NS–Beamtenbud)* National Socialist Civil Servant Union
NSBO	*(Nationalsozialistische Betriebszellenorganisation)* National Socialist Company Organisation
NSDAP	*(Nationalsozialistische Deutsche Arbeiterpartei)* National Socialist German Workers Party
NSKK	*(Nationalsozialistisches Kraftfahrer-Korps)* National Socialist Motor Vehicle Corps
NSV	*(NS-Volkswohlfahrt)* National Socialist Public Welfare
OKH	*(Oberkommando des Heeres)* Army High Command

OKW	(*Oberkommando der Wehrmacht*) Wehrmacht (Armed Forces) High Command
OT	(*Organisation Todt*) Todt Organization
RDI	(*Reichsverband der Deutschen Industrie*) National Federation of German Industry
RFSS	(*Reichsführer SS*) Reich Leader SS
RKF	(*Reichskommissar für die Festigung des deutschen Volkstums*) Reich Commissar for the Strengthening of Germandom
RM	Reichsmark
RMO	(*Reichsministerium für die besetzten Ostgebiete*) Reich Ministry for the Occupied Eastern Territories
RSHA	(*Reichssicherheits-Hauptamt*) Reich Security Main Office
RuSHA	(*Rasse- und Siedlungshauptamt*) Race and Settlement Main Office (of the SS)
RSI	*Repubblica Sociale Italiana*
SA	(*Sturmabteilung*) Storm Troopers (of the NSDAP)
SD	(*Sicherheitsdienst*) Security Service (of the NSDAP)
Sipo	(*Sicherheitspolizei*) Security Police
SPD	(*Sozialdemokratische Partei Deutschlands*) Social Democratic Party of Germany
SS	*Schutzstaffel*
SS-TV	(*SS–Totenkopfverbände*) SS Death's Head Formations
SS-VT	(*SS–Verfügungstruppe*) SS Special Service Troops
VJP	(*Vierjahresplan*) Four Year Plan
WVHA	(*Wirtschafts- und Verwaltungshauptamt*) Economic and Administrative Main Office (of the SS)

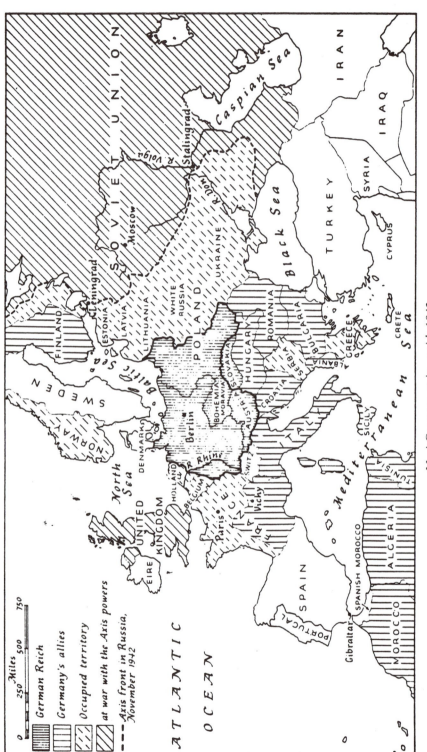

Nazi Germany at its zenith 1942

Introduction

There are many ways of learning about the period of National Socialist rule in Germany and Europe. Commemoration days for the victims of National Socialism usually direct public attention to particular aspects of that time; exhibitions, lectures, works of art, editorials, reports and many other events in the media focus from various perspectives on the different facets of the period between 1933 and 1945. This is, on the whole, a good and important thing. However, there are now some commentators who are warning that such a flood of information might lead to saturation and psychological resistance. Others are still not only discovering new sources and materials, but also changing their perspectives and trying out new models of interpretation.

Given this situation, such a concise synopsis of the period as this book aims to give may be helpful; there are not very many usable general surveys available. But even a general study cannot cover all areas. It, too, can only hope to select from the great variety of possible topics, and inevitably must emphasize certain aspects of the overall subject in preference to others. In making this sort of choice, several factors have seemed to me especially important.

Our growing distance from the events of 1933–1945 suggests new ways of viewing the subject. The generation already adult at that time is slowly dying out. The two following generations, to one of which I belong, can no longer base their opinions on personal experience of the period. Instead they draw their information from many other sources, such as what they have learnt in school, from personal acquaintances, or the media. But from this there follows a twofold danger: either ill-matching fragments of information are bundled together and incorporated into a distorted overall picture, or concepts are constructed out of stereotypes, giving a simplistic but rarely more comprehensible view of history.

This study, then, endeavours to provide in part a narrative and factual account, focusing on political crimes committed between 1933 and 1945, which were greater and more numerous than during any other period of German history. But it is also my intention to create an awareness of the lives and living conditions of the Germans of that time, made strange and remote to us by the enormity of those crimes. Not all Germans were perpetrators, of course, or even accomplices, and it is part of my aim, wherever possible, to indicate clearly the coexistence (often in the same locality) of normal every-day life with events quite out of the ordinary, and to signal, in general political developments, the tensions that arose as a result.

With growing self-awareness of European 'identity' in the wake of the dissolution of the Soviet bloc, and increased political co-operation among the countries of Western Europe in particular, it is important not to lose sight of National Socialism's former domination of Europe. It should not be forgotten that the memory of the Second World War, not only as a military struggle but also as occupation and oppression, is still very much alive in most parts of Europe. It is, after all, generally true that people tend to remember their own suffering best and most deeply. This is certainly true for many Germans, whose suffering was frequently most acute in the second half of the war and in the post-war period, and who hardly remember the preceding persecution and occupation by Germans in other countries as being worthy of reflection. Of course, I will seek to present successive and often parallel experiences of suffering against a background of structural contexts and developments. Important as the distinction is between those who experienced National Socialism as persecutors and those who knew it as victims, each person's view can only encompass a part of the range of experiences, whether of restraint or freedom, of the whole. And the fabric of relationships was different for each individual and social group. The same people and groups were sometimes to be found in the roles of victims as well as persecutors, and the dividing-line in a European context was by no means always between Germans and non-Germans, or between fanatical National Socialists and those who were politically or racially ostracized by the regime. Only when all dimensions of National Socialist rule in Europe are sufficiently known and accepted for discussion can the future be embraced. But the acquisition of such knowledge has to be an individual intellectual and psychological process. This is why catch-phrases often heard in Germany, such as 'dealing with the past' (*Aufarbeitung*) or 'mastering the past' (*Bewäl-tigung*) have little meaning.

Although this book is intended as a narrative history of the National Socialist period, it also attempts to explain and analyse. General theories, however, are avoided – valuable as they can be, there are clear limits to their usefulness in a study of this sort. The focus of my book is on the Führer dictatorship, its mental preconditions, the decisive, radical action to which it gave rein, its combination of individual intentions and structural constraints, and the relationship within it between polycratic structures, unleashed dynamism and psychological radicalisation.

For a long time much attention was devoted to the question of how the National Socialists came to power, to what extent full National Socialist rule was established and how its crimes came about. The aim was to provide insights for the generation involved or caught up in these events, who wanted to understand the causes of developments which turned out to be so negative, as well as the behaviour that had contributed to them. The main concern was to prevent a repetition of history, to nip any recrudescence of National Socialism in the bud. These questions are also discussed in the present work, but the way to 1933 is treated less extensively than elsewhere. On the other hand, more attention is devoted here to the after-effects of the National Socialist period on German and European history and its intended and, even more, its unintended consequences. Or, to put it differently, we are concerned with the continuity, however broken it may be, of German history after 1945, for which the use of such labels as 'of National Socialist origin' or 'membership in the Nazi party' serves little purpose. This book represents an attempt to present, in the limited space available, the years from 1933 to 1945 within the continuum of German history before and after that period. This will not be to ignore differences, but it should make it possible to place the enormity of German crimes in their proper context.

For although it is right to trace and explain the Nazi aberration in terms of German and general history, it was not a predetermined and inevitable development. Hitler's becoming Chancellor in 1933 was a mixture of chance and necessity. And by no means all supporters of his government were advocates of war preparations as a means of solving external problems; or of persecution and restructuring of domestic politics to the extent that they were actually carried out. Likewise, the Second World War and genocide can be explained as resulting from these conditions, but not without qualification. It is as illogical to say that preparations for war, and the Second World War itself, were the inevitable results of power politics and German efforts to revise the Treaty of Versailles as it is to argue that the ostracizing of certain groups was the inevitable result of discrimination, or mass murder the result of pogroms. Possibilities did become real history under conditions certainly comparable to those which may exist in future, but those conditions, which will be described here, were also unique constellations of circumstances, structures, and individuals.

|1|

Weimar and the Rise of National Socialism

THE WEIMAR REPUBLIC

From the very beginning the Weimar Republic did not have an easy time in winning acceptance as a political and social order for all Germans. After the collapse of Imperial Germany, the chances of instituting structural reforms were greater than was actually realized at the time. The influence of the military, the civil service, leading businessmen and financiers, and various other elements represented a certain continuity, and these groups were accepted as guarantors against an external and internal collapse of society. Indeed, the radicalism of the left developed only as a result of the absence of reforms in 1919, while the dismemberment of the German state had never been seriously envisaged as a goal by the victorious Allied powers. In the National Assembly, which worked out a constitution at Weimar during 1919, there was a broad majority in favour of a parliamentary, democratic system; 76.1 per cent of the voters supported democratic parties in January 1919 – the liberal German Democratic Party (DDP); the Centre, a Catholic party; and the Social Democrats (SPD).[1] Thus Weimar had a good chance of success at the beginning, and it retained that chance almost to the end.

Participation in the government by National Socialists (the *Nationalsozialistische Deutsche Arbeiterpartei* or NSDAP) was made necessary neither by the constitution, the will of the voters, nor political sense. Of course, it was a period of tension in almost all areas of political life, creating a potential for conflict that grew over the course of time. This becomes easier to understand if we remember that Germany had been almost the last country in Western Europe to achieve unification, doing so only in 1870–1; and it was a state which needed time to develop a sense of identity. At about the same time as Germany was unified, rapid industrialization began there, as had happened in Britain, France and Belgium earlier. By around the turn of the century, Germany had taken the lead in economic development, science, and many other areas, and had developed a momentum greater than that to be found in any other nation, except the United States. By contrast, the German political system, including the development of political awareness and political participation on the part of a large proportion of the population, remained behind that of the rest of Western Europe. This was the essence of what was called the German 'special way' (*Sonderweg*) – a rather problematic term, given that a 'normal' path towards a modern society, an industrial state, was difficult to discern even in western states. But compared with the authoritarian multi-ethnic state of Russia and the new nation states of East Central Europe, some of which came into being only as a result of the First World War, Germany offered a relatively large part of its population a high level of participation in the political process. The German 'special way' thus consisted specifically of the relatively large gap between socio-economic and political development. A similar gap existed between Germany's growing size and strength and its political maturity – a gap in which its population, its economic strength and its military power all played an important part. The peace established by the victors of the First World War in Europe in 1919–1920 had, in essence, attempted to reduce Germany's power by reducing its territory – without, however, really affecting the substance of its position as a great power – and had tried to limit its military and economic power until it had demonstrated its good behaviour in future. These actions, however, gave rise to a revisionism in Germany that prevented broad acceptance of the newly established order in Europe.

The Weimar Republic had to withstand severe strains in practically all areas. The authoritarian systems and ways of thinking that had characterized the Wilhelminian state still lingered on, particularly in the civil service, the armed forces, and the judicial system. Most of the political parties were more interested in consolidating their own positions than in political compromise; economic and socio-political reform was constantly undermined by the continuing influence of the great landholders and the power of heavy industry. Anti-parliamentary thinking turned only too quickly into anti-democratic politics. Generally speaking, during this time there was an impressive movement towards modernity in German culture and politics. But wherever right-wing tendencies became directly involved in politics, they all too easily found a new strength in authoritarian unity. Left-wing groups and individuals, on the other hand, exposed and sharply attacked the democratic and social shortcomings of German political reality in the 1920s in such a way that they often produced little of the political awareness they desired, and contributed instead to the destabilization of the Republic. Each of these stress factors was in itself normal, and could perhaps have been dealt with, but together they produced an increasingly explosive mixture.

Above all, Weimar needed time. Whatever had not been reformed in the initial phase immediately after the First World War could be reformed, if at all, only over a long period of time. There was obviously a great deal of continuity with the past, especially with the War, in the lives of individuals and in institutions; but that it should have had the effect it did requires explanation. For, in time, Weimar was able to show some successes, such as compromises in the area of social policy between labour and capital, an economic upswing and, in the area of foreign policy, a restoration of Germany's position as a recognized great power. But, on the whole, the feeling of living in a crisis and, in the end, a real crisis itself, proved decisive.

A considerable part of the burden imposed on the new republic came from abroad, as an understandable consequence of military defeat in total war. None the less, that very defeat was one which many Germans refused to accept, and they viewed its consequences only with a sense of outrage. This was especially true of war reparations, of the occupation of German territory in the west, particularly the Ruhr in 1923 (going even further than Versailles), and above all, of the world depression after 1929. The conflicts, amounting almost to civil war between left- and right-wing groups, and the actions of the governing moderate parties, which tended to be directed more against the left than the extreme right, came to an end only superficially in 1923, and thereafter became more frequent, especially in the economic crisis after 1929. In this way Weimar became a republic which few Germans could support unreservedly. Domestic political opponents were considered enemies by large sections of the public; foreign-policy conflicts were considered to be denials of German claims.

As early as 1920, in the first elections to the Reichstag, the parties that had supported the Weimar constitutional compromise (the SPD, the Centre, and the German Democratic Party or DDP) lost their majority and never regained it. By the mid-1920s the parliamentary system did seem to be functioning, in that the conservative-liberal German People's Party (DVP) and the German National People's Party (DNVP) occasionally participated in governments, although the latter refused to participate in a government to which the SPD belonged, a detestation that was reciprocated. Nevertheless, the SPD often lent its support to governments in providing parliamentary majorities against the right-wing parties in foreign-policy questions: the final occasion on which a 'grand coalition' extending from the German People's Party to the SPD had the support of a majority in the Reichstag was 1928–30. But, especially in social policy, these parties could not overcome their differences, which led to the fall of their government in March 1930.

THE DRIFT TO THE RIGHT

Especially in the middle class and among right-wing groups, the view was widespread that parliamentary government as it had existed up to that time was finished. In 1925 the election as president of Germany of Field Marshal Paul von Hindenburg, who had already retired from the army even before the

First World War, gave new impetus to those forces already striving for a 'change of leadership' (*Führerwechsel*). Even before the start of the world depression, influential persons and groups in the business world, the media, and the right-wing and moderate parties, as well as parts of the Reichswehr, sought to promote a new political order which had nothing to do with the Republic as it had been up to that time. They were intent on establishing a 'Hindenburg cabinet', which they hoped would result in a sharp turn to the right. The extensive presidential powers provided in Article 48 of the constitution were now to be used deliberately to create a new state. Chancellor Heinrich Brüning, who in the long term was contemplating a restoration of the monarchy, accepted this framework. Until his fall in May 1932, he deliberately risked losing parliamentary support, becoming increasingly dependent on the president and his inner circle.

In those years almost all parties, including those moderate parties of which most of the governments were made up, moved increasingly to the right in terms of their leadership, political orientation or political style. They sought to present themselves as fighting organizations and thus to demonstrate a militant readiness to accept political conflict, whether for or against the Republic. This tendency extended to the 'Iron Front' formed by the SPD, the socialist unions, the republican defence organization, Reich Banner Black-Red-Gold, and the workers' sports organizations in December 1931. In 1930 the originally left-wing liberal German Democratic Party merged with the Young German Order to form the German State Party, a change of name that clearly demonstrated the fate of the party's previous liberal orientation. As early as 1928, the Centre Party demonstrated the growing strength of its right wing with the election of the prelate Ludwig Kaas as its chairman. After the death of Gustav Stresemann in 1929 the interests of heavy industry, which had always been present, clearly gained the upper hand in the German People's Party. And the German National People's Party adopted a course of consistent opposition to the Republic as early as 1928, when Alfred Hugenberg took over its chairmanship and placed his powerful press concern in the service of his political ideas. The traditional moderate non-socialist parties shrank to insignificance. Voters left them not because of, but in spite of, the general turn to the right. For one thing, in 1928 and 1930 there was a strengthening in the small special-interest parties such as those of the small businesses, artisans, or the farmers, the protest parties. But by 1932 they too had collapsed. Only the Catholic Centre Party and its more conservative offshoot, the Bavarian People's Party (BVP), were able to maintain and strengthen their positions. But the State Party and the German People's Party, each of which had already sunk to below 5 per cent of the vote in the election of 1930, saw their shares of the vote decline to between 1 and 2 per cent in the Reichstag elections of July and November 1932. Nor were the Social Democrats unscathed: after reaching a relative high point in 1928, they lost almost 2 million voters by November 1932, when they only received 20.4 per cent of the vote. Although there was not necessarily a direct exchange of voters, this corresponded to a growth in the strength of the German Communist Party (KPD) by 2.7 million voters in the same period. Thus at the end of 1932 a trend began to appear: in future the Communists (with 16.9 per cent of the vote) might become the stronger of two bitter political and ideological rivals, both of which claimed to be workers' parties. And even the National German Trade Union Federation (*Allgemeiner Deutscher Gewerkschaftsbund* or ADGB) adopted a more strongly nationalistic course when it attempted to support Brüning.

In Prussia, which comprised almost two-thirds of Germany's population (61.2 per cent) and territory (62 per cent), a Weimar coalition which occasionally included the German People's Party governed almost without interruption in the 1920s under Social Democrat Otto Braun. But this coalition lost its base in the regular election of April 1932: all parties between the SPD and the German National People's Party lost votes, especially those parties of the middle. The victors were the National Socialists, whose strength rose from 9 to 162 seats in the state parliament, an accurate reflection of the generally favourable trend in their fortunes. The presidential election in the spring of 1932 clearly showed that a new development had already begun, with the prospect that, in future, parliamentary democracy would no longer reflect the wishes of large groups of the population. Hindenburg, the man whose dictatorial authority was supposed to provide the vehicle for further reshaping the Republic, barely failed to achieve an absolute majority in the first round of voting, though he was elected in the second. But the Protestant field marshal was the candidate of the moderate parties, which this time included the Centre and the SPD. His main opponents were Ernst Thälmann of the Communist Party and Adolf Hitler. All three men advocated models of society that led away from Weimar. For the former mainstay parties of Weimar, Hindenburg had become the candidate who seemed to offer the best chance of preventing a right- or left-wing dictatorship.

It should be emphasized that the turn towards an authoritarian state was a real goal and not a temporary measure to cope with an emergency situation. When the political course – certainly still reversible then – was set in 1929, there was neither a manifest economic crisis, nor did the National Socialists represent a significant political force. Both these mutually reinforcing conditions only became really important as the turning away from democracy was already in full swing. The real possibility of a breakthrough by the National Socialists to the status of a mass party was evident, however, as early as 1929 or the beginning of 1930, and was reflected in the increase in their seats in the Reichstag from 12 to 107 in September 1930. In Thuringia the first National Socialist ministers, among them Wilhelm Frick, were already in office at the beginning of 1930; they entered the government in Brunswick that same year. In the spring and early summer of 1932 National Socialists were participating in the governments of Saxony-Anhalt, Mecklenburg-Strelitz, Oldenburg, and Mecklenburg-Schwerin. But in all large German states their bid for power was unsuccessful for the time being. In spite of all the increases in the number of votes they received, the National Socialists were never able to achieve an absolute majority in a free national election in Germany. The high points of their election successes were 36.8 per cent for Hitler in the second round of the presidential election (April 1932), and the 37.3 per cent which the party received in the Reichstag election of July 1932. Even in the small German states the NSDAP never received an absolute majority of the votes in a free election, although its share of the vote was occasionally only slightly below that.

THE NSDAP AS A MASS PARTY AND EXPECTATIONS OF SALVATION

The landslide election successes of the National Socialists can only be explained when it is clearly understood that the NSDAP was two different things at the same time: on one hand it was a mass party, on the other an ideological protest party.[2] To put it differently, the radical protest of the Hitler movement was more capable of integrating all social groups than any other party yet. Setting aside its Bavarian beginnings, we shall concentrate on its membership and voters after 1930. Before the Reichstag election of that year the party had 126,523 members; by 30 January 1933, according to official party statistics, the figure had risen sevenfold to 849,009 members, even though a considerable number had left the party. By January 1933 the membership number 1,435,530 had been issued (though we know that not *all* previous numbers were in fact assigned to members by that date). By 1930 the NSDAP had already succeeded in building up a relatively efficient apparatus under Reich Organization Leader Gregor Strasser, who had been in office since 1928. The paramilitary organization of the Storm Troopers (*Sturmabteilungen* or SA) was strictly – but not always willingly – subordinate to the political apparatus. In 1932, however, the SA achieved a division of labour with the political organization. It embodied in populistic fashion the militant violence of the streets, and thus gave the party an image as a preserver of order against the left. The NSDAP built up its own organizations for numerous professional and cultural areas and specific age groups, and was also able to influence, infiltrate and, in some cases, take over the leadership of traditional social-interest groups as early as 1933. For example, in industrial centres, especially in Berlin, National Socialist Company Organizations (*Betriebszellenorganisationen* or NSBO) were established after 1928, and their total membership rose to between 300,000 and 400,000. To be sure, these organizations were neither able to infiltrate the traditional trade unions nor did they have any influence on the party programme. Richard Walther Darré developed the agrarian political organization of the NSDAP after 1929. And, independently of his own personal views, his organization was able to achieve a decisive influence at all levels in the traditional German Agrarian League (*Reichslandbund*) as early as 1932. The same was true of the conservative employees' German National Shop Clerks' Organisation (*Deutschnationaler Handlungsgehilfenverband*). National Socialist organizations were also established for jurists, doctors, teachers, and civil servants; although public officials, at the national level particularly, and in most German states, were forbidden to be active Nazis, making it less than easy to profess loyalty to the 'movement'.

The National Socialists were especially successful in attracting young people. In 1930 almost 70 per cent of the members were under 40 years old; 37 per cent were under 30. And this relative youthfulness was typical of the rank and file as well as party functionaries, forming a strong contrast to all other parties except the KPD. The courtship of the rising generation was conducted in part through the Hitler Youth, the Union of German Girls and, last but not least, the National Socialist Student Union. This last organization achieved its breakthrough in 1928 and 1929, and had for the first time an absolute majority in the general student committees of the Universities of Erlangen and Greifswald the following year. As early as 1931 a member of the National Socialist Student Union became chairman of the German Student Association (*Studentenschaft*).

Men in particular became active National Socialists. According to Michael Kater's calculations, only 7.8 per cent of the new members between 1925 and 1932 were women, a figure that declined until 1936 and rose strongly to a third of new members, only in the last phase of the Second World War. The broadest samples taken by the same author indicate that 35.9 per cent of the new members between 1930 and 1932 were from the lower classes, 54.9 per cent from the lower middle class, and 9.2 per cent from the upper classes. In comparison with the population as a whole (the corresponding figures in the population statistics in the summer of 1933 were 54.56 per cent, 42.65 per cent and 2.78 per cent) the lower middle class and the upper class were clearly over-represented; the lower class, on the other hand, was under-represented. But still, it furnished a third of the new members, and among the skilled workers and artisans (unlike the unskilled) it corresponded to the average for the population. In rural areas its representation was even above average. In comparison with the population as a whole, lower-middle-class specialists without academic training, salesmen, primarily in large and medium-size cities, and farmers were strongly represented in the NSDAP, and not only, as is often assumed, lower- and middle-level employees.

What seemed to be true of especially active National Socialists, the party members, was also true, with slight shifts, of National Socialist voters. They came from all groups of society, even from the workers. It was not so much the unemployed and the less-qualified voters who saw a solution to their problems in the party of the radical right, but skilled workers who were still earning their living. Much evidence indicates that many of them had earlier voted for the parties of the political centre. In contrast, the organized industrial workers still tended to vote in their majority for the KPD or the SPD, without, however, being completely immune to National Socialist tendencies. The NSDAP became the third strongest workers' party. On the whole the rural population voted early for the NSDAP, especially in the predominantly Protestant parts of Germany. This development began in Schleswig-Holstein and continued in Oldenburg and both states of Mecklenburg, spreading to Pomerania and East Prussia in 1932. This fact itself refutes the long-held belief that the NSDAP attracted the middle class and thus was an 'extremism of the centre'.

Nevertheless, it is true that 'the small farmers, salespeople and independent artisans of the old middle class formed the core of NSDAP followers and were the most stable and durable components of the National Socialist electorate between 1924 and 1932'.[3] With the start of the world depression, 'this hard core of National Socialist voters consisted of protest voters from the new middle class and the pensioner middle class [among others retirees and pensioners], all of whom were affected by the economic crisis of the time'. Falter and others have noted that there was a preponderance of housewives and non-professionals in this group.

But in the upper class too, however, that term may be defined, there was a very strong inclination to vote National Socialist. Especially in the residential areas of the very wealthy in the large cities, the NSDAP achieved good election results, although this trend had already begun to wane in 1932. 'The NSDAP,' Childers concludes, 'found a surprisingly large number of followers in established circles of society.' To summarize in a rather graphic way, in terms of its social composition 'the NSDAP was a people's party with a large middle class belly' (Falter). Among the voters, unlike the party members, women were slightly under-represented, but this underrepresentation had become a small majority by 1933. Another distinction is important in understanding the National Socialist election successes: that between the different churches. Significantly fewer persons voted for the NSDAP in Catholic than in Protestant areas. Although a slightly increasing number of Catholics tended to vote National Socialist, on average in the Reichstag elections from 1930 to 1933 only half as many Catholics as Protestants supported them. What were the earlier political preferences of National Socialist voters? There are several indications that many from the established parties of the centre, which for their part were not supported by the middle class alone, came to the NSDAP via small protest parties. Many had not bothered to vote at all earlier. But most NSDAP voters did come from the established parties of the centre or the right, though the SPD, the Centre Party, and the Communists all lost a number of voters to the NSDAP. For its part, the NSDAP was not able to win the lasting loyalty of many of those who supported it, and floating voters were common.

These data only suggest why the NSDAP grew to be the strongest party. The reasons were as varied as the voters themselves. The numerous National

Socialist organizations could only develop because they reflected the manifold preferences of individual social groups, appealing to already-existing wishes and fears. Generally the National Socialists usually promised, in very vague phrases, the elimination of all specific grievances; but their various organizations concerned themselves with providing concrete help – from soup kitchens to management consulting – for their specific groups of supporters. As early as February 1930, Hitler wrote:

> The great work of the first years after I regained my freedom is now beginning to bear its first fruit. One must plough and harrow, sow and work unceasingly until at last the time comes, within a few weeks, when the crop will be visibly ripe, and finally in a few days the fruit can be gathered in. With [political] movements it's no different. We have laid a solid foundation. We have ploughed [the field of] our nation as does no other party.[4]

He was referring to propaganda and advertising, areas where the professionalism of the NSDAP was far ahead of the efforts of all other political parties. This was primarily the work of its propaganda leaders, Heinrich Himmler and, after 1930, Joseph Goebbels. Thanks to the comprehensive reports on the mood of the population from the lower-level organizations of the party, by 1932 Goebbels was the first to develop educational and spoken material aimed at certain social groups. Compared with other parties, the NSDAP was also superior in the permanent mobilization of its followers to attend assemblies and demonstrations outside normal election periods. Here the most important speakers, and above all Hitler, were sent to address specific groups or speak on particular occasions throughout Germany. For assemblies in closed buildings the party was able to charge admission and thus earn a considerable amount to finance its other activities. In each of the election campaigns between April and November 1932 aeroplanes, the most modern means of transportation, were chartered for the party leader, who was thus able to speak in several widely separated cities on the same day. He made a total of almost 200 such speeches. The party published a book of photographs under the title *Adolf Hitler über Deutschland (Adolf Hitler over Germany)*, which showed the Führer 'coming from on high' giving him a quasi-religious grandeur. It was not the first time modern technology would be used to mobilize support for the charismatic leader.

But all this, however new it may have been, was only effective in connection with a protest against the existing political order itself. 'Weimar' was attacked as such, as 'the system', and was denounced using that particular term. This meant, too, that the National Socialists considered themselves to be primarily an extra-parliamentary opposition, as reflected in Goebbels' remark that, in addition to the possibilities for agitation in the Reichstag, parliamentary immunity and free tickets on the national railways were the most important things. Such a willingness to be led upward from the depressing present to new greatness contributed more than any individual statement to the popularity of the National Socialist movement. Within a few years it succeeded in creating something of a political environment of its own, one which was marked by an extraordinary dynamism. The message was understood only too well that the main issue was not this or that individual reform, not the elimination of supposed or real social hardship or injustice, not revision in small steps of the peace established by the Treaty of Versailles; the core element was the appeal to national, ethnic unity as a precondition for something completely new and future-orientated. People's willingness to accept such appeals was widespread and grew even stronger, especially under conditions of economic crisis. Not only their current loss of social status, but also the fear of much broader groups that they would be caught in the maelstrom of social decline increased the longer the economic crisis lasted. Especially prominent persons in rural areas and small towns professed their allegiance to National Socialism early, and often assumed the role of local trendsetters. The appeal of National Socialism to young people points in the same direction. The escape from the monotony of everyday routine, the feeling of starting out for a bright future, was made, through an act of faith, into a political guideline.

The revolutionary claim expressed in many speeches and printed declarations contradicted the principle of legality proclaimed at the same time. This principle was first stated solemnly by Hitler in his testimony as a witness in the trial of several young Reichswehr officers in Ulm charged with involvement in National Socialist infiltration of the military; and it immediately acquired the status of a tactical guideline. During the referendum on the Young Plan in 1929, and then at the meeting of the Harzburg Front in 1931, which in itself produced few results, the National Socialists appeared as allies of the German National People's Party and the paramilitary *Stahlhelm* (Steel Helmet), the Union of Front Soldiers, and thus demonstrated their acceptance by the existing political parties of the right. For their part, however, these parties increased their attacks on the Republic. Friction in relations with them resulted from the simple fact that Hitler claimed the leading role for his own movement. The radical friend–enemy thinking, which played an important role, especially in circles of the 'conservative revolution', was practised most consistently by the National Socialists and produced results that snowballed. 'I have sunk my teeth into my enemy, and I shall not let him go,' Hitler proclaimed in an election speech on 15 March 1932.[5] His opponents 'would have to kill me before they can drag me away from this enemy of Germany'. With the same radicalism Hitler attacked traditional political interest-groups and their organizations.[6] 'Either we shall succeed in hewing a nation hard as iron out of this hotchpotch of parties, federations, associations, world views, caste feelings and class madness, or the lack of this internal unity will ultimately destroy Germany' (speech to the Düsseldorf Industrial Club, 27 January 1932). Clearly aiming to win round to his listeners, he explained that he intended to overcome the differences between the middle class and the proletariat, to infuse society as a whole with a new quality of social solidarity. Historical comparisons with Bismarck's work and with the overcoming of the fragmentation of Germany after the Thirty Years War not only used history as a source of arguments, but also had as their aim the authenticating in history of a revolutionary process. The rejection of the multi-party state and social divisions, indeed of all existing conflicts, was a widespread phenomenon around 1930 and could be used to political advantage. But the very certainty of salvation that Hitler proclaimed for himself and his movement indicated a deep-seated psychological predisposition for this movement on the part of his followers. 'Remove the last bit of faith in the possibility of deliverance from the human heart . . . and you will observe that people consider the reduced portions [of food] to be the most important thing in life,' Hitler explained. His intention was to give his listeners the impression that they would be able to determine their own destiny secure in the idealistic future goal of German greatness, and that they would overcome the feeling of being at the mercy of forces they could not influence and weighed down by material interests. The 'march into the Third Reich' (Goebbels) thus acquired the status of a necessity of world history.[7]

Adolf Hitler was the most important person in the NSDAP. This was first of all true of his formal position as leader of the party. Refounding the party in 1925 after his imprisonment in Landsberg, he had reserved for himself the right to appoint party functionaries and to decide personally the frequent personal or programme conflicts in dictatorial fashion. This position of the Führer was also part of the party programme. As the programme proclaimed on 24 February 1920 was declared to be unchangeable in 1927, it was gradually pushed into the background. Hitler was then able to set new goals unchallenged. This real power was augmented by the emphasis, perhaps more important for propaganda purposes, on the role of Adolf Hitler himself, which served to strengthen the internal cohesion of the Nazi movement and illustrated, when the election came, the spread of the Führer cult in large parts of the population. 'Heil Hitler! That's our greeting in the new year, just as it was our last greeting in the old one. Heil Hitler!' was the way Gregor Strasser expressed his sentiments as early as the turn of the year from 1926 to 1927, and this religious form of address was increasingly accepted in the party after 1930.[8] 'It is necessary to give listeners an apodictic faith. Only then will it be possible to lead most of the followers in the desired direction. Then they will follow the Führer even when setbacks occur. But [they will do this] only if they have received an absolute faith in the absolute rightness of their own nation,' Rudolf Hess realized as early as 1927. And Joseph Goebbels was the decisive man in the spreading of this form of faith by means of all available media. It consisted first of all of the 'Hitler factor' (Broszat), in which the eagerness to believe was focused on a single person.[9] There are numerous reports of such Messiah experiences, either at a first meeting or, as it were, as a habitual drug: 'I didn't come to Hitler by accident; I was looking for him . . . The rebirth of Germany can only come about through a man who was not born in a palace but in a hut.'[10] Indeed, in 1925 Joseph Goebbels placed Hitler on a level with the founder of the Christian religion: 'I read Hitler's book from cover to cover, with rapacious excitement! Who is this man? Half plebeian, half god! Really the Christ, or only John the Baptist?' (14 October 1925). Half a year later Goebbels had achieved the certainty he sought: 'Adolf Hitler, I love you, because you are great and modest at the same time' (19 April 1926). As such a mass longing became focused on one man, Hitler himself accepted the adoration shown him and identified himself more and more with it. It is true that, since the beginning of his political career in 1919 and 1920, he had often proclaimed himself as a radical either–or choice. But probably only after the 1920s had Hitler, who gave the impression of a rather unpolished man when he appeared socially, gained the certainty that he was not simply a prophet making straight the way for some other national leader, but that he should fill that role himself. In 1932 he was still flirting only tactically with the term 'drummer boy'. Although Germany's acceptance of a doctrine of salvation as a political programme had deep causes within its society, it was not clear at the very beginning that Hitler himself would become the embodiment of such a programme. However, his position as Führer gave him a certain freedom of action; and this enabled him to present himself as the man who could fulfil the wishes and solve the problems of various social groups.

The axioms of Hitler's programme assumed a relatively rigid form very early and developed an unusual degree of consistency. As is often typical of self-educated people, he had acquired a view of the world whose components could only be changed to a limited extent by new perceptions. In its constitutive parts this conglomerate of ideas was neither new nor original. Nevertheless it did acquire a new significance, especially in its combining of images of a universal enemy with action. And, publicly advocated during the years of struggle by leading National Socialists, it extended beyond the causes of NSDAP election successes outlined above. It is doubtful, however, whether all or even the majority of active National Socialists or voters for the party took seriously the specific slogans about future policy or completely understood their full significance. And even if the slogans were understood, they often had so little relevance to the present that they simply seemed unrealistic. But that was precisely Hitler's special quality: he held fast to his basic ideas, not only for propaganda reasons but also with a personal tenacity. Several points will suffice to outline his basic views here:

1 His world view and his view of politics were dualistic, distinguishing only between absolute evil on one hand, which had to be exterminated, and the absolutely good and desirable on the other.
2 This distinction was based on the view that human races were the central factors in the development of world history. The Jews, who at that time lived in almost all countries, represented the extreme negative. In Hitler's view they sought, as 'parasites', 'bloodsuckers', 'bacilli' and 'corrupters of nations' to achieve, through infiltration, domination over their 'host

peoples' and, in the final analysis, over the entire world. In contrast, the opposite extreme was represented by the Germanic, Nordic or Aryan race, whose largest, uniform racial core was to be found in the German people.

3 Because of this universal racial conflict, permanent struggle was inevitable. Civil wars and wars between states were only two manifestations of the same battle, in which the stronger, superior races would assert themselves at the expense of the weaker. 'Every being strives for expansion, and every nation strives for world domination. Only those who do not lose sight of this final goal will find the right path.'[11]

4 For Hitler the striving of the Jews for domination manifested itself in various forms, especially in Bolshevism, but also in Marxism, Socialism, and – a somewhat lesser threat – in democracy in general. From this point of view were derived ideologically determined perceptions of enemies at home and abroad. Taken seriously, they seemed incredible and astonishing, but subsequent developments showed that these seemingly fantastic dreams were in fact the determining factors in Hitler's own personality and the basis for his policies, which he would stop at nothing to realize. His contemporaries conceded that his view of the world did not lack a certain internal coherence, but most of them did not believe that the objective political conditions existed in which world domination based on a racial, not to say racist, ideology could be achieved.

THE STRUGGLE FOR POWER

Two additional goals resulted logically from the National Socialist mission of salvation for Germany. Firstly, the promised exodus from national disgrace and desperation had to take place in the not-too-distant future. In numerous speeches Hitler constantly expounded variations of the claim that the National Socialist movement would grow exponentially until it achieved its aims. The stereotypical story of the growth of the party from modest beginnings in back-room meetings of a handful of men to a movement attracting millions in the present was repeated to tens of thousands of people, showing that the party was dynamically driven and aimed at quick success. 'The way from seven men to 15 million was more difficult than the way from 15 million to the German nation,' the New Year's proclamation of the party announced in 1932.[12] Of course, these figures were not accurate. 'We want to march into the new year as fighters, so we can conclude it as victors . . . Germany, awaken!' The belief that success and the taking of power were imminent mobilized the energies of party members in every election campaign. But in spite of all the increases in the Reichstag election of 1932 compared with the election of 1930 (though only a slight increase compared with the presidential election), it was obvious that an end to the impressive growth was in sight. It was Goebbels who articulated the Nazis' second goal. 'We won't get an absolute majority this way. So we'll have to take another approach.' In his eyes that could only mean turning away from the policy of attaining power legally and/or from attempts by the National Socialists to take complete control of the government. The NSDAP was at the crossroads.

Earlier, at the end of May 1932, the Brüning government had fallen. Various factors had come together which in part concerned the content of the government's policies, but in part also the ill feelings of the Reich President and his inner circle towards Brüning. Among the causes of such feelings was Brüning's plan to 'resettle' hopelessly debt-ridden country estates. One of the organizations opposing this plan was the conservative German Agrarian League, whose representatives had Hindenburg's ear. An end to the economic crisis was not in sight, and Brüning's foreign policy, which was subordinate to his economic policy of national recovery, had not yet achieved any success. Thus he was not toppled '100 metres from the finish line', as he himself thought. In addition, Hindenburg was re-elected president as candidate of the centre left. The prohibition of the National Socialist paramilitary organizations ordered by Brüning and his interior minister, Groener – for foreign policy reasons but even more to maintain peace and order in April 1932 – had little effect on the situation in the streets. On the other hand, it did threaten to prevent a rapprochement between the government and the National Socialists. But that was increasingly what General Kurt von Schleicher, the string-puller behind the scenes and head of the Ministerial Office in the Reichswehr Ministry, wanted. It was his influence, and that of other advisers without responsible positions, rather than the lack of a parliamentary base or the withdrawal of support by various interest groups, which led to Brüning's fall. One can describe the development of the presidential cabinets in the spring of 1932 as a power vacuum, although it should also be stressed that for the exercise of the dictatorial powers of the Reich President (based on Articles 48 and 25 of the Reich constitution) various instruments of state power were available, including the Reichswehr. Moreover, individual politicians, as well as the parties and interest groups, had not abdicated. Rather, they often engaged in complicated activities outside the established institutions. Essentially they were no longer interested in achieving a majority consensus on the basis of parliamentary principles.

Few signs of this change were more typical than the fact that the new Chancellor, Franz von Papen, was solely Schleicher's 'invention'. Papen's function was to enable Schleicher and the Reichswehr to avoid having to assume direct political responsibility. Schleicher wanted to be the 'head' of the new cabinet; he needed a chancellor who would assume the function of a 'hat'. But, especially in the circle of influential and powerful people in the government and by winning the confidence of Hindenburg himself, Papen quickly acquired a weight of his own. Two developments during Papen's brief chancellorship were of particular importance for the further course of German history: his attempt to secure power by considering the wishes of the NSDAP, and the fact that many measures taken during those months created the immediate preconditions for the National Socialist dictatorship. Papen's policies gave the authoritarian presidential regime a new quality: his chancellorship became a constitutive link between Brüning and Hitler. Seen in this light, Schleicher's chancellorship (from December 1932 to 30 January 1933) represented only an interlude, a deviation from this basic tendency.

The fact that after 1930, and even more so after 1932, the National Socialists represented a political force actively or passively involved in all discussions of how new arrangements for effective German policies could be constructed in future, makes statements about their radical demands relative only to a certain extent. Because the NSDAP, due to its mass support, was expected to play an important role in politics, various analyses of the situation and strategies for the best use of the presidential system to transform the existing order were developed within the party itself. All National Socialists wanted to get into power, but the views of some as to how that was to be accomplished differed from those of Hitler who, however, overcame all internal resistance to his plans in the end. Conservative and right-wing nationalist circles were primarily interested in 'taming' and using the National Socialist movement, which they considered in some respects dangerous, for their own purposes. In conversations with Schleicher, Hitler declared his readiness to tolerate a new government under Papen on two conditions: the withdrawal of the order banning the SA, and new elections. (He does not seem to have expressly demanded a change of the power relationships in Prussia.) For reasons of their own, the policy-makers in Schleicher's circle found these demands acceptable and even desirable. In spite of increasing objections from the south-German states, the ban on the National Socialist paramilitary organizations was lifted in June 1932. The elections took place at the end of July in an atmosphere marked by violent clashes in the streets, primarily between National Socialists and Communists. The NSDAP became by far the strongest political party; theoretically, in co-operation with the Centre and the German National People's Party, it was now in a position to form a parliamentary majority, although in practice disagreements between the parties made this impossible. Moreover, the Communists and the National Socialists had a negative majority, and this situation was not changed by the following election. Apart from the lack of will of the parties of the political centre, it was no longer even theoretically possible to form a majority coalition of parties loyal to the Republic. For a while it seemed that the Centre Party and the National Socialists were attempting to form a majority coalition in Prussia; but the internal debate among the National Socialists soon closed off this way to power. Papen, who had earlier occupied a Centre Party seat in the state parliament of Prussia, resigned when he became Chancellor in order to demonstrate that he was above partisan political considerations.

After their election victory, which they considered a defeat because of their failure to achieve an absolute majority, some members of the NSDAP began to demand that the party should participate in a government in order to gain influence. Gregor Strasser, Hermann Göring, who was now President of the Reichstag, and probably also Joseph Goebbels, seem to have pushed more or less forcefully for such participation. But in Hitler's view this would have deprived his movement of its dynamism by integrating it into the existing political structure and subjecting it to the wear and tear of daily responsibility. For this reason he demanded that he be made Chancellor and that his party also be given the Labour, Interior, and Aviation Ministries as well as a new Ministry of Popular Education. First soundings quickly showed that Schleicher, who took over the Reichswehr ministry and with it the acting government, was not prepared to accept these demands. Hitler decided to go for all or nothing. He concentrated SA units – it was said a total of 60,000 men – around Berlin, where expectations that the Nazi movement would prevail seem to have been especially widespread. Dreams of a 'March on Berlin', which had failed so miserably in 1923, suggested themselves in analogy to the Italian fascist model of a seizure of power in 1922. This time the chances of success were better than they had been nine years earlier. Nevertheless, this attempt to take power remained only a threat, as Hitler realistically assessed the situation and shied away from a confrontation with the government. On 13 August Hindenburg refused to entrust the office of Chancellor to Hitler, and in an aggressive press statement Schleicher made this rejection into a humiliation. Disappointment spread in the SA, which had wanted to attack but was held back by Hitler and its Chief of Staff, Ernst Röhm. But Hitler was also deeply depressed. He seemed to have reached the end of his possibilities, and in the following months he let political matters drift; his only plan for getting into power, that of dynamic increases in party membership and political blackmail, had failed.

Consequently, subsequent discussions about the tactical means (though not the ultimate goal) of a coalition were conducted primarily by Gregor Strasser, whose name also appeared on relevant lists of possible ministers. In the end these talks came to nothing. On 12 September 1932, in a grotesque scene in the Reichstag, two events took place at the same time. In accordance with Article 25 of the constitution, Papen presented a constitutionally valid order from the Reich President to dissolve the Reichstag; while Göring, as president of the Reichstag, refused to recognize the order and instead had the chamber express its lack of confidence in Papen, a move which under the circumstances was without constitutional validity. Only the German National People's Party and the German People's Party voted for Papen; 90 per cent of the other deputies present (from the Communist Party to the NSDAP) voted against him. Hitler placed his hopes in a new election campaign and the mobilization of all resources to achieve a complete victory for his radical alternative. For this reason his débâcle in the Reichstag election of 6 November 1932 was all the more serious. Voter participation did sink from 84.1 per cent to 80.6 per cent, but the NSDAP lost 4.6 per cent and its share of the vote sank to 33.1 per cent. Two million voters had turned away from the party in the preceding two months. Within the party, whose financial reserves were almost exhausted, a 'rotten mood' (according to Goebbels) began to spread. After this setback, Hitler's determination to continue the struggle almost sounded like a voice crying in the wilderness. But, in spite of the slight gains of the parties supporting him, Papen was also finished. He shied away from an open break with the constitution, or a civil war, and resigned on 17 November.

THE GOVERNMENT OF FRANZ VON PAPEN

In Papen's short term as Chancellor, the course for the future had been decided in many respects. Firstly, there was the composition of his 'cabinet of the barons'. Schleicher, the Defence Minister, has already been mentioned. Konstantin Freiherr von Neurath, a career diplomat, became Foreign Minister and remained in that post until 1938. Lutz Count Schwerin von Krosigk, a high finance official, took over the Ministry of Finance and remained in that position until the end of the Third Reich. Franz Gürtner, since 1922 Bavarian Minister of Justice, received the corresponding position in the national government and stayed there until his death in 1941. Two other nobles served only under Papen: Freiherr Wilhelm von Gayl, previously in the Reich Senate (*Reichsrat*) for East Prussia, took over the key post of the Interior Ministry, and Magnus Freiherr von Braun became head of the Ministry of Agriculture and Food Production. Paul Freiherr Eltz von Rübenach, an independent, presided over the Ministry of Postal Services and Transport until 1937. In addition, Hermann Warmbold served as Economics Minister and Hugo Schäffer as Labour Minister; both had also been members of the previous cabinet. Most of these men of the political right, who could only operate by using the emergency decrees of the Reich President, were prepared in principle to join a National Socialist government; they did not find it difficult, therefore, to continue in their positions under Hitler later. Only von Gayl and Schleicher refused to accept National Socialist support in forming a majority under circumstances as they existed. That meant a readiness to break openly with the constitution and establish, at least temporarily, a dictatorship. Such a right-wing cabinet without any mass support could be saved only by disregarding Article 25 of the constitution, which required that the Reichstag be convened within 60 days after an election. Such ideas, which were generally accepted in Hindenburg's inner circle, were not put into practice, but the readiness to accept them prepared the way for the completely different remodelling of the constitution in 1933. After Hindenburg's rejection of Hitler the National Socialists attacked Papen's government of the time as reactionary.

Papen's *coup d'état* in Prussia marked a decisive change, first in the federal structure of the country, and then also in the personnel of the Prussian bureaucracy. On 20 July 1932 the Chancellor issued an emergency decree removing the minority government in Prussia, temporarily took over the office of Prussian minister president himself, and appointed the mayor of Essen, Franz Bracht, as deputy Reich commissar for the Prussian ministry of the interior. These actions eliminated *de facto*, if not on paper, an element of the federal structure of the country. On 25 October 1932 the state court, to which the legitimate Prussian government under Otto Braun together with the political parties and the south German states had appealed, rendered a decision against Papen in a crucial point: the representation of Prussian interests in relations with the national government had to remain in the hands of the old government. But the court declared Papen's action against the Prussian government itself to be legal. Until March 1933 two centres in Prussia claimed the right to exercise the powers of government, but in questions of concrete policy the commissar had the upper hand. It is questionable whether this coup-like act was actually in accord with the power of the president to issue emergency decrees. More important was the fact that the most powerful German federal state had been eliminated as a political factor. The political parties in Prussia and the policies of the governing Weimar coalition there, especially of the Social Democrats, fell victim to the fundamental struggle of the right-wing groups against 'Marxism'. With the loss of this last republican-parliamentary bastion, 'the SPD ceased to be an influential force in German domestic politics. In the following months the party was completely isolated politically.'[13] The question has often been asked as to whether the SPD could have prevented this surprise attack by calling a general strike or by using the Prussian police. But not only the SPD leadership under Otto Braun had already given up the struggle; party members and other supporters were hardly able to form a closed front, especially as they had to expect a possible civil war against the Reichswehr and/or the SA, together with continued hostility from the KPD and the NSDAP. The question thus has to be answered in the negative. This was one aspect of Papen's 'Prussian coup'.

Another aspect was the fact that Prussia had the most important bureaucratic and police apparatus in Germany. Papen justified his emergency decree, not without reason, as necessary for the 'restoration of public safety and order'. But this was only one of his reasons; fighting in the streets was also frequent in other German states, and it continued in Prussia. It could not be stopped with police measures. None the less, in the internal Prussian administration so many officials were removed or transferred that one might call it a political purge, the first wave of a *Gleichschaltung*, a technical term meaning synchronization but which under the National Socialists acquired the meaning of bringing everything into line in support of the existing regime. For the time being, this *Gleichschaltung* was carried out in accordance with the aims of right-wing conservatives. Three of the four highest Social

Democrat provincial administrative officials (*Oberpräsidenten*) lost their offices; state secretaries, senior officials of government districts (*Regierungspräsidenten*), police chiefs and a large number of ministerial officials at all levels were replaced. Others were transferred to unimportant positions. 'In this way, the Republican changes in the Prussian administration that had been pushed through in twelve years were reduced to nothing in a few months.'[14] These changes had not been simple party politics, but had rather constituted an attempt – of only very limited effectiveness in Prussia – to widen social access to the traditional civil-service élite inherited from Imperial Germany.

The changes in the top police positions were especially important. Until Papen's coup, Social Democratic police chiefs had, as a matter of course, proceeded against National Socialists as well as Communists, as they did, for example, in the May disturbances in Berlin in 1929. The accusation that they had protected or spared left-wing groups was absurd. But it was believed, and after July 1932 measures were taken in Prussia to make sure that only groups and organizations on the left were considered to be enemies. In this way the Berlin police chief and former Interior Minister Albert Grzesinski, a Social Democrat, his deputy, Bernhard Weiss, a member of the State Party who had been the main target of Goebbels's propaganda, and the head of the uniformed police in the capital were replaced. Numerous occupants of positions in the political police were also replaced. Senior Executive Officer Rudolf Diels, who became the first head of the Gestapo in 1933, had already distinguished himself as an informer in the preparations for the coup against Prussia, and now began his rapid rise; and the police began to overlook crimes and provocations on the right.

The significance of Papen's government was not limited to its organizational and personnel decisions; its stated goals also prepared the way for the future. Papen announced his programme not in a speech to the Reichstag, but in a radio speech on 12 September, 1932: 'The system of formal democracy [had for him] led to ruin in the judgement of history and the eyes of the German nation.'[15] The main task now was to establish a government independent of the parties, based primarily on the authority of the Reich President 'chosen by the nation'. The future Reichstag was to be combined with self-administering bodies, made up of various co-determination boards and organizations in the economy. And the voting age would be raised. Moreover, the authority of the Reichstag was to be reduced and its powers limited by an Upper House appointed by the Reich President. Prussia would be 'organically' united with the whole of Germany. Papen envisaged an authoritarian and potentially dictatorial state; but he lacked the time and power to realize his plans. None the less such a programme, although it had no chance of being accepted in the Reichstag, had its supporters. It was welcomed in broad sectors of industry and also met with some approval from agrarian groups, although they were not happy about the economic policy of the government as far as it affected their material interests.

Moreover, the authoritarian reforming of society was to be begun from below. In 1932 it was decided to establish a Reich Curatorium for the Physical Training of Youth. This was a demand of Schleicher's from the previous year and was now begun under the supervision of a retired general. The aim was, on one hand, to deprive the parties, including the right-wing ones, of their paramilitary groups and to concentrate the organizations in the hands of the state, and on the other to begin personnel preparations for the large-scale rearmament now being accelerated, to 'guarantee an adequate national defence through the creation of large groups of healthy, strong and well-trained young men'.

More effective, and of greater immediate importance, was an 'Emergency Decree of the Reich President to Revive the Economy' (4 September 1932), which did not meet with energetic opposition from the trade unions, although together with another decree it marked the beginning of a reduction of the social services provided by the Weimar state. These decrees were designed to reduce radically wage and arbitration rights, and they also made additional wage-cuts possible. Moreover, the decrees rejected Brüning's austerity policy in favour of energetic job-creation programmes based on tax relief for industry and state-financed investment, and they introduced voluntary labour service, which was well received even by the free trade unions. Although he continued to enjoy Hindenburg's confidence, Papen's days as Reich Chancellor were numbered after the November elections. It had not been possible to win Hitler's support, and his party mounted increasingly sharp attacks on Papen. The dilemma continued: as long as the Reichstag remained, it could topple the government at any time. But if, contrary to the constitution, new elections were not called for the time being after the Reichstag had been dissolved, this would lead to a situation similar to a civil war. In the end Papen came to envisage such a course. But when Schleicher, motivated by tactical considerations, explained that the Reichswehr would probably not be able to deal with internal disturbances from the left and the right, the final decision was taken against Papen, again in the small circle close to the president.

THE GOVERNMENT OF KURT VON SCHLEICHER

On 3 December 1932 von Schleicher took over the office of Chancellor with a slightly changed cabinet, reluctantly and as it were as the last alternative to Hitler. But he had a different plan. He referred to himself as the 'general with a social conscience' who did not want to base his power on bayonets. As his original plan to 'tame' Hitler had failed the previous summer, he tried a new way to win mass support, a way which at first glance seems rather odd. His aim was to attract the free trade unions on one hand and the co-operative parts of the NSDAP on the other to support his government; and he therefore offered Gregor Strasser the Vice-Chancellorship. From a programmatic point of view his undertaking was not entirely without prospects of success. Papen's socially reactionary emergency decrees of 4 and 5 September were immediately rescinded. And in his inaugural speech of 15 December – again broadcast by radio – Schleicher proclaimed 'creating jobs' to be the main aim of his programme.[16] He rejected conflicts between socialism and capitalism, between private and planned economies, as senseless, and proclaimed his determination to promote private investment and public programmes to create jobs. Indeed, he presented an emergency programme for public works costing 500 million Reichsmarks. Plans for the construction of settlements for small farmers in the east, and immediate aid measures for the winter, underlined the social element in his programme. The fact that the Reichstag did not topple Schleicher immediately, although he had no prospects of obtaining the support of even one of the larger parties, must be considered one of his successes. He aimed to establish, at least temporarily, a military dictatorship based on the powers of the Reich President. But the mass support he sought for his non-partisan front simply could not be achieved. His negotiations with the National German Trade Union Federation (ADGB) did give some grounds for hope, but the SPD, which for its part was concerned about being overtaken by the Communists in future if it tried to move closer to Schleicher, persuaded the unions to reject his offer. Gregor Strasser, who had just reformed and tightened up the organization of the NSDAP and seemed to be the rising strong man and an alternative to Hitler, took the negotiations seriously, but on 8 December he accepted Hitler's uncompromising course, resigned from all party offices, and went on leave. Thereafter he no longer played a significant political role. He had given up. In spite of subsequent developments, it was already clear at the end of 1932 that Schleicher's plan had failed.

There were several individuals whose decisions were partly responsible for this; but it must also be stressed that both the trade unions and the National Socialists had taken risks in supporting him. If they had co-operated further with Schleicher, they would also have been responsible for his failures, and would have had to abandon, for the time being, their most important goals. Above all, the big interest groups did not like the general's strategy. Concessions to agrarian interests, such as in the question of the mandatory addition of butter to margarine, could not moderate the protectionist course of the German Agrarian League against the Chancellor; and it was precisely this kind of measure which met with criticism from the workers. After mid-January 1933, influential representatives of agrarian interests made a co-ordinated effort to turn Hindenburg against Schleicher, and some of them even advocated a right-wing coalition under the leadership of the National Socialists. And even more important was the fact that a large part of German industry, and especially heavy industry, was seriously concerned about

Schleicher's 'socialist' course. On 19 November, when Papen had to resign, a small group of industrialists, though not the most influential ones, had caused a sensation by declaring their support for the appointment of Hitler as Chancellor. But most industrialists still preferred policies such as those which Papen had pursued.

In this situation the newly toppled Chancellor regained a key role based on Hindenburg's continued confidence in him. After the losses in the Reichstag election, the crisis in the NSDAP had become more acute. In the subsequent municipal elections in Thuringia (even before the Strasser crisis) the party also suffered considerable losses, and had to mobilize its entire propaganda apparatus and organization to achieve a modest success in the parliamentary election in the small state of Lippe on 15 January. Moreover, the party coffers were empty. The liberal economist Gustav Stolper was certainly not being unrealistic when he wrote at the time, 'The year 1932 marked the high tide of Hitler's fortunes and [also] his political demise . . . [Since August 1932] the Hitler movement has been collapsing, and the extent and speed of that collapse can only be compared to his rise.'[17] Papen, however, began negotiations behind Schleicher's back to include the National Socialists in a government; however, this immediately became public knowledge. On 4 January 1933 he had talks with Hitler in the house of the Cologne banker, von Schröder, one of the signatories to the industrialists' declaration of 19 November 1932. Although Hitler was prepared, for a time, to renounce his all-or-nothing demand that he be Chancellor, and to be satisfied with the 'ministries of power', namely the Interior and Defence, in the final analysis Papen's intrigues were successful only when Hitler was offered the chancellorship.[18] In fact, everything was open until the final moment, and even in this situation there was no real need to make the leader of the NSDAP Chancellor. In spite of the services of an intermediary such as von Schröder, the fact that Hitler did become Chancellor was not due to pressure from industrial circles. Opinions there were divided, and most of those who did attempt to influence the choice of Chancellor favoured Papen as the strong man. Nor was the ultimate choice of Hitler due to any attempt to create a cabinet with majority support in the Reichstag, although that was ostensibly the aim of the negotiations with various political parties. Nor was it due solely to Hitler's undoubtedly dynamic will to power, which no-one could ignore in the long term. It was rather simply that, in the view of the power centre that had formed around the Reich President, all other political solutions had been exhausted. A series of occasionally grotesque intrigues, with secret meetings at various places, with obscure and scheming intermediaries, finally produced the alternative which Hindenburg reluctantly accepted. It is even possible that blackmail played a role, to prevent the discrediting of the Reich President as a result of the exposure of scandals such as the illegal use of funds for the Eastern Aid (*Osthilfe*) Programme, which occurred at that time. Schleicher was denied the full authority and support of the President, and resigned on 28 January 1933. Two days later the new cabinet of 'national concentration', which had been planned for three weeks, was sworn in. The new Chancellor was Adolf Hitler.

If one considers what real alternatives to this solution were actually available at the beginning of 1933, it becomes clear that, for various reasons, under circumstances as they existed none of them was feasible. A left-wing government of Communists and Social Democrats, perhaps formed after a general strike, never had a chance in the Weimar Republic because of the irreconcilable antagonisms dividing those two parties. There was no longer a majority in the Reichstag for a government of the centre, even if it had extended from the SPD to the German National People's Party; and such a government was in itself inconceivable. On the whole, the ability and will of the parties to reach compromises had shrunk even further as a result of the economic crisis. No possible minority government with a combination of individual parties had any prospect of success. The only choice was between an authoritarian government with and one without the National Socialists. It was precisely this that had been the dominant fact in German politics since 1929; all other possibilities had been deliberately discredited or excluded.

Such a solution required presidential support. Although it was not very probable that Hindenburg would complete his term of office, the prospect of his departure and a new presidential election campaign was not welcome. As long as he remained in office, however, his values and preferences determined the concrete application of his presidential powers. It is thus pointless to speculate about whether, in view of later developments, Schleicher's policy would have been the lesser evil, or whether other new chances of a conservative dictatorship without the National Socialists, which briefly seemed possible, would have been better. Of course there was some resistance and scepticism among conservatives, but the decisive circle around Papen and Hindenburg still did not understand, on 30 January 1933, what had now become possible. Papen's exclamations: 'We have hired him,' and 'In two months we shall have pushed Hitler so far into the corner that he'll squeak,' show this most clearly.[19] In his eyes, even though they had entrusted Hitler with the office of Chancellor, he and the other members of the cabal around Hindenburg had at last achieved what Brüning had strived for: they had won the co-operation of the National Socialists as a broad, plebiscitary base, as a junior partner for their own plans; they had created the conditions for taming the National Socialists by giving them responsibility. Now it would at last be possible to construct the new, anti-democratic state. These circles did not think that they had given the new Chancellor a chance to begin dynamic pursuit of the power which he had always proclaimed as his goal. Rather, they believed that they had taken the necessary precautions to make him nothing more than a peripheral figure. Indeed, he himself had promised not to infringe upon the position of the Reich President, and they thus assumed that they would be able to get rid of him easily if that should become necessary. Hitler even accepted the fact that he would have no direct control over the armed forces; before the new cabinet was sworn in, Hindenburg filled the office of Reichswehr Minister with General Werner von Blomberg, who was, however, favourably disposed towards the National Socialists. In Prussia not the Chancellor, but the Vice-Chancellor, Papen, was made commissar. Finally, for the first time in years it had apparently been possible to persuade the German National People's Party again to accept political responsibility. Outwardly Alfred Hugenberg, the Minister of Economics and Agriculture, functioned as a strong man in the new cabinet. The same was true of the *Stahlhelm*, whose leader, Franz Seldte, became the new Minister of Labour. Most members of the cabinet believed that the 'Nazi battalions' were not the only support of the government. On the other hand, contrary to later National Socialist legend, Hitler had not seized power as a result of his single-minded pursuit of it, but had grasped the last straw to prevent his own political decline.

|2|

The Conquest of Power

MOBILIZATION AND TERROR

In formal terms, the government of which Hitler was Chancellor was a presidential government like its predecessors. Apart from the new Chancellor, only two other National Socialists belonged to it; Wilhelm Frick as Minister of the Interior and Hermann Göring as minister without portfolio. Göring, however, was also the provisional Prussian Minister of the Interior (and Reich Commissar for Aviation). The conservatives thus had a clear majority in the new government; but they never had a chance to use it. This was not because the National Socialists took out their draft laws and economic policies and immediately tried to realize them: they hardly had any policies, and even those they had seldom played an important role. Two other basic factors of German domestic politics were responsible, against which the National Socialists' partners and opponents were unable to defend themselves: on one hand, a widespread feeling that a new beginning was being made, the dynamism of the movement, and its mobilization of human energies; and on the other, the use of intimidation, terror, and deprivation of rights. The first group of factors was directed essentially towards one part of German society, while the second group was aimed at the remainder, whose members were ostracized. Political opponents of the National Socialists such as the Social Democrats, as well as groups that the National Socialists themselves had declared to be hostile – and above all, the Jews – were labelled as enemies and attacked. 'The extermination of Marxism, root and branch' was one internal party slogan;[1] 'A war of extermination against the [whole] stock of democratic ideas' was another. It was simply impossible to prohibit six million people who supported the Communist Party, Hitler observed as he rejected a corresponding suggestion from Hugenberg on 30 January 1933. He thus applied a carrot-and-stick approach, but the stick was rather a mild metaphor compared with what was actually taking place. Both aspects of the

National Socialist tactics were directed against the whole of German society. At first some people wanted to see only the new beginning; those who were threatened were given the chance to avoid further intimidation by joining in the jubilation.

And there was, to be sure, much jubilation from the very beginning. When the National Socialists themselves still could not quite believe that they had succeeded, Joseph Goebbels organized a torchlight procession in Berlin of militant paramilitary organizations – the SA and the SS (*Schutzstaffel*), and also the *Stahlhelm*. It began at around 5 o'clock in the afternoon and lasted long into the night. Tens of thousands (although probably not the 500,000 men the National Socialists claimed) marched in military order through the Brandenburg Gate and the area where most government buildings were located, to pay homage to Hitler and Hindenburg. In other German cities similar and, if anything, more spontaneous torchlight processions took place: in Hamburg the SA, the *Stahlhelm*, and students marched under the slogan: 'A Threefold Hail to Our Führer, Our Reich Chancellor Adolf Hitler!'[2] But this did not represent the entire nation. There was indifference and much scepticism, especially in the middle classes.

Nevertheless, the National Socialists knew how to present this and subsequent events as a seizure of power, and how to propagate this view in the media. In cinemas, people all over Germany were able to witness and experience that march through the Brandenburg Gate. On 30 January 1933, for the first time, German radio changed its programme schedule to cover a change in government. And this new medium was to play an important role in the future propagation of this and other myths. On 10 February a campaign speech by the new Chancellor was broadcast by all stations from the Berlin Sport Palace. Goebbels himself served as the reporter at the event, and vividly described the 'mass of people' standing solid and united together, the visual impressions, and the rhythmic chants of 'Hail!' 'What a turn of events through an act of Providence!'[3] he commented. Hitler spoke of his 'conviction that this nation will one day arise again' and appealed: 'People of Germany, give us four years. I swear to you, when we and I entered upon this office, I did not do it for the salary, for pay. I did it for your sake alone!' He ended his speech with a religious 'Amen', which was immediately followed by the solemn music of the Egmont Overture. Hitler thus presented his approach to politics not primarily as a grappling with or discussion of concrete issues, but as an act of identification, a mobilization of will, and even more, a religiously exaggerated, fateful rite. Even at this early stage he therefore appeared as the executor of a divine will, at least for those who were prepared to believe in him.

The opening of the Reichstag, held in the Garrison Church in Potsdam on 21 March 1933, was aimed more at the Prussian-conservative part of the population; Hitler wore a morning coat and, facing the uniformed Reich President, bowed in respect to the Hohenzollerns over the coffin of Frederick the Great in an act intended to symbolize a link between the old and the new

Germany. This ceremony was preceded by a church service, also broadcast on the radio, in which the Protestant pastor, Otto Dibelius, delivered a pertinent sermon. The celebrations on 1 May, the traditional holiday of German workers since 1890, were aimed at other social groups. But the means were similar. Not only was the first day of May made a legal holiday on which the free trade unions and the National Socialists marched together, but the hanging out of flags and the use of banks of searchlights in a vertical position imitated and exaggerated religious symbols. The festive illumination was intended to evoke the impression of a 'cathedral of light' incomparably greater than real churches; indicating the insignificance of the individual, it also suggested the possibility of his or her participating in the great cause of national revival. 'You are nothing; your nation is everything' later became the corresponding slogan. On 1 May Hitler concluded his speech: 'Lord, we shall not leave you! Now bless our struggle and our freedom and with them our German nation and fatherland!'[4]

One should certainly not conclude from these outwardly staged appearances that such events necessarily achieved sweeping success; but they did serve to weaken people's private reservations towards National Socialism wherever they existed. Those who had earlier voted National Socialist because of their particular situations were strengthened in their choice: the nation now had a future, the will to believe found a goal in the new beginning. Of course, this basic mood of enthusiasm, which had previously appeared, in different guises, perhaps half a dozen times in Germany in the twentieth century, was at first artificial. But gradually it had a real effect. Especially in contrast to the governments of the Weimar period, the new cabinet radiated to German society a new feeling of energy centred on Adolf Hitler.

Together with the use of terror, this fact constituted from the very beginning another reason why the National Socialists' conservative political partners were never able to consolidate their position. In the final analysis they wanted to institutionalize the anti-parliamentary developments by passing an enabling law. But even before he took his oath of office, Hitler pushed through a plan within the new government not to dissolve the Reichstag immediately but to hold one more election, the last one. Its purpose, of course, was not to change the composition of the government or to make possible a return to a parliamentary system, but to extend the momentum of the National Socialist movement to the whole of German society and to lay the plebiscitary foundation for the elimination of all elections. It was an aim which was never achieved. Although on 5 March the feeling of experiencing a new beginning made itself evident in the highest level of voter participation in any general election in Germany up to that time of 88.8 per cent, and although, in this still partially free election, the NSDAP did receive 8.8 per cent more votes than 4 months earlier, none the less with only 43.9 per cent it clearly failed to obtain an absolute majority. Nevertheless, together with the vote for the German National People's Party (8.0

per cent), which now demonstrated its rejection of the black, red and gold colours of the Republic by changing its name to the Fighting Front Black-White-Red, this was still enough for a small majority; and that was the important thing. The parties of the political centre remained splinter groups; the SPD and the KPD, whose participation in the election was obstructed in varying degrees, suffered slight losses. For the first time, the National Socialists succeeded in obtaining a significant number of votes among Catholics. But the largest group of new votes came from people who had previously not voted at all. Hitler himself was already more popular than his party. Technically Germany now had a majority government, but no-one would venture to draw from this the logical political conclusion that it would govern on the basis of its own majority. The powers of the President were sufficient to govern, at least as long as the conservative partners of the National Socialists co-operated.

The political system had been fundamentally changed by a presidential decree before the election under the pretext of Communist subversive activities. It is true that on 30 January the KPD had called for a general strike, and had described the National Socialists' activities as an 'unveiled declaration of war on the German working class and population';[5] but the strike was successful in only a few places, such as in the port of Hamburg. The KPD had been unable to co-operate with the Social Democrats and the free trade unions because of their own policy of confrontation with the 'Social Fascists', which they were still practising a few days before the strike. The SPD and the free trade unions, on the other hand, pleaded for 'keeping cool and calm'; they wanted to reserve a general strike as a final weapon to be used as soon as the new government openly resorted to illegal measures. Consequently the Communists resumed their policy of attacking the democratic left. In an appeal, the trade unions warned, 'The vital interests of the whole working class are at stake,' and the SPD proclaimed its desire to 'defend the political and social rights of the people ... with all means against any attack'. But this verbal demonstration of determination was based on an underestimation of the situation. 'Adolf Hitler is permitted to speak; Alfred Hugenburg will act', the SPD deputy Kurt Schumacher proclaimed in a speech. The Social Democrats did not want recklessly to start a civil war, and an important factor in their position was also the fear of being no match for the Nazis and the instruments of force available to the state.

In the first days after 30 January 1933, the Centre Party permitted itself to be put off with negotiations about entering the new government, although the civil war-like terror of the past months continued, with the important difference that the SA and SS now knew that the power of the state was on their side. The war against the left by all available means was openly proclaimed as official policy. Because of this alleged fight against Communist atrocities, Hermann Göring promoted some 55,000 members of the National Socialist paramilitary organizations and the *Stahlhelm* to the status of auxiliary police on 22 February 1933, thus making many of those who had contributed to the violence and terror of the past months responsible for keeping peace and order. Several days earlier he had ordered the police to establish 'best relations' with these organizations and, contrary to all law, had issued an order for the police to make use of their firearms.[6]

> Police officers who make use of their firearms in carrying out their duties [against subversive organizations] will be protected by me irrespective of the consequences of that use. On the other hand, anyone who fails [to make use of his firearm] because of misguided self-restraint can expect disciplinary action.

Here Göring expressed himself more bureaucratically and with more restraint than in a speech a few days later:

> Fellow Germans, my measures will not be weakened by any kind of legalistic reservations . . . Here it is not my task to exercise justice, but to annihilate and exterminate, nothing more. This struggle, fellow Germans, will be a struggle against chaos, and I do not conduct such a struggle with police measures.

To put it more clearly, from the very beginning illegal measures were cloaked in a veil of legality. This was in part due to consideration of the National Socialists' coalition partners, but beyond that it was also a question of tactical expediency.

Such an outbreak of private warfare in the name of a national new beginning cannot be understood by describing it simply in terms of decrees and laws enacted in a formally legal manner. Much was done improperly; but the external appearance of legal forms did remain a feature of the rapidly expanding practice of arbitrary rule. On 4 February Hindenburg issued a 'Decree for the Protection of the German Nation', which had already been prepared the previous year,[7] and which contained the authority to prohibit assemblies and printed material. On paper it was due to 'an immediate danger to public peace and safety', and was a reaction to the call by the Communist Party for a general strike. But the prohibitions could be expanded at will. Not only political rallies and newspapers of the KPD and the SPD, but also those of the Centre were affected; the 'battle against Marxism', which Hitler and the entire new cabinet had proclaimed as their election slogan, could be extended to include all persons and groups opposed to the regime. As early as February many Social Democrats abandoned hope of carrying on any effective political opposition, as they had good reason to fear for life and limb. By the time the election was held, 69 people had been killed (among them 18 National Socialists, who were then honoured as martyrs), and hundreds of others had been injured. A pogrom atmosphere began to spread; only a provocation or excuse was lacking for a real witch-hunt.

THE *GLEICHSCHALTUNG* OF THE POLITICAL SYSTEM

On 27 February 1933 the Reichstag burned. This was probably the work of one individual, someone with anarchistic convictions; in any case it was not the beginning of a Communist counter-revolution, as many people were only too ready to believe. 'Now we'll act. Göring immediately forbids all Communist and Social Democratic publications,' Goebbels noted in his diary.[8] More important, however, were a speedily drafted emergency decree 'for the protection of the Nation and the State' and another (prepared) decree 'against treason against the German nation'. This last decree stiffened the punishment for treason, as the military leaders had wanted, to include the death penalty. The first decree, which soon came to be called the Reichstag Fire Decree, suspended the state of law as a whole and itself remained the 'basic law' of the National Socialist regime until 1945. It suspended the most important basic rights of the Weimar constitution: personal freedom, the free expression of opinion, the freedom to form organizations and to assemble, and the privacy of correspondence. Unreasonable searches, the seizure of and restrictions on property – all became possible 'outside the otherwise applicable legal limitations'. 'If measures necessary to re-establish public peace and safety within a state [*Land*] are not taken, the national government itself can take the initiative.' This was a general authorization for 'measures' which it was now possible not to define closely, and which became a characteristic feature of the National Socialist system. The decree was completely at variance with traditional law, as it did not threaten punishment based primarily on certain circumstances and factual findings, but was aimed at achieving an ideal state of society, a harmonious national community, and that aim was considered to justify all means, however arbitrary they might be. But this first became apparent only in practice. Even before the Reichstag Fire Decree was issued, for example, all Communist deputies and functionaries who could be found were taken into 'protective custody', to be joined the following day by left-wing intellectuals associated with the *Weltbühne*, especially its editor, Carl von Ossietzky. After the Reichstag election of 5 March this campaign was intensified. The SA auxiliary police began a hunt for all Communists; some were turned over to the police. Others were brought to improvised imprisonment and torture chambers and unauthorized concentration camps, as the prisons were already full. In Prussia alone there were 20,000 people in 'protective custody' in March 1933, and not all of them were Communists.

To be sure, there was a newly elected Reichstag, and it could abrogate the presidential emergency decree. Of course that was only a theoretical possibility, but as a matter of principle an enabling law had to be passed, and this was done by the Reichstag on 24 March 1933. To secure the necessary two-thirds majority required by the constitution, the National Socialists resorted to illegal, grotesque perversions of the standing rules of procedure. After receiving vague promises about future constitutional guarantees, the Centre Party and, with reservations, the remaining delegates of the moderate parties voted for the law; it passed with 444 votes of the 642 deputies present. The Communist and some of the Social Democrat delegates had already been arrested. Before the vote, members of the Reichstag were physically intimidated by terror. The SPD chairman, Otto Wels, defended the 'no' vote of his party with a courageous statement of faith in 'the principles of humanity and justice, of freedom and socialism'.[9] It was to be the last free opposition speech in Germany for 12 years. Hitler could afford to heap scorn on his political enemy and once again to settle accounts with the 14 years of allegedly Marxist rule: 'Germany shall be free, but not through you!' In the Law for the Relief of Hardship of the People and the Reich, the government was given permission to make laws by decree 'in so far as they are not concerned with the rights of the Reichstag and the Reichsrat [Senate] as such'. Indeed, the Reichstag continued to exist and new elections were held, usually combined with plebiscites. But it now served only as a sounding-board, and had the task of regularly extending the Enabling Law, which at first was limited to 4 years; and, although its continued existence had been expressly promised, the Reichsrat soon disappeared.

The uses of the new Reichstag became evident in the session of 17 March 1933. In a foreign-policy crisis, in which Hitler's conservative partners, in particular, pressed for a hard line, the Chancellor made a moderate, statesmanlike speech, soon described as a 'peace speech', which received applause from all sides from left to right. The Communists were no longer present, but the threatened SPD too, after some internal debate, expressed its support for the Chancellor in foreign policy. This shows how widespread was the partial consensus for a national new beginning, in spite of the sometimes fatal persecution to which opponents of the National Socialists were already being subjected. In London, *The Times* commented: 'This support of all parties for Hitler's policy is not subjugation to his rule; rather Hitler has actually spoken for a united Germany in all these things.'[10]

In the spring of 1933 the parties not only lost their right to participate in German political life; with the exception of the NSDAP they ceased to exist altogether. Election meetings of the left-wing parties were broken up, their newspapers forbidden. In street clashes the Communists were no match for the National Socialist organizations, which now appeared as auxiliary police. Considering the intensity of persecution to which the Communists were exposed, the 81 Reichstag seats they won on 5 March 1933 represented an astonishing success; in Berlin they actually remained the strongest party, with 30.1 per cent of the vote. But the Communist Party deputies could not take their seats in the Reichstag, which were regarded as legally non-existent. On 31 March the Communist victories in the Reichstag and the state parliaments were declared invalid. Most of the Communist deputies had been in a concentration camp or prison since the Reichstag fire, or had fled abroad. Their party offices were plundered and occupied by the SA and the SS. In order to avoid strengthening the SPD, the Communist Party had not been formally banned before the election; later, a ban was not necessary. The Communists, who had also appeared on the scene as a revolutionary party against 'Weimar', were the best-prepared party for the illegal work and resistance which began in the summer of 1933, after their suppression. The SPD, on the other hand, staked everything on a strategy of legality; but, in spite of some readiness to resist in its own ranks, it was not able to effectively oppose the terror. Even before the election, defeatism, resignations, and the dissolution of entire local party organizations had begun. The election results – the SPD lost only 70,000 votes compared with the previous election – were celebrated as a success, and the party still waited for a chance to resume political activity some time, somehow, even in a state dominated by National Socialism. At first the party leaders refused to accept the idea of illegal activity. But in the expectation of persecution such as the party had experienced under the Socialist Law in Imperial Germany, part of the leadership moved to Prague with the party treasury and the archive at the beginning of May 1933. In this way tactical differences concerning the right future course developed; they were an inevitable result of cautious party activity in Germany in consideration of persecuted or arrested members on one hand, and of the more forceful statements and greater loyalty to principle displayed by party leaders in exile on the other. On 10 May the government confiscated the assets and printing shops of the SPD; on 22 June Interior Minister Frick banned all activity by the party and defended his action by pointing to the activities of its executive committee in exile. All party leaders still in Germany were arrested; legal activity became impossible; and the remnants of Social Democratic organizations in Germany continued to exist only under conditions of conspiracy.

Shortly thereafter the smaller moderate parties dissolved themselves. The State Party, which had moved towards the SPD, yielded to pressure. The German People's Party gave its approval to the 'national unitary state'. Not wanting to be left behind, Hugenberg's German National Front announced its affiliation with the NSDAP in a friendship agreement on 27 June. This development had been preceded by numerous changes of allegiance, but there was also persecution. As early as 29 March evidence of anti-National Socialist views had been confiscated in the house of Ernst Oberfohren, the arch-conservative parliamentary chairman of Hugenberg's party; even the German National paramilitary organizations were forbidden on the basis of the Reichstag Fire Decree, formally directed against the Communists. And Hugenberg had so discredited himself, even among conservatives, with his radical demands for colonies and expansion in Eastern Europe at the World Economic Conference in London that he resigned his ministerial post on 29 June.

On 5 July the Centre, the last independent party, dissolved itself. Here, too, there was persecution, but there was also much support for the new government. At the Fulda Bishops' Conference on 28 March the Catholic Church, which had earlier condemned National Socialism as anti-Christian, appealed for loyalty towards the new government. The Vatican entered into negotiations for a concordat with the Hitler government, and Papen made this matter his own personal concern. In the Centre Party opinions were divided as to the best political tactic for the future; but those members advocating loyalty towards the government and the Vatican prevailed. Ludwig Kaas, the party chairman, went to Rome at the end of March and agreed in the negotiations for a concordat that clergymen (like himself) would be forbidden to participate in politics in future. Under massive pressure and police persecution the Centre abandoned politics, as the Bavarian People's Party had done a day earlier. Brüning himself was the most prominent *émigré* of this political persuasion. The Reich Concordat, which was initialled on 8 July, provided formal safeguards for Catholic social and cultural institutions in future. This was more than the Weimar Republic had been prepared to concede. A report on the mood of the population in Middle Franconia spoke of a 'complete pacification of public life', but years of work would still be necessary to impart to the 'broad masses of previous voters for the Bavarian People's Party the meaning and content of National Socialism with sufficient emphasis' so that they would become 'conscious and convinced supporters of the new idea of the state'.[11] On 6 July Hitler told the Reich governors (*Reichsstatthalter*), 'We are proceeding slowly with the completion of the total state.' But at the same time he also announced the end of the revolution, which must 'not become a permanent process, as if the first [revolution] now must be followed by a second, and the second by a third'. On 14 July a law was enacted by decree that made the founding or maintaining of political parties a punishable offence, the only exception being the NSDAP. That same day public officials were instructed to use the Hitler salute (the words 'Heil Hitler' and a raised right arm) to show their loyal sentiments.

Joseph Goebbels celebrated this 'greatest revolution of all time'. Did the event which the National Socialists described as 'their revolution' deserve that name? There is no doubt that the German political landscape had been radically changed within a very short time. Six months earlier no-one, not even the NSDAP itself, could have imagined such a development taking place with such breathtaking speed. The party had over-estimated not only its political enemies on the left but also its compliant allies among the moderates and on the right. Of course, the Weimar constitution was set aside (although not formally), a very specific kind of dictatorship was established, and the polarization of society was carried to such an extreme that it acquired a new quality and led to a new kind of ideological consolidation. All these things are classic features of a revolution. But Hitler's speech against a second revolution in particular showed the limits of this change. Briefly speaking, from the very beginning an alliance developed between the new mass movement and important parts of the old German bureaucratic, economic, and military élites. By mid-1933 the claim to leadership had clearly shifted in favour of the National Socialists and their Chancellor. Towards the traditional leadership groups in particular – the military and bureaucracy – the National Socialists proceeded at first with extreme caution and consideration. It was no accident that Hitler's first visit as Chancellor was to a Reichswehr barracks, and at a private social gathering on 3 February 1933 he sought to enlist the support of the military leaders in a speech lasting several hours. By assuring the generals that the Reichswehr would remain the sole external power-instrument of the state, and that the battle against Marxism would be carried out by his party army, he created the basis for an alliance which, though at first unstable, lasted 5 years. And in questions of foreign policy, together in part with domestic political matters, men like Hugenburg and Papen especially, and in some respects Blomberg and Neurath, were inclined to favour measures more radical than Hitler himself, for tactical reasons, considered sensible. Business leaders, many of whom were not exactly pro-democracy, had made their contribution to ending the Weimar Republic. But although it is true that some of them, like the banker von Schröder, had supported Hitler as a candidate for Chancellor, as a group they did not take a uniform position on the events of 30 January 1933. Paul Silverberg, an industrialist, though he had supported Hitler for Chancellor the previous year, would have preferred to keep Schleicher in that office in January 1933. These differences of opinion among business people explain why the National Federation of German Industry (*Reichsverband der deutschen Industrie* or RDI) and the Union of German Industry and Commerce (*Deutscher Industrie- und Handelstag* or DIHT) at first displayed what was clearly a reserved attitude towards the deliberately vague economic programme of the new government, which did not go very far beyond the election slogan 'Create Jobs!'. Business was concerned, above all, about the increasing demands for economic autarchy. On 20 February 1933, at an informal meeting, more than twenty industrialists expressed these reservations to Hitler, Göring, and the newly appointed president of the Reichsbank, Hjalmar Schacht. Primarily domestic political promises – no new elections, rearmament – caused these industrialists to make new and generous donations to the NSDAP's election campaign. In June an 'Adolf Hitler Fund of the German Economy', suggested by Gustav Krupp von Bohlen und Halbach, not only institutionalized this financial assistance but also clearly established an alliance with the new men in power.

The fact that on 1 April 1933 SA units had already occupied the offices of the National Federation of German Industry, probably not spontaneously, and the National Socialist economics expert, Otto Wagner, had forced both the immediate resignation of Jewish managing committee members such as Ludwig Kastl and Silverberg and the installation of a National Socialist representative on the directing board, did not change this support. After a conversation between Hitler and leading industrialists on 29 May, agitation against corrupt business leaders was stopped. A week earlier the National

Federation of German Industry had formally dissolved itself; on 19 June it was revived, together with the employer organizations, under the leadership of its old chairman, Krupp, as the Reich Estate of German Industry (*Reichsstand der deutschen Industrie*). In autumn the business organizations formally reorganized themselves, in a strict hierarchical fashion, into Reich groups according to corporative principles. But in spite of all opportunistic slogans – or rather, perhaps, because of them – important sectors of big industry were able to keep their own interests largely unaffected. Of course, this was officially proclaimed as a *Gleichschaltung* in accordance with National Socialist views, which replaced the dominant policies pursued by a majority of the members of the National Federation of German Industry. But at the same time it became clear that neither revolutionary action against property nor a promotion of middle-class interests was a top National Socialist priority. Hjalmar Schacht and, for a year, the Economics Minister and general director of the Allianz Insurance Company, Kurt Schmitt, were able to function as spokesmen for business within the government.

Hugenberg, who was supposedly the strong man in the cabinet, was able to set priorities neither in the relationship with large industrial concerns, nor in the area of agriculture. In agricultural organizations this was done rather by Richard Walter Darré, the head of the agricultural policy apparatus of the NSDAP, who became Minister of Agriculture in June 1933. Even earlier, the National Socialists had been strongly represented in most agricultural organizations. In part voluntarily and in part as a result of media pressure, the German Agrarian League and the farmers' organizations merged, and Darré took over the office of 'Reich leader'. In May the agricultural boards (*Landwirtschaftskammer*) were included. Darré became Reich Farmer Leader, and thus controlled everything relating to agriculture in the party, the state, and the formerly free farmers' organizations. Even large landowners who were well disposed towards the NSDAP were pushed aside, by the use, for example, of accusations of corruption; but large landholdings as such remained intact. Darré himself was a supporter of the 'blood and soil' ideology, a romantic exaltation of the soil as the source of national strength; and by the end of 1933 he began to work for the realization of his ideas in the most comprehensive, specifically National Socialist law up to that time, the Reich Hereditary Farm Law. This was based on an even more radical Prussian law, and was enacted on 29 September 1933. In only a few other areas was National Socialist ideology transformed so rapidly into actual policy. In addition, the Reich Food Estate (*Reichsnährstand*) was established that same autumn. This also marked the introduction of a new form of organization, in which members of a given professional group or class were put into corporations, as did the National Socialist Fighting Union for the Commercial Middle Class (*NS-Kampfbund für den gewerblichen Mittelstand*) for artisan and retail organizations. The leader of the latter, Adrian von Renteln, also became the head of the Union of German Industry and Commerce.

This Nazification of organizations which continued to exist contrasts sharply with the methods used in dealing with the free trade unions which, even during Schleicher's brief tenure as Chancellor, had moved away from the SPD and also resorted to a tactic of strict legalism. They no longer dared to openly support the SPD in their election proclamations, but attempted to reach an understanding with the new government. They protested emphatically, but without success, against attacks on union offices, which increased after March. Nevertheless, they also attempted to stay in existence by adapting to the new situation. One trade-union editorial, which called upon the 'national revolution' to 'translate its will to socialism into socialist deeds', stated: 'Socialist Germany will never become a reality without the nationalization of the socialist movement'.[12] The chairman of the free trade unions, Leipart, even offered to help Hitler in achieving an 'economic peace'. Of course, this opportunism was noted with approval in leading business circles. The German National Trade Union Federation joined with the Christian and the liberal Hirsch-Duncker unions in an informal 'Leadership Circle of the United Trade Unions' and demonstrated together with Hitler on 1 May, the 'Day of National Labour'. But all these efforts did not help the unions. By 17 April Joseph Goebbels, who had become Reich Minister for Popular Enlightenment and Propaganda, together with Hitler and the Reich organization leader of the party, Robert Ley, had already set the course they intended to pursue:

> We'll make 1 May into an overwhelming demonstration of German national will. On 2 May, trade union offices will be occupied. Here, too, everything will be [subjected to a] *Gleichschaltung*. There may be a lot of noise for a few days, but then they [the trade unions] will belong to us.[13]

And the National Socialists did proceed in this fashion, although in some cases this only involved confirming in a populistic manner the influence which already existed of the National Socialist Company Organizations (*Nationalsozialistische Betriebszellenorganisationen* or NSBO). Often trade union leaders were taken into protective custody after being mistreated, whereupon other trade unions submitted to the new line. However, the company cell organizations were given control of the facilities of the free trade unions only for a short time. On 10 May, without previous planning, the establishment of a new organization was announced, with Robert Ley as its head. In the German Labour Front (*Deutsche Arbeitsfront* or DAF) employers and employees were supposed to work together in a corporative structure.

Gleichschaltung, or 'bringing everything into line', was the catchword used by the National Socialists for events in the first half of 1933. This German technical term, meaning synchronization, was in itself quite neutral and even suggested a certain harmony; but from the very beginning of its use by the National Socialists a connotation clung to it of marching in step, of

adjusting to the mixture of force, new beginning, and opportunism which
were the new signs of the times. As far as civil servants were concerned, the
loss of their professional organizations and their merging them in the
National Socialist Civil Servant Union (*NS-Beamtenbund* or NSB) was less
important than preserving continuity in all sectors of public administration,
from the administration of justice to the diplomatic service and the schools.
Very few civil servants resigned voluntarily. Everywhere they tended to keep
on working under the new conditions, and this was made easier by the fact
that the National Socialists' actions during their conquest of power were still
formally legal. The preservation of legal forms was reassuring, even though
it often involved nothing more than a sanctioning of acts already committed
outside the law. As the key ministries of the interior in Germany and Prussia
in particular were in the hands of the National Socialists, the purge of
personnel there which had been started under Papen was accelerated. As
early as February 1933 fourteen police chiefs in large cities in Prussia were
relieved of their jobs, and previous office-holders were replaced at all levels,
from district administrators and the highest provincial administrative officials to ministerial civil servants. Most of the new functionaries were not
registered National Socialists but conservatives close to the German
National People's Party. Certainly, the National Socialists' coalition partners
were taken into account during this development; but what was more
important was the realization that hardly enough qualified National Socialists were available.

   This personnel shake-up bore fruit. Hardly had the direction of the new
government become clear after the election than a real boom in new members
began for the NSDAP. Taking developments in 1848 as an analogy, National
Socialists spoke ironically of 'March casualties' (*Märzgefallene*) when referring to those who joined the party for opportunistic reasons after the March
election. As Goebbels observed, for many people the letters NSDAP had
come to stand for *'Na, suchst Du auch ein Pöstchen?'* ('Well, are you looking
for a job, too?') To prevent this tendency from getting out of hand, a
membership stop was decreed at the beginning of May, which, however, still
permitted the acceptance of new members in special cases, often with a
seemingly honourable 'low' membership number. The demonstrative process of forcing Social Democrats, Liberals and – from the very beginning –
Jews out of positions in public and private life, in which the Nazis had been
turned loose against all Jews, from business people to judges, as early as 1
April, was diverted into formally legal channels on 7 April. A law with the
innocent-sounding title of 'Law for the Restoration of the Professional Civil
Service' was intended to 'create again a national civil service' by a 'ruthless
purge [of] all alien elements', Communists and other 'foreign bodies'.[14] The
law was soon applied in all areas of public employment, and then, by
analogy, in the independent professions and in culture, and deprived 'several
hundred Jewish university teachers, approximately 4,000 Jewish attorneys,
3,000 doctors, 2,000 civil servants, and an equal number of actors, actresses,

and musicians' (Thamer) of opportunities to practise their professions. There were hardly any 'party-book civil servants'. In the cabinet discussions of this law, Hitler expressly promised that members of the Centre Party would not be affected in future and that, in addition, membership of the NSDAP would not be made a requirement for public office. After the end of the political parties, the alliance between National Socialists and the conservatives continued to develop, in public offices and administration, a tendency towards a uniform élite loyal to the state. Party membership became a matter of expediency in advancing one's career.

THE TRANSFORMATION OF GERMAN SOCIETY WITHOUT A 'SECOND REVOLUTION'

'What we are now experiencing is only the transfer of our own dynamism and legality to the state. This is taking place with such breathtaking speed that one scarcely has any time to call his own,' Goebbels noted in his diary as early as 6 April.[15] The dynamism of the effort to synchronize everything in support of National Socialist aims affected almost all areas of society, the traditional pluralistic professional organizations and the various associations, even those in cultural and seemingly non-political areas. What has been said of the large interest associations was true, with variations, everywhere, at the national and regional levels and in individual cities and communities. In all organizations there were already more or less conspicuous National Socialist members, whose number now increased rapidly and who began publicly to demand positions of leadership. Representatives of the political left were chased away; a diverse, pluralistic social fabric of societies and associations was transformed into a single, uniform organization. Often assisted by intimidation, National Socialists took over leading positions as the victors of the hour. Finally, each organization restructured itself. Instead of a chairman, there would now be a 'leader'. Formal structures for conveying the wishes of rank-and-file members to the leadership were eliminated. The principle of leaders and followers was introduced, according to which the leader possessed all authority and responsibility.

Some developments were only seizures of power on a small scale; others were at first and occasionally only camouflage: old functionaries changed their titles, 'National Socialist' appeared before an organization's name, the statutes were changed, a swastika was added to the emblem. But the party organizations were constantly trying to expose such purely external acceptance, and this in turn offered abundant opportunities for denunciations and personal intrigues. The policy of bringing all organizations into line in support of National Socialist aims was often formulated in corporative terms, but this did not necessarily mean that it was made strictly uniform. What changed was the possibility of free organizational activity. Legitimation by state and/or party offices became necessary and, especially in the growing number of authority conflicts, offered opportunities for interference from outside. Formal acceptance of being brought into line gave protection not only from further interference by the party; occasionally it was repeated several times. The important thing was to demonstrate loyalty to and acceptance of the 'new state' at the organizational level.

The parliamentary political system was one of the first institutions in Germany to be modified in support of the new state; in other areas this process took several years, and in the end included the taking of power by National Socialists in the states and local communities, which resulted in the elimination of constitutional federative structures and the establishment of a centralized state. Most important at first was the elimination of the dualism in Prussia between the government of Otto Braun, formally still in office, and Reich Commissar von Papen. On 4 February 1933 a majority of the Prussian parliament rejected the suggestion that the parliament should dissolve itself, as did the majority of a three-man committee empowered to take such a step, in which Otto Braun and Konrad Adenauer out-voted a National Socialist. But with an emergency decree obtained by Papen and a second coup in Prussia the remaining powers of the Social Democrat, Braun, were transferred to the commissar, who then dissolved the Prussian parliament only 2 days later. In the other states (*Länder*), and in cities and local communities, this was done a day earlier. Only a few other German states already had National Socialist governments (Thuringia, Brunswick, Oldenburg, and Anhalt), but several had governments with minority cabinets whose function was merely that of caretaker; and developments in Prussia caused them considerable concern about their own position. As Hitler had formally promised to retain federalism, the Reich Senate (*Reichsrat*) made only a weak protest, on 16 February, against the methods used in Prussia. From then on, however, little was heard from the representatives of the German states in Berlin.

In the Reichstag election campaign the pressure on the state governments from the NSDAP increased, especially because of allegedly inadequate enforcement of emergency decrees which were, in fact, often obediently applied as the national government desired in anticipation of such pressure. In most cases immediately after election day, 5 March, the power of the state governments was broken within a few days. Usually this was achieved by the well-known dynamism of the National Socialist movement operating under directions from Berlin. National Socialist mass rallies and SA and SS parades served to celebrate the election victory. The conflict escalated when the National Socialists raised a swastika or a black, white, and red flag over city halls or government buildings. The police, who were occasionally pushed aside by the National Socialists, yielded to the pressure and in some cases even actively co-operated with them. Under the pretence of maintaining peace and order, Interior Minister Frick installed police commissars where that was still necessary. Most of them were leading regional National Socialist or SA functionaries in the states.

The most open confrontation took place in Bavaria, where Minister President Heinrich Held first secured the support of Hindenburg and then, following the pattern of 1923, attempted to mobilize the state police and the Reichswehr for his own protection. But his efforts were in vain. On 9 March he was forced to accept, under protest, the appointment by Frick of the former general and National Socialist, Franz Xaver Ritter von Epp, as General State Commissar. Under pressure, the state parliaments in Hamburg, Hesse, and Württemberg elected new governments led by National Socialists. In the other German states the recently named Reich commissars themselves took the initiative. In some cases they took over the state governments; in others other leading National Socialists, often Gau leaders,[16] were appointed; in many other cases, the commissar appointed additional ministers. Conflicts within the NSDAP about new sinecures were frequent; functionaries of the German National People's Party were considered only occasionally. Similar methods were used in the Prussian provinces, which were under Göring's authority. There Gau leaders and/or SA leaders were appointed as the highest provincial administrative officials, and at the same time the lower hierarchy was streamlined. Although the national government had promised in the Enabling Law to retain the Reich Senate, within a few days this promise turned out to be worthless. On 31 March 1933, following the model of the Enabling Law, a first law to subordinate all authorities to the National Socialist state transferred legislative authority to the governments and ordered a reconstitution of the state and communal parliaments, with seats distributed in proportion to the Reichstag election results.

As such, the German states with National Socialist governments could have strengthened the federal principle *vis-à-vis* Berlin. But at Hitler's initiative a law was issued a week later creating Reich governors (*Reichsstatthalter*) charged with maintaining the authority and carrying out the policies of Berlin in the states. Occasionally several small states were combined under Gau leaders in the following months, who then gave the position of Minister President to their party comrades. The Reich Governors were given informal general authority; each was 'a kind of viceroy of the Reich' (Hitler).[17] At first, conferences of the Reich Governors formed an important executive instrument of the Reich Chancellor. Given Hitler's aversion to bureaucracy, such a system could not possibly create clear administrative law and legal distinctions. In Prussia, Hitler himself took over the position of Reich Governor, and Papen resigned ignominiously from the central office of temporary Minister-President, thus marking another step in the political decline of Hitler's conservative backers. Hitler delegated his authority as Reich Governor of Prussia to Göring, who had already taken over the office of Prussian Minister-President. In an additional step the Prussian and Reich ministries were combined, both in fact and in the person of Göring. Because of Hitler's preference for active, dynamic individuals a Reich administrative reform in a National Socialist and bureaucratic spirit, such as Frick attempted to promote for years, had no chance of success. Absurd hierarchies, such as the one the Munich Gau leader Adolf Wagner described in a letter to Frick on 23 June 1934, were characteristic of the developing National Socialist system, but they had no practical significance:

> According to the present legal situation, the Reich governors are subordinate to you as Minister of the Interior. Adolf Hitler is the Reich Governor of Prussia. He has delegated his authority to the Prussian Minister President. You yourself are, however, also Prussian Minister of the Interior. Adolf Hitler and the Prussian Minister President are, however, legally subordinate to you as Reich Minister of the Interior. As you, the same person, are also Prussian Minister of the Interior, you are on the other hand subordinate to the Prussian Minister President and to yourself as Reich Minister of the Interior.[18]

The formal end of German federalism and the last remnants of parliamentary government took place on the first anniversary of Hitler's coming to power. On 30 January 1934 the Reichstag and, somewhat later, the Reich Senate passed a law whose content was still to be determined by the actual distribution of power in practice: 'The parliaments of the [German] states are abolished. The powers of the states are transferred to the Reich. The state governments are subordinate to the Reich government . . . The Reich government can enact new constitutional law.'

At first glance the triumph of Hitler and the National Socialists seemed complete. But the limits become clearer if one considers which forces within the National Socialist movement were not able to have their way, at least for the time being. Certainly before 1933 the movement had developed neither the organizational nor the ideological unity it claimed to have. Not every wish could be satisfied after the National Socialists took power in 1933. The Baltic German Alfred Rosenberg laid claim to being the NSDAP's chief ideologue and had even developed, among other ideas, a new Germanic, anti-Christian religion that might serve as the basis for imperialistic expansion. At first his ambitions were concentrated on the state Ministry of Foreign Affairs, but he had to be satisfied with the establishment of a Foreign Policy Office (*Aussen olitisches Amt*) of the NSDAP, with which he was able to pursue, to a very limited extent, his own policies towards other countries, like Great Britain and the northern European states. His Fighting Union for German Culture, founded in 1929, was not able to gain any influence in a Reich Chamber of Culture dominated by Joseph Goebbels.

The engineer Gottfried Feder also belonged to the early National Socialists. His thesis of the need to break 'interest slavery'[19] – 'the con lition of the nations under money or interest slavery of all-Jewish high finance'– embodied an important current of feeling within the NSDAP, as its anti-capitalist slogans appealed primarily to workers, farmers, and owners of small middle-class businesses. Although, according to this view, normal entrepreneurs, as 'exploiters' and 'blood suckers', did make profits, they at least also created jobs. Department stores, on the other hand, enticed people to senseless consumption by 'awakening completely unnecessary needs'. Like the big banks, they constituted the enemy of the economy. From this perspective, Hugenburg, Schmitt, and Schacht were quite the wrong people. But Feder and his like never had a chance to put their ideas into practice. In the economy, the introduction of the Führer principle and the corporative order were completely sufficient. Feder himself continued in office for a year as State Secretary in the Ministry of Economics, but remained without any influence there, and dedicated himself subsequently to theoretical studies of city construction and planning.

In the period of the conquest of power, the National Socialist Fighting League for the Commercial Middle Class took Feder's theses seriously: consumer co-operatives were boycotted, as were department stores, especially if they belonged to Jews. On 1 April 1933 this was only co-ordinated by the state, but by August the league was already dissolved. Its successor, the more traditionally inclined German Retail Federation (*Gesamtverband des deutschen Einzelhandels*), was merged with the German Labour Front. The postponing of additional actions against the department stores until further notice, and the fact that their activities were hampered by only minor restrictions, were generally not accepted in the NSDAP. A 'Jewish' concern, Hertie, was even reorganized with state funds. On the whole the department stores recovered; only the 'Jewish' ones fell victim to 'organized popular anger' in 1938. All this was typical. In 1939 the *Völkischer Beobachter* observed: 'With middle-class ideologues one can't create a national community with a real national economy.'[20]

In themselves the NSBO, since the beginning of 1933 under the leadership of Robert Ley as successor to Gregor Strasser, seemed incompatible with the Führer principle. They were intended to be the arm of the SA in businesses and factories and, through their opposition to both employers and 'Marxist' unions, they developed more and more into representatives of the interests of workers (including agricultural workers) and employees. They became a rallying-point for socially revolutionary forces that played a major role in the violent actions against the free trade unions, including their dissolution, in the spring. The events of 2 May were, therefore, an act of spontaneous terror that went beyond the will of the organizations. In the elections to works councils (*Betriebsräte*) in March 1933 the NSBO did achieve respectable gains in mining and the chemical and steel industries compared with the previous year, but on the whole the support they received, 25 per cent, remained disappointing for the National Socialists. This led to a postponement of further elections to work councils for the time being. Thereafter the NSBO belonged to the German Labour Front but retained a certain independence. Nevertheless, its organizational capacity was often inadequate for the task of taking over the property of the trade unions.

The main reasons for the growth in NSBO membership from the old parties of the left and the trade unions probably varied from opportunism to subversion. Membership rose from 372,000 in March 1933 to 727,000 in May. In November 1934, the NSBO had 1,336,000 members.[21] But they lost the right to collect dues, and their claim to formulate social policy was effectively eliminated by the installation of state trustees of labour on 19 May 1933. The intention was to confine the NSBO completely to its propaganda function as the 'SA of companies and factories', as Robert Ley put it. Many would-be revolutionaries among NSBO functionaries showed 'to a frightening degree . . . a spirit of pure class conflict', one trustee complained. There were threats against the 'great gentlemen of the concerns' as 'parasites in power' who would 'have to be removed by force'. Another trustee spoke of the NSBO as 'disguised Marxists'. This indicated a trend, and Ley set himself the task of reducing the influence of the organizations by personnel purges, among other means. 'The German Labour Front is the organization of all working people regardless of their economic and social position. In it the employee stands next to the employer', a proclamation claimed in November 1933. The Law for the Regulation of National Labour of 20 January 1934 remained vague in many areas, but it did serve as a kind of basic social law of the Third Reich. In companies and factories it made the Führer-and-follower principle the norm, and gave the works councils and shop stewards the power to participate only in internal social questions. The discontent in large parts of the NSBO continued to smoulder in the first half of 1934.

Like the members of the NSBO, those of the SA did not necessarily have to belong to the NSDAP when they joined.[22] Fluctuations in membership, which were rather high in the other two organizations, reached almost 50 per cent in the SA by 1933. After the National Socialists came to power, the SA, unlike the NSDAP, continued to accept new members. From 700,000 in January 1933 it grew to 2.9 million by August 1934 (without the SA-Reserve II). This was an impressive figure, even if one considers that the *Stahlhelm* had already been incorporated into the SA in the summer of 1933 and was integrated into the active formations, or the SA-Reserves I and II, according to age and thus fitness for service. Not including these groups – approximately 1.4 million additional men – 750,000 to 950,000 former members of the *Stahlhelm* were probably involved. Of course, as a result of this growth, the SA was no longer a uniform paramilitary organization, and internally it was divided into various groups such as the SA cavalry, the SA naval units, and the SA flyers. But there remained a core of old fighters who believed that they had borne the brunt of the street fighting and had thus conquered power. They wanted no consolidation, but rather asserted that the real revolution had still not taken place. As early as March and April 1933 the National Socialist leadership had been forced to admonish its followers to proceed in a lawful manner. Occasionally this was directed at certain party activities, but primarily it was at the civil war mentality of the SA, many of whose members believed, 'We've won; now it's our turn.' Often they also believed that they were now in a better position to settle personal feuds or to become richer. 'Individual business sense and a search for government jobs' were indeed factors, but 'unclear, anti-capitalistic resentment viewed from the perspective of middle-class interests' (Jamin) were probably the dominant factors here.

Business circles increasingly complained about this, as did the party leadership. Hitler, nominally the highest SA chief, and Ernst Röhm, his Chief of Staff and the SA's actual leader, had been close friends since the 'time of struggle' (*Kampfzeit*); indeed, it was Röhm who had discovered Hitler's political talents. This was why his appearances with his followers were marked by increasing self-confidence, even towards Hitler. As Röhm clearly stated in June 1933:

> The SA and SS [will] not permit the German revolution to lose its momentum or be betrayed by the non-fighters halfway to the goal! Not for their sake, but for Germany's. For the brown army is the last defence of the nation, the last bulwark against Communism. If the German revolution fails because of reactionary resistance, because of incompetence and inertia, the German people will be plunged into despair and will be easy prey for the blood-stained madness from the expanses of Asia. That is why the idea that keeping peace is the first duty of the citizen, which today dominates the thinking of some people who have been brought into line and even the thinking of some worthy gentlemen who call themselves National Socialists, is a betrayal of the German revolution.[23]

'Whether they like it or not,' he wrote, 'we'll continue our fight. If they finally understand what it's about, with their help; if they don't want to understand, without them! And if necessary, against them!' This was indirectly aimed at Hitler, who thereupon proclaimed the end of the revolution on 6 July:

> More revolutions have succeeded at the first attempt than have been slowed and then stopped. Revolution is not a permanent condition and it must not become one. The free flood of the revolution has to be channelled into the safe bed of evolution . . . One must not therefore remove an economist if he is a good economist but still not a National Socialist, and especially not if the National Socialist one puts in his place doesn't understand anything about economics. In the economy, ability alone should be the decisive consideration.

The conflict could not be decided at this purely verbal level. Röhm and Rudolf Hess (for the NSDAP) were appointed Reich ministers without portfolio in December 1933, and on many occasions Hitler praised the self-sacrificing activity of his brown-clad battalions. But all that did not change the fact that 'the SA man will soon not know if we are really in power'. The SA auxiliary police were dissolved, in Prussia on 2 August and in the rest of Germany on 31 December 1933. Unemployment among SA men was above average for the country as a whole. Unlike other National Socialist leaders, higher leaders in the SA had received few sinecures. Given the demand for a change in the élites of German society, the armed forces were basically the only possibility remaining for the SA. Röhm expressed this in a metaphor of the 'grey rock' (the Reichswehr) that had to be submerged by the 'brown flood'. This suggested that the best solution would be a dissolution of the Reichswehr in favour of a militarily restructured National Socialist people's army in the form of the SA. At the very least this would involve taking over a large number of SA officers at all levels into the expanded armed forces. But for Hitler there could in principle be no question of such a thing: he needed a powerful instrument of aggression for his foreign-policy goals, and even greatly improved discipline could not make the SA into such an instrument. At best the SA could become a militia, as Hitler implied to the Reichswehr, the SA, and the SS on 28 February 1934.

It was thus practical necessity, and not primarily loyalty, that bound Hitler to his initial promises to the still-powerful Reichswehr. And from their privileged position the generals certainly made efforts to achieve co-operation with the SA. After all, the SA did constitute a mass of 'valuable human material', which should be enlisted in the support of the state. Indeed, this had been part of the conservative programme that had brought Hitler to power. But, unlike the programme for other sectors, this one succeeded. In the discussion already mentioned, Hitler approved Blomberg's proposal 'to use the SA for frontier protection and preliminary training . . . In other areas the armed services must be the only bearers of arms for the nation.'[24] But this did not stop the infighting. Neither Röhm nor even less his non-commissioned officers intended to abide by this agreement, which would have reduced the SA to insignificance. As in the previous year, talk of a second revolution began to be heard with concern in business circles. Judging by all that we now know, Röhm himself did not plan a *putsch*. He still intended to realize his claim to power through and with Hitler. It can be considered an outward indication of this that he sent the entire SA on furlough on 8 June 1934, without instructions for the future, and only repeated his threats against all enemies of the SA once.

But discontentment and anger were not confined to those who wanted to accelerate the revolution; their feelings were also shared by those conservatives who had envisaged a very different kind of authoritarian state. Continued unemployment, economic and supply problems, corruption, and lawlessness formed the general background for this development in the winter of 1933–1934. This dissatisfaction crystallized around Vice-Chancellor von Papen. Because only informal or conspiratorial opposition was now possible, there was no co-ordinated action. As Hindenburg's death seemed imminent, attempts were made in vain to induce him to express in his will a wish for the restoration of the monarchy, an idea that had been repeatedly aired in various circles for Germany or Prussia or Bavaria since the previous year. It was hoped that the increasing gravity of the SA crisis might trigger a conservative reaction and, with Reichswehr support, lead to a typical military dictatorship. On 17 June 1934, at the University of Marburg, Papen made a speech written by his close co-worker, Edgar Jung, a leading neo-conservative thinker, in which he openly criticized the 'unnatural totality claims of National Socialism'.[25] He was concerned about re-establishing a state of law, about a clear separation of state authority from the 'constant dynamism' [of National Socialism], 'lack of principles, untruthfulness, ungentlemanly behaviour and arrogance'. The speech was not publicized; the speaker was arrested; and Papen submitted his resignation, which Hitler rejected.

To be sure, Papen and his followers did not have any power base, nor did he enjoy the support of influential groups. The armed forces were only interested in the elimination of the SA. A strange coalition of interests developed which, in addition to leading figures of the regime, included jealous functionaries of the NSDAP and of the SS, formally subordinate to the SA. Some members of the coalition probably believed rumours that the SA was organizing a *putsch*, and a pogrom atmosphere developed that seemed to demand immediate action. Göring and Goebbels, Himmler and Reinhard Heydrich, as well as military leaders such as von Blomberg and his Chief of Staff, von Reichenau, and the Commander-in-Chief of the army, von Fritsch, were all involved or at least informed, and this was also true of many regional functionaries. The armed forces provided weapons and transportation, and were prepared to intervene if necessary.

FROM THE 'RÖHM *PUTSCH*' TO THE 'BLOMBERG CRISIS' IN 1938

The actual operation was carried out by the SS and the police. On 29 and 30 June, Hitler himself participated by personally arresting the SA leaders, and in particular Röhm, who had been invited to Bad Wiessee under the guise of attending a conference. Even earlier, Göring, Heydrich, and probably also Blomberg had drawn up death-lists, to which they added names on an *ad hoc* basis. Until 2 July senior SA leaders were killed without any legal authority in Munich, in other places in Bavaria, and also primarily in Pomerania and Silesia. Murder squads frequently confused the names of their intended victims. In addition to General von Schleicher, his wife was also shot, as was his predecessor in the office of Reichswehr Minister, General von Bredow. Vice Chancellor von Papen was placed under house arrest; Jung and one of his co-workers were killed. Moreover, old accounts from the failed *putsch* of 1923 were settled. A total of 89 people fell victim to the conspiracy of the Reich leadership. On 3 July a terse law declared the 'measures taken' to be legal, and somewhat later Hitler appeared before the Reichstag. 'In that hour', he proclaimed, 'I was responsible for the fate of the German nation and was therefore the highest judge of the German people.'[26] One of Germany's most renowned experts in constitutional law, Carl Schmitt, justified the action as an extra-legal emergency situation under the title 'The Führer Protects the Law'. The Reichswehr placed its bureaucratic interests above its very real horror at the murder of two generals. The fact that persons outside the SA had been killed was criticized, too, in the general population. But 'people are aware that these incidents were excesses carried out without the knowledge and against the will of the Führer and [other] leading persons'. This was just as untrue as the imputation of a *putsch*, which was embellished with tales of the homosexuality of Röhm and other SA leaders to increase feelings of popular revulsion. In any case the opinion generally prevailed that 'the crushing of the Röhm revolt has had the effect of a cleansing thunderstorm. The nightmare oppressing the people has been followed by a great sigh of relief.' Thus the general feeling was one of stabilization, of the long-hoped-for beginning of normal conditions.

This series of developments was concluded by the expected death of Paul von Hindenburg on 2 August 1934. A day earlier a law had been decreed which united the offices of Reich President and Reich Chancellor in the single person of Adolf Hitler. And the armed services themselves seized the initiative for an oath of loyalty to their supreme commander, the 'Führer and Reich Chancellor', as he was now called. Hindenburg's funeral at the Tannenberg Memorial for the hero of the First World War, which dated from the Weimar Republic and was decorated with swastika flags for the occasion, marked the end of an epoch and the burial of one of the gravediggers of the Weimar Republic. Papen was sent as ambassador to Vienna.

However one may assess the ideological orientation and the social positioning, together with the alliance possibilities, of the conservative reactionaries around Papen; a return to a state of law with an authoritarian structure was now no longer possible without the elimination of the entire National Socialist regime. There could no longer be any question of an open organization of conservative forces. But in spite of the more or less complete control over all social and political organizations established by the National Socialist regime in 1934, the fact that certain conservative élites were indispensable for the National Socialists as alliance partners enabled them to maintain a certain independence, and in some respects their position was even strengthened. For the killings were followed by lengthy disciplinary purges of the SA. Its activism and revolutionary morale were broken, to be unleashed only once in the following years, on 9 November 1938. As with the SA, the NSBOs were also eliminated as independent and potentially activist organizations, being basically brought into line through complete incorporation into the German Labour Front. This perhaps explains the murder of Gregor Strasser who, as Ley's predecessor, would have been best suited to strengthening the position of the 'left' wing of the party.

Thus the multi-directional, mobile phase of the National Socialist regime ended in mid-1934. Of course, the 'blood and soil' ideology sponsored by

Darré was formally carried out in agricultural policy. The Reich Hereditary Farm Law of November 1933 was intended to lay the foundation for a new farmer class and a renewal of agriculture by defining who was a farmer, establishing inheritance rights, and by other means. But this involved only minimum interference in property relationships. More important was the unification of all aspects of agriculture, including distribution, in the Reich Food Estate as a mass organization which, however, essentially led to a greater bureaucratization and not to a real restructuring. The limits of this policy soon became evident in the appearance of supply problems for the population. Unlike the agricultural sector, the conservative élites were able to maintain the basis of their positions in business and the armed forces. Only their traditional opportunities to articulate their views were restricted. The violent settling of differences at the highest levels of state authority was approved in a plebiscite by 89.9 per cent of those participating, with 95.7 per cent of eligible people voting. Possible falsifications of the vote notwithstanding, this figure shows not only a consolidation of the regime, but also, above all, the popularity of Adolf Hitler.

From this point on, the questions of who had been a National Socialist for a long time, who had become one only recently, and who did not belong to any party were no longer so important in German politics. The pressure to conform was stronger in the state sector than in industry. In any case, soldiers were not permitted to belong to a party. The important factor now was how individual groupings and their representatives participated in what was called 'the great reconstruction work of the Führer'. Here there were more heated discussions about the course, means, and pace of the policies of the regime. All these disputes, however, were marked by, and took place within the context of, preparations for war. In the economy, Hjalmar Schacht acquired the influence of an economic dictator after mid-1934. But in a raw-materials and foreign-currency crisis, after the spring of 1936, he preferred to take a slower course and reintegrate Germany into the world economy. As a result, Hermann Göring was able to build up his own apparatus and claim comprehensive authority in certain areas of economic policy after September 1936. His Office of the Four Year Plan pushed Schacht's Ministry of Economics more and more into the background. At the end of 1937 Schacht resigned as Minister of Economics and, at the beginning of 1939, as President of the Reich Bank.

In the Foreign Ministry, the traditional diplomatic corps played an essential role in defending the legal change of government in relations with other countries, and was able to maintain its internal unity under Foreign Minister von Neurath and State Secretary Bernhard Wilhelm von Bülow (who died in the spring of 1936), although numerous diplomats joined the NSDAP. More important was the substance of German foreign policy, which increasingly came to be conducted outside the Foreign Ministry. This was not so true of special interests, such as the Foreign Organization of the NSDAP which assumed responsibility for Germans abroad and which, under its leader

Ernst Wilhelm Bohle (carrying, after 1937, the rank of State Secretary), was incorporated into the Foreign Ministry, or of the Foreign Policy Office of the NSDAP under Rosenberg. It was more often individual National Socialist leaders such as Göring or Goebbels, together with Rosenberg and, above all, Joachim von Ribbentrop, who intervened in the area of foreign policy, sometimes on special missions for Hitler but also on their own authority. On 4 February 1938 Ribbentrop, who had already been German Ambassador in London for 2 years, actually became Foreign Minister. He was given Ernst von Weizsäcker, a career diplomat, as new State Secretary, who for his part hoped to turn back the purely bureaucratic apparatus the Foreign Ministry had become into the 'motor' of German foreign policy.

The situation in the armed services was more complex. In the 1920s the Reichswehr had secured a position as one of the more important élites supporting the state and, in spite of parliamentary control, had largely been able to define itself and its professional aims independently of the democratic system, which it disdainfully described as a 'state of parties'. This was at first due to the limitations placed on the German armed forces by the Treaty of Versailles in 1919, which made it possible to keep the élite relatively homogeneous. For example, the number of officer candidates from the traditional source, the nobility, once more increased. Together with the murders of June 1934, Hitler's assurance to the leaders of the Reichswehr that it would remain the sole bearer of arms for the nation strengthened their alliance with the new rulers. It was hardly noticed that, almost as an expression of thanks, the Reichswehr (officially called the Wehrmacht after 16 March 1935) for the first time permitted the SS to assume certain military responsibilities, thus creating a new rival for itself in the long term. The metaphor used by Hitler, that the party and the armed services were two columns supporting the new state, corresponded fairly closely to the self-image of the military leaders, who consequently issued a large number of internal decrees, especially in the areas of training and indoctrination, promoting the adjustment of the military establishment to National Socialism. Of course there were, at first, opportunistic reasons why the military leaders around Blomberg and Reichenau had to prevent a strengthening of the SA and bring the military establishment into line behind the National Socialist regime, thus avoiding the process being forced upon them from outside. But the policy of maximum rearmament, which will be described later and on which they completely agreed with Hitler, was decisive.

A critical change of personnel and reorganization in the military establishment became possible not because of any difference of opinion with Hitler over the Policy of maximum rearmament and the foreign-policy risks it involved, but for other, incidental reasons. Through his marriage to a former prostitute Blomberg had offended the traditional views of the officer caste. Von Fritsch had been expected to be his successor, but because of a fabricated accusation of homosexuality he was also morally discredited. But it was not the pro-Nazi Reichenau who became the chief of the Wehrmacht, nor the dynamic National Socialist, Göring, who commanded the Luftwaffe. Rather, Hitler chose not to allow the positions to be strengthened of people who were, after all, conceivably potential rivals; and, after some hesitation and improvisation in accordance with his supreme-command authority as head of state, he himself assumed the title of Commander-in-Chief of the Wehrmacht on 4 February 1938, which for the first time gave him direct powers of military command. The office of Minister of War itself was abolished, and Wilhelm Keitel, a general from the military bureaucracy, became head of the new Wehrmacht High Command (*Oberkommando der Wehrmacht* or OKW), which functioned as Hitler's military office. At the same time, comprehensive personnel changes were carried out within the Wehrmacht and in other areas.[27] Six senior generals of the Luftwaffe and ten of the army were retired, and at least forty-four other generals were transferred. In addition to a reshuffling in the Foreign Ministry itself, three leading ambassadors were retired. Other organizational and personnel changes affected the Ministry of Economics, the propaganda ministry, and the Reich Chancellery.

There seems to have been no uniform line in these changes. Of course, several conservative military leaders and diplomats were removed who were considered critics of the regime. But their successors were not necessarily convinced National Socialists. More important was the trend to rejuvenation and thus, in Hitler's view, to a new push of dynamic energy for the regime to move forward, especially in its consistent policy of preparing for war. To screen this particular motive from the public, and probably also to calm those affected, a 'Secret Cabinet Council for Foreign Policy Questions' was appointed under the direction of the previous Foreign Minister, von Neurath. In addition to leading National Socialists, the council also included the top military leaders. It suffered, however, from one shortcoming: it never really existed, as it never met.

On 4 February 1938 the consolidation of National Socialist power was concluded. After that date the National Socialist dictatorship had sufficient influence for its purposes over the military, and thus over the last potential instrument of conservative power. Especially in a regime based upon and orientated towards the use of force at home and abroad, this constituted a central element in the stabilization of its rule.

|3|

Preparing for War

HITLER AND THE SECOND ATTEMPT TO MAKE GERMANY A WORLD POWER

After the failure of Germany's attempt to become a world power in the First World War, the country's position as a great power was reduced, but not eliminated as such, by the Treaty of Versailles in 1919. German colonies were placed under League of Nations mandates. North Schleswig, Eupen-Malmedy, Alsace-Lorraine in the north and west, and parts of the provinces of Posen, West Prussia, and Upper Silesia in the east formed the core of the territorial cessions usually justified on ethnic grounds. Germany's military strength was limited to 100,000 men for its land forces and 15,000 for its navy. In addition, there were other partly temporary limitations. The most serious of these seemed to be reparations. Because of the refusal by large parts of the German population to acknowledge the country's military defeat, and selective agitation directed at the treaty's claim of German war guilt, the prevailing reaction to reparations was one of moral indignation.

'Revision' of the treaty became a buzz word behind which the most varied intentions could be concealed: they could be aimed at a particular restriction in the treaty, or at all of them together; they could make use of economic means or be based only on diplomatic negotiation, or they could include military elements. At the beginning of the 1920s some advocates of revision sought quick successes – which would have meant a new war – but others envisaged a long effort, by peaceful means if possible, to achieve their goals. And revision was not necessarily limited to re-establishing Germany's frontiers of 1914. Some revisionists promoted a state of all Germans, including, for example, the annexation of Austria; others supported a German economic and perhaps even political hegemony in Central Europe and beyond. Their demands culminated in the catchphrase of the 're-establishment of

Germany's position as a great power', which at its most extreme could also mean finally realizing the expectations of victory in the First World War in a second attempt. Few Germans realized that in comparison to 1914 the chances of achieving this aim had actually improved, as the United States, the world's leading economic power, was also interested in an economically strong Germany, the new Soviet Union was still in a phase of internal consolidation and not a significant factor in international politics, and the world-power positions of Great Britain and France had been weakened as a result of the First World War.

The second dominant line of Weimar foreign policy, represented by Foreign Minister Gustav Stresemann, placed its faith in the economy, and sought as a first aim to achieve international integration through diplomacy. But it encountered difficulties even before the world economic crisis which began in 1929. Nevertheless, Brüning was able to build on this foundation in his policy of deliberately using the collapse of the world economic system as a lever to achieve complete international freedom of action for Germany. In July 1932, under Papen, this policy led to an end of reparations with agreement on a final sum, which was never paid; on 11 December 1932, a five-power declaration accepted future German military equality in principle, although no provision was made for turning the declaration into reality. In the threefold crisis of the European system of nations, the world economic order, and German democracy, German foreign policy thus won considerable successes in its policy of revision, and gained more room to manœuvre. And these successes opened new possibilities for any German government, possibilities which were completely independent of the later National Socialist assumption of power, and which improved with signs of an easing of the world economic crisis.

Hitler advocated the most radical policy. His views were based on his conception of international politics as a permanent struggle – including, in the final analysis, war – and he had always considered the world to be a challenge cup belonging to the strongest power. Since 1930 he had often spoken publicly of his aim of German world domination. This was meant literally, although it did not seem to have any relation to the reality of international relations in the twentieth century, and was based solely on his conviction of a numerically superior 'Aryan' racial core and his absolute determination to fight for his aims. Within a few days after he became Chancellor he attempted to obtain the support of his conservative political partners for his broader goals. The heads of the army and navy, and also Foreign Minister von Neurath, probably listened with friendly scepticism to Hitler's remarks about immediate domestic conquest and consolidation of political power. These remarks extended from the education of youth and the nation to the struggle to achieve a relative economic recovery on an agrarian basis, and to the build-up of the armed forces, which constituted the 'most important precondition for achieving the goal: regaining political power'.[1] But agrarian settlements would not produce any decisive success in the final analysis, as 'the territory for natural expansion (*Lebensraum*) for the German people' was 'too small'. 'How is political power to be used when it has been achieved?' Hitler asked, according to the summary notes of a general who was present. 'That [cannot be] said now. Perhaps to win new export possibil[ities]; perhaps – and probably better – to conquer new *Lebensraum* in the east and [carry out] its ruthless Germanization. [It is] certain that with political power and struggle, the present economic conditions can be changed.' This sweeping programme was in complete agreement with his spoken and written statements of the past decade, and implied a clear sequence of steps to be taken: first, psychological, economic, and military preparation at home for war; then a war to solve the supposedly existing problems of *Lebensraum*, which could not be solved otherwise. An integral part of this programme was to be a war to enslave Eastern Europe and especially the Soviet Union. Between these two aims, however, several connecting links were still necessary, which could be described straightforwardly as practical policy. To most of Hitler's listeners this programme probably seemed a quite utopian fantasy that had little to do with the realities of power politics and international relations in 1933. Nevertheless, his visions formed the guiding principles of his actual policies. It is thus clear that National Socialist dynamism did not represent a mobilization of popular energies as an end in itself, or solely for purposes of social integration, but rather, it reflected a self-imposed historical mission that envisaged preparation for a war unlimited in principle, and it attempted to awaken and satisfy widespread longings in German society as a way to achieving that aim.

THE CHANGE OF COURSE, 1933

In his views about the proper future aims, or at least the proper course, of German foreign policy, Hitler was not without his critics. In mid-March 1933, in reaction to Hitler's remarks, State Secretary von Bülow of the Foreign Ministry produced a long memorandum on future options for German foreign policy, the essential points of which Neurath presented to the cabinet.[2] But the differences of opinion with Hitler were not resolved. As Neurath observed rather defensively, Germany would not have to renounce dealing with broad political questions in future, but it should emphasize economic and financial policy tasks in the medium term. 'Obtaining advantages for Germany from the continuing changes in Europe and the world' should be given only second priority. The most important thing – and here the foreign ministry agreed with Hitler – was to push forward the 'revision of Versailles', and in that regard there was still much to be done.

Because of Germany's military weakness, a military balance, even with Poland, could be achieved only in 5 years. As a debtor country with a large market for consumer goods, Germany would find considerable international support in overcoming its economic crisis. For this reason the exploitation of step-by-step possibilities for revision was to be left to the diplomats, who would apply an 'artichoke theory' and 'avoid political and economic danger zones'. A good relationship with France was impossible, but it was desirable to have such a relationship with England. However, both powers had common interests, so that Germany should co-operate with fascist Italy against France. The United States could not be counted on in the long term, but conflicts in trade and financial policy had to be expected. Neurath carefully weighed small, individual revisionist steps for the Chancellor. Only the recommendation that 'an understanding with Poland' was 'neither possible nor desirable' pointed to aims beyond this gradualist approach. Interim solutions in the revision of Germany's eastern frontiers were to be rejected; 'only one more partition of Poland' was ultimately acceptable. But to achieve it Germany would need the Soviet Union as a partner; this could be combined very well with anti-Communism at home. Thus, as Bülow's memorandum and Neurath's presentation showed, a National Socialist and a traditional Wilhelminian line confronted each other in German foreign policy. But in the area of practical politics, at least in the short term, the two tendencies were in general agreement; moreover, ministers such as Hugenberg advocated publicly, as did Papen internally, an anti-Bolshevik foreign policy that was in many respects similar to Hitler's long-term aims.

In May 1933 von Neurath and von Blomberg placed Germany on a course of international confrontation at the Disarmament Conference of the League of Nations in Geneva, when they planned Germany's withdrawal from the Conference and the League, in order to prevent the military 'equality' which had already been conceded to Germany in principle from being restricted for a further long period in a general disarmament convention. Such a frontal attack, against which Neurath had warned Hitler earlier, gave the latter the chance to show that he had taken the lesson to heart. With his 'peace speech' to the Reichstag on 17 May 1933 he presented himself as a co-operative political leader. Although he clearly indicated his future aims with his words about satisfying Germany's 'honour and rights', he had ignored more militant suggestions for his speech from his experts. Moreover, on 5 May 1933 the German government extended the German-Soviet neutrality treaty of 1926, which had long been under discussion. Just as readily, Germany accepted the suggestion of the Italian dictator Mussolini to create a kind of directing committee of the European great powers by concluding a four-power treaty, to include Britain and France (but excluding the Soviet Union). This treaty, however, was not developed beyond the point of being initialled, for in the meantime events in Germany – the terror, incidents in the streets, and the persecution of the Jews – began to create serious problems for the preservation of German interests abroad. Nevertheless, the cover provided by the Foreign Ministry for these allegedly purely domestic political measures helped to prevent other countries from fully comprehending the real extent of the changes taking place in Germany. The tendency to consider Germany under Hitler as still a normal, predictable state in the world community, or at least to believe that it could be induced to become such, did not change.

The British in particular made efforts to keep German military strength low by establishing a generally low level in the proposed armaments convention. But France which, in view of the changed political situation in Germany, wanted to impose an additional probationary period of several years before permitting a limited German rearmament, resisted this plan. Thereupon, on 14 October 1933, in agreement with his advisers, Hitler, in a new great speech to the Reichstag, took advantage of the situation to proclaim Germany's withdrawal from the disarmament conference and from the League of Nations. In Germany, this very popular decision was confirmed by a plebiscite (and a Reichstag election), and it demonstrated German unity to other countries. But it was not entirely without risk; the Reichswehr made plans for emergency operations in case military sanctions were introduced against Germany. However, because of the differences between Britain and France, the German gamble succeeded. The other European powers reacted only with protests, if at all. In past years the League of Nations had served increasingly as a sounding-board for German revisionist demands, but in Germany itself it enjoyed little popularity. Hitler's decision to withdraw from the League marked an important, fundamental change: a rejection of a policy based largely on multilateral obligations in favour of one of power politics and national egoism.

Against the resistance of the Foreign Ministry, Hitler pushed through a first, fundamental change of course in relations with Poland and the Soviet Union. As late as the spring of 1933 there were signs of an imminent military confrontation with Germany's eastern neighbour, whose authoritarian government encouraged the spreading of rumours that it was planning preventive military action against Germany. This was intended to prevent an accommodation of the Western Powers with Germany and even involved a threat to seize certain areas to be used as pawns. In view of Germany's relative military weakness, these plans were not unrealistic. But Hitler did not worry about this when he used diplomatic channels to offer Poland a settlement at the beginning of May. After several hesitant feelers, the hostile press campaigns were moderated, a renunciation of force was announced, and finally, on 26 January 1934, a non-aggression pact for 10 years was concluded. Apart from the concordat with the Vatican in July 1933, this was the first significant foreign-policy success of the new government. The agreement was all the more remarkable because it was concluded after Germany had left the League of Nations, and thus marked not only Poland's attempt to pursue an independent great-power policy between Germany and the Soviet Union, but also indicated her turning away from reliance on collective security as advocated by the Western Powers and, a short time later, by the Soviet Union.

On the other hand, German-Soviet relations rapidly deteriorated. This was not necessarily a direct result of the anti-Communist terror in Germany, which also extended to Soviet establishments there; Stalin was able to disregard that. German-Soviet economic relations, which had developed especially during the world depression, could not slow this deterioration. Meanwhile, the co-operation between the Reichswehr and the Red Army which had been important for both sides in the 1920s – the Germans had tested weapons prohibited by the Treaty of Versailles on Soviet territory while the Soviet Union profited from German know-how – had outlived its usefulness as a result of the German rearmament and was ended by the Reichswehr by August 1933, when the development of weapons and the training of personnel for tanks, gas warfare, and the Luftwaffe had created some of the preconditions for German rearmament. However, not only did the Soviet government regret the end of this co-operation, but in other areas, too, Stalin indicated that he was prepared to continue normal relations with Germany, quite along the lines proposed by Neurath and Bülow.

After the end of 1933, however, the National Socialists succeeded in bringing about a turning-away from Moscow motivated by their anti-Bolshevik ideology. The German rejection of a joint guarantee for the independence of the three Baltic States proposed by Soviet Foreign Minister Litvinov on 28 March 1934 marked in essence the end of the Soviet role as an active factor in German foreign policy until 1939. Economic relations between the two countries were also reduced. As of 1936, German domestic anti-Communism was intensified in the form of increased propaganda against Bolshevism for the purposes of foreign policy.

Several points should be noted about the change of course in German foreign policy in 1933. After consolidating his domestic political power, Hitler concerned himself increasingly with foreign policy. While he continued to advocate the most radical long-term concepts, at the level of concrete policy he nevertheless insisted, for the time being, on a course which was in many respects moderate, and which went against the views of the Foreign Ministry and the Reichswehr. This strengthened the domestic political alliance under the slogan 'The Struggle against Versailles'. Not all the measures that followed can be explained as preparations for war; many simply used existing possibilities pragmatically to strengthen Germany's position, especially in foreign trade. But the fact that the Chancellor made and controlled foreign policy (though not its every individual step) wherever he wanted to do so made German policy in diplomacy, economics, and armaments compatible with his absolute determination to prepare for war. What were goals in themselves for many of the German conservative élite – such as regaining by Germany of a position as an independent great power – were for the new rulers only necessary interim steps to war. When, however, the course towards war became generally clear after 1935, the army leaders were quite prepared to accelerate it in areas for which they were responsible. It is therefore basically wrong to distinguish between the years of pure revisionism after 1933 and the following period of preparations for war. Rather, the course towards war had already begun in 1933 (and in some respects even earlier), but it was still ambiguous and, as presented in public, it could be interpreted as reintegration in a normal community of states based on co-operation and competition for power.

WAR PREPARATIONS AT HOME: THE ECONOMY AND REARMAMENT

In accordance with Hitler's wishes, foreign policy, economic consolidation, and rearmament served to prepare for a new world war. Not only were there great differences in the degree of awareness of this aim among the National Socialists' conservative coalition partners, some of whom did not understand it at all, but the aim itself had to be denied in order to delay as long as possible the initiation of counter-measures by the international community. For this reason demands for a revision of all peace-treaty restrictions continued to play a major role in German foreign policy, and they were pursued with a certain objective, rational logic. Increasingly this was done in a triumphalist manner, through unilateral declarations, coups, and threats, despite the fact that multilateral agreements, like those reached by Stresemann, were perfectly feasible. For other countries these actions constituted constant provocations. But Hitler and his National Socialist underlings knew how to conceal the real aims of their policy for a long time. On one hand German demands for revision, whatever advantages they offered in preparing for war, were presented in terms and ways that made them seem reasonable and understandable for the international community rather than as links in a chain; each time they appeared as final demands rather than as steps to potentially unlimited aggression. On the other hand, Hitler took advantage of numerous opportunities to stress his love of peace, to organize meetings of German war veterans with their counterparts from France and Great Britain, and to emphasize that his own experiences in the First World War had taught him to place great value on the preservation of peace. After almost every German coup Hitler made a peace speech and offered far-reaching but vague apparent concessions, which did in fact help to prevent decisive counter-measures by the European Western powers.

From the very beginning German peace propaganda had the aim of mollifying, even blackmailing, the international community. From Hitler's point of view, however, this had the disadvantage that his professions of peaceful intentions were largely accepted by the German population too, who generally applauded any expansion of German power but did not support the idea of a new war. German propaganda in speeches and the controlled press did not speak mainly of war, territory for natural expansion (*Lebensraum*), or world power, but of unacceptable restrictions on German freedom of action or of Germans beyond Germany's borders. In November 1938 Hitler privately described this dilemma:

> Only by constantly stressing Germany's will to peace and peaceful intentions was it possible for me to gain piece by piece freedom for the German people and to give them the weapons that were always necessary for the next step . . . This was why I had to talk only of peace for years. It was, after all, necessary gradually to prepare the German people psychologically and to make clear to them that there are things that . . . have to be achieved by means of force. For that purpose, however, it was necessary not only to propagate the use of force as such, but it was [also] necessary to explain certain foreign policy developments to the German people in such a way that the inner voice of the people itself gradually began to demand force.[3]

In practice, however, there were limits to this form of indirect mobilization.

It was in itself an insane undertaking to prepare an unlimited war of conquest under the conditions of military technology and its enormous powers of destruction in the twentieth century. If this war was to be fought against a possibly worldwide coalition of states, German chances of winning, in so far as they existed at all, consisted in exploiting for as long as possible the interest of other nations in preserving peace, in order to expand German power and change the balance of forces in Germany's favour. Although Hitler described his aims internally in this very comprehensive fashion, the final aim of a war of conquest could not be proclaimed openly or serve to mobilize direct support for his programme in Germany. It is also true that, in the area of international relations as a whole, the fundamental principle of conflict arbitration in the League of Nations had not completely replaced traditional power politics.

Nevertheless, especially in the world economic depression, whose effects in some countries lasted until 1938–9 and in some cases even into the war, preserving the general peace was the main interest of most states. This very longing for peace was exploited not only by the Third Reich but also by fascist Italy and authoritarian Japan – all powers which, in the eyes of their own leaders, possessed too few territorial or economic resources or other symbols of power – to realize through aggression their respective, differently motivated, expansionist goals. With its invasion of Manchuria in 1931 Japan preceded the other two have-not powers and shattered the unstable political order established in East Asia after the First World War. In 1932 Japan conquered and in 1934 created a satellite empire there, Manchukuo, and withdrew from the League of Nations, which was not significantly strengthened by the entry of the Soviet Union the following year. In 1934, Italy began an attempt in Ethopia to expand its colonial empire in Africa, which led to an open war there in 1935–6, the annexation of that independent state, and finally also Italy's withdrawal from the League after it had been the target of sanctions decreed by that organization. The expansionist aims of both states – in the Mediterranean and in the area of South-East Asia and the Pacific – were indeed ambitious, but neither in terms of their national potential nor in terms of the intentions of their respective leadership groups did they constitute a threat to the stability of the international system as a whole, as did the ambitions of National Socialist Germany. In principle this was also the view of the other great powers, above all in London, where Britain's own world-power position was considered to be threatened by all three revisionist states, and in Paris and Washington, where one or the other of the three was regarded as a danger.

The main threat to the post-war order – which had largely disintegrated in the world economic depression after 1929, resulting in stronger tendencies towards national economic or imperial isolationism – was the possibility of co-ordinated action by all three have-not states; however, it never materialized. In the first place this was because of the strong national and yet personal egoism of the dictators, Hitler and Mussolini, strengthened, in the case of Germany, and of Japan, by a pronounced racism. But each action of one of the expansionist states gave the others the chance to challenge and overtax, with little risk, the limited defensive forces of those countries interested in preserving peace and the status quo.

And that is precisely what happened. Until 1936, and in some respects until 1938, the fate of the Republic of Austria, protected by Italy, constituted an obstacle to co-operation between Italy and Germany in other questions. The two have-not powers also competed in the Balkans. And they were kept apart by Italy's less determined expansionist policies; for a long time Mussolini preferred big gestures to big deeds, and at first he strove for an acceptance of Italy as a great power in a restored and united Europe by practising a see-saw policy between Germany on one side and France or Great Britain on the other. In East Asia, German foreign policy gave top priority to good relations with China, as the sending of military advisers for the regime of Chiang Kaishek showed in particular. In the military conflict resulting from the Japanese expansion on the Chinese mainland, the German foreign ministry and the armed forces long sought to continue the priority given to China. The mainly declamatory Anti-Comintern Pact concluded with Japan in the autumn of 1936, which Italy joined a year later, and the new priority given to better relations with Japan, were the results of the unofficial activities of Joachim von Ribbentrop. Against the strong opposition of conservative forces, German military advisers were withdrawn from China on Ribbentrop's initiative after February 1938; and Germany recognized Manchukuo as an independent state.

THE ALLIANCE WITH GREAT BRITAIN: UNATTAINABLE

Basically National Socialist foreign policy aimed at complete national freedom of action, and thus sought to shake off or avoid all supranational or multilateral commitments. Hitler sought alliances on the basis of their value in war, and in addition to Italy he considered Great Britain above all to be the ideal partner. In Hitler's view, common racial characteristics and the absence of conflicts of interest due to geography made Britain a desirable ally. At least until Germany hegemony had been established on the European continent, and Germany was in a position to conduct foreign policy as a world power, competition with what was formerly the strongest naval power in the world had to be avoided. And for this reason any German colonial and naval claims such as had been made by Imperial Germany had to take second place in order to make possible in Europe, and especially in the East, a partnership with Britain on the basis of mutually complementary interests: Britain's desire to maintain her far-flung empire and position as a world power, and Germany's wish to establish an empire on the European continent. Additional arguments to convince the British of the desirability of such a partnership were Britain's weakness, especially in relation to the growing power of the United States, and a widespread anti-Bolshevism in parts of the British governing classes, which gave reason to expect that Britain would be prepared to give Germany a free hand for a war to conquer (*Lebensraum*) in the East. Neurath in the Foreign Ministry, however, and broad groups of the German conservative élites, had no faith in such a special relationship with Britain; and it is true that from the British point of view there was no real basis for it, although the British government was fully aware of Hitler's tireless efforts over the years to achieve the revolutionary alliance despite all obstacles.

All the leading political groups in Great Britain were interested, for domestic political, economic, and social reasons, in the preservation of peace. Any major war into which Great Britain might be drawn would inevitably strain her resources, reveal the economic weakness of the country, and further endanger the cohesion of an Empire consisting of independent nation-states bound together in the Commonwealth. Because the international order of the post-war period had largely collapsed it was thought especially necessary to accommodate – to a limited extent – the wishes of the revisionist states in order to construct a new order dedicated to preserving peace, which would satisfy their legitimate interests through reasonable compromises. This was called a 'general settlement' or 'appeasement', and it had economic as well as important military aspects together with those of power politics. Even after the final collapse of the Geneva Disarmament Conference in April 1934, the British attempted, partly in co-operation with France (which for its part also continued to cultivate traditional alliances) to bring about new general international agreements. This involved, on one hand, the Eastern Pact, which was in reality more of a French project, together with an effort to guarantee frontiers in Eastern and Central Europe in a form similar to that embodied in the Locarno Pact of 1925 for Western Europe. On the other hand, the British supported an 'Air Pact' to prevent an arms race in that area; for the development of military aviation, with its possibility of a strategic bombing-war, represented a threat greater than any other weapon to the security of the island empire. Both efforts, which were also in the interest of most small European states, were blocked to a considerable degree by German foreign policy in the years 1934–5.

On the other hand, Hitler considered British co-operation to be an indication of the possibility of achieving a valuable bilateral alliance, as had also been explored (unsuccessfully) with France in 1933–4. Especially in talks with the British, Hitler sought to suggest new future German armaments limits as a basis for bilateral agreements. In each case these represented the minimum figure of his actual plans and, from a National Socialist perspective, they did not affect Britain's interests as a world power. This had been especially true for German land forces at the end of 1933. In March 1935 Hitler proceeded to shock the British Foreign Secretary, Sir John Simon, by informing him that Germany had already achieved parity with Britain in air armaments (still forbidden for Germany by the Treaty of Versailles). But the most serious German offer concerned naval armaments, an area where rivalry like that with Britain at the beginning of the twentieth century was to be avoided. Hitler's reason for making this offer was that the British government was attempting to achieve at least minimum provisions against a general naval arms race for the period after 1936, when the agreements reached between the five strongest naval powers in Washington in 1920 and in London in 1930 were due to expire. The earlier attempt to set ratios for the most important categories of ships (Great Britain 5, the United States 5, Japan 3.5, and France and Italy 1.75 each) had led in practice to efforts to take full advantage of the upper limit in each category, and to complaints, from France and especially from Japan, about discrimination in the form of low assigned ratios.

This was the starting-point for Hitler. Instead of beginning any discussion of the British aim of building confidence through an exchange of information about naval programmes, in November 1933 he ordered the Commander-in-Chief of the navy, Raeder, to offer to construct a German battleship squadron to support the British against the United States. In the following year he developed the idea of limiting the German fleet to 35 per cent of the British navy and thus creating the basis for a historic alliance through this renunciation of world-power rivalry. Hitler insisted on his figure as the basis for bilateral naval talks with Britain in spite of Raeder's vigorous arguments that, with an eye on France, 50 per cent should be the minimum German limit. And the talks did indeed lead to the signing of a corresponding agreement between Ribbentrop and the British Foreign Secretary on 18 June 1935.

By signing the agreement the British government created difficulties for itself in relations with France, as it marked the first time it had approved unilaterally a German violation of the Treaty of Versailles; but it also felt it had obtained definite advantages by securing a permanent, almost threefold superiority compared with the German fleet. For the existing German fleet, on the other hand, the agreement allowed a fourfold increase in warship tonnage. It is reported that the conclusion of the agreement caused Hitler to speak of his 'happiest day'; Ribbentrop considered it to be a very important event in world history. Both men believed that they had taken the decisive step towards a comprehensive war alliance. The British Foreign Office and the Royal Navy, however, had signed the naval agreement only as a preparatory step for a general naval conference, at which there would have been no chance of Germany being allowed unlimited naval rearmament. But even with the Anglo-German agreement, the existing system of naval armaments control collapsed; a new London naval conference in the first months of 1936 resulted only in a meaningless exchange of almost unlimited naval construction programmes.

In fact Hitler failed to realize his grandiose alliance plan in 1935. Securing his policy of expansion through another great power of similar quality was impossible, although he continued to court Britain in the following years and Ribbentrop attempted, in his own fashion (albeit unsuccessfully in the end), to realize Hitler's aims while he was German ambassador to London from 1936 to 1938. At the beginning of 1938 he concluded that his mission had failed and viewed Britain thereafter as a certain future enemy; but Hitler in practice changed his policy only to a course 'without England', which, however, did not solve his dilemma of how to prepare for war against the majority of the other countries.[4]

THE REARMAMENT OF THE WEHRMACHT

Only a few days after assuming office in 1933, Hitler had presented 're-establishing Germany's ability to defend itself' *(Wiederwehrhaftmachung)*, the primacy of rearmament, as the guideline of his policy in the cabinet, and this remained his primary short-term aim. He was aware that such a course, openly proclaimed, would inevitably lead to decisive counter-measures and possibly even to a preventive war by France. It was therefore necessary to exercise the utmost caution while passing through this danger zone, until the forced pace of rearmament permitted him to proceed with less restraint and more self-confidence. In military circles it had been realized as early as the mid-1920s that any future war would be a total one. Not only did a military war have to be conducted, but a 'fighting nation' as a whole had to be mobilized. Thus a psychological and economic preparation of the entire peacetime population, with all the implications of such a barracks state, constituted a necessary condition for waging any future war. The question of whether these means were still desirable at all was either not asked in the individual departments and ministries concerned, or the answer was axiomatically assumed to be positive. Beyond planning, Weimar offered few chances to give these ideas concrete form. The situation changed only with the proclaimed national 'new start' after 1933. It was, however, typical that, because of the dominant position of the National Socialists, the armed forces did not take the lead either in the psychological or in the economic mobilization of the country, but essentially confined themselves, as they had earlier, to preparations of material and personnel, although in a total war these would be only two parts of an overall mobilization.

Independently of this long-term planning, the Reichswehr had already drawn up an armaments plan at the end of the 1920s which was to be secured by international negotiations and which went beyond the limitations imposed on Germany by the Treaty of Versailles.[5] Instead of the previous 7 divisions in a 100,000-man army, it envisaged material provisions for equipping 16 divisions by 1932, but without any increase in personnel, as in the event of war it was intended to call up veterans of the First World War. In the spring of 1932 a second armaments programme was developed for the years 1933 to 1938, in a domestic and foreign situation fundamentally changed by the world depression, which envisaged the creation of a 21-division field army in the event of war. It was modified the same year by Schleicher for tactical negotiating and domestic political reasons, and became a 'remodelling plan' that envisaged an enlargement of the active army to 144,000 men by 1938 and which was intended to achieve a 21-division army of 570,000 men through shorter, militia-like training, the inclusion of border guard troops, and pre-military instruction. Thus in 1932 the course was set for a rearmament programme that would exceed the limits of the Treaty of Versailles in any case, regardless of whether or not it was sanctioned by an international armaments convention. This was the reason for the intransigent position taken by Neurath and Blomberg in the disarmament negotiations: the effects of German rearmament had to be noticeable abroad during 1933. The military perspective was reduced to the problems of what was technically feasible in rearmament. Moreover, the personnel build-up soon came to the fore; equipping the army for a war was given second priority.

Only the National Socialist paramilitary formations could have forced changes in Hitler's consensus with the armed forces; but even before the murders of the SA leaders the course had been set for a future army based on general conscription, especially as the SA were considered to be of only limited value as reserves in the event of war. In December 1933 the decision was taken to create a 300,000-man army of 21 divisions by 1938. In that year the wartime army after mobilization was to be able to comprise 63 divisions; the question of how they were to be properly equipped was left completely open. The aim was to be able to fight 'a defensive war on two fronts with some chance of success'. This defensive formulation did indeed take into consideration the existing international relation of forces, if an attack by France and Poland (until January 1934) or Czechoslovakia was expected. In this connection, military leaders like Chief of the General Staff, General Ludwig Beck, complained that Hitler should have announced Germany's intention to rearm immediately after his foreign-policy coup on 14 October 1933.

Beginning in 1933, the army started accepting more volunteers for short periods of up to one and a half years, and pressed for the proclamation of general conscription. But Hitler delayed taking this step until March 1935, because of the imminent referendum in the Saar. The Treaty of Versailles, which Germany constantly violated in its armaments programmes, envisaged such a referendum after the Saar had been under a League of Nations administration, dominated by France, for 15 years. On 13 January 1935, after an extraordinary German propaganda effort, but in an essentially free election, almost 91 per cent of the Saarlanders voted to return 'home to the Reich'. Of course national feeling was the dominant factor, but such overwhelming support clearly also represented approval of reunification with Germany under the National Socialist regime. Broad national approval greeted the reintroduction of general conscription, unilaterally announced on 9 and 10 March 1935, and together with a public statement of the existence of the Luftwaffe, whereas the German naval rearmament was sanctioned bilaterally in the agreement with Great Britain only 3 months later. At the same time the vague designations previously used to conceal the activities and nature of German military authorities were all replaced with terms reflecting more clearly their real functions (such as General Staff instead of Troop Office).

German rearmament was determined by the dynamism of its own constantly increased pace and by the expansion of its aims. This was due in part to Hitler, but it was also an expression of the purely military perception of Germany's increasing international isolation and, as of 1937–8, of the forced rearmament of Germany's neighbours. In this process of action and reaction, the army leadership around Generals von Fritsch and Beck did not realize either that the latter development was primarily a reaction to their own rearmament; and they attempted to increase the pace and quantity of their rearmament even more. As early as 1934 it was planned to create the organizational framework for a 21-division army that same year; as of 1935 the aim was an army of 36 divisions, which was then announced publicly in the Law for the Build-Up of the Wehrmacht on 16 March 1935. Although several senior officers expressed reservations, the army leaders were none the less prepared to accept any decline in the quality of the army that would result from the extremely rapid pace of rearmament: For example, the percentage of officers in the army as a whole was only 1.7 in the autumn of

1935, whereas the desired figure was 7; and supplies were sufficient for only a few months in the event of war.

In the course of this extremely rapid rearmament, the 50-kilometre zone east of the Rhine, demilitarized under the Treaty of Versailles and expressly confirmed again in the Treaty of Locarno in 1925, acquired a key role. German leaders were interested in full access to the reservoir of young men it contained and in securing the region, especially the Ruhr, Germany's most important armoury, with combat-ready divisions against a feared French attack. Although it was certainly possible now to reach a mutually acceptable international settlement, Hitler decided to take advantage of the still-undecided war in Abyssinia, in which Italy was involved and which also bound the Western Powers politically, to stage a spectacular entry of a limited German troop contingent into the demilitarized zone on 7 March 1936. In view of the dissatisfaction that prevailed in the German population because of economic problems and the struggle within and with the churches, this step had a socially integrative effect typical of National Socialist policies and, as Hitler and his advisers were aware, it involved a high risk. But the coup was successful: France missed its last military opportunity to stop Germany's defiance of the international community. The operation was approved in a plebiscite and was accompanied by Hitler's rhetorical proclamations of his peaceful intentions, even including his readiness to return to the League of Nations; and international reaction was confined to diplomatic protests.

Although arms production could not keep up with the personnel build-up, the Wehrmacht was still determined to push forward the technical development of the most modern equipment and weapons. As one aim of the Treaty of Versailles had been to prevent that very thing, the Reichswehr in the 1920s had come to view preparation for the day when Germany would regain the freedom to rearm as one of its most important tasks, to be fulfilled in secret at home and abroad. But in view of the pace of German rearmament from 1933 onwards, these illegal preparations turned out to be of only limited usefulness in many sectors. Until March 1935 Germany relied on camouflage. The actual definition of the function of weapons, their testing, and their mass production often coincided. The weapons acquired were modern, but it would have been preferable to test them first instead of immediately putting them into mass production. But because speed and quantity were important, weapons were produced which had often been prepared only on the drawing-board. As will be seen, such weapons often suffered from shortcomings or were hardly suitable for a large-scale war; but they still had to be put into service.

This conflict of aims can be seen most clearly in the Luftwaffe. The army as well as the navy had been able to circumvent the prohibition on German military aviation in the Treaty of Versailles. Officers officially trained for 'air-raid protection' were taken over into the newly formed Ministry of Aviation in 1933, which became the Luftwaffe High Command in 1935.

Göring's dynamism and forcefulness and his position in the National Socialist hierarchy resulted in his branch of the Wehrmacht receiving a disproportionately high share of available resources. At that time the idea of a strategic air force, which would guarantee victory by bombing the 'sources of the enemy's strength' such as industrial installations and transportation routes or even by spreading death and terror among the civilian enemy population and thus helping to avoid a long war of attrition on the ground, reflected most clearly the concept of total war. Corresponding images of war as an opportunity or a nightmare were widespread in most countries, especially as there seemed to be no completely effective defensive measures against bombers. In May 1933 the most important person in such matters, State Secretary Erhard Milch in the Reich Ministry of Aviation, requested Lufthansa director Robert Knauss to work out plans for the rapid build-up of a fleet of approximately 390 four-engine, long-range bombers which would deter any enemy from risking an attack on Germany. Such ideas were not completely rejected, but the construction programme of the Luftwaffe was determined by other factors. Firstly, the argument could not be dismissed out of hand that, because the level of German armaments was considered inadequate, air power should be used for home defence and direct tactical support of the army and navy in the event of war. For this reason, too, great importance was attached to defeating the air force of any country with which Germany might be at war. Moreover, the men who had been taken over into the new Luftwaffe were trained specifically for such tactical missions and thought primarily in terms of them. For reasons of prestige it was also considered important to produce a large number of aircraft as quickly as possible, so that they could be used in relations and confrontations with other countries as a deterrent or for purposes of bluff.

Thus the aim of German rearmament in the air was not at first to create a latent threat by preparing for a total air war; the development of a long-range bomber was begun only in 1936. Only 18 such bombers had been delivered to the Luftwaffe by the outbreak of war in 1939. In 1936, in a grandiose deception, the French air attaché in Berlin was taken on a tour of numerous airfields, to each of which the same newest aircraft had been flown before his arrival. In many respects, therefore, the development of the Luftwaffe for purposes of political propaganda and deterrence was given priority over its development as an instrument of real military power. Nevertheless, there can be no doubt that, in view of the fact that the starting point was almost zero, within 6 years a formidable instrument of aggression with over 4,000 aircraft was created in spite of constantly expanding programmes, an initially excessive variety of models, and increasingly frequent bottlenecks of all kinds within the armaments industry. But, to a far greater extent than the propaganda of the totalitarian state suggested, this instrument was designed for tactical air warfare and not to achieve victory in a total war.

Though not to the same extent as that of the Luftwaffe, the development of the navy was also marked by constantly expanding armaments targets that went beyond all previous plans. The navy's view was that the weight and influence of nations in the world were determined essentially by their naval power; but this was important for Hitler only as part of a later phase of his plans to make Germany a world power, after the conquest of territory for expansion (*Lebensraum*) on the European continent. Prior to 1933, under the limitations of the Treaty of Versailles, the navy had commissioned in the large-ship category only three 'pocket battleships' of nominally 10,000 tonnes each. These ships were inferior to the corresponding vessels of the other powers, which were not bound by the Treaty of Versailles. Nevertheless, it was expected that such vessels would be effective against enemy trade in a war on the high seas. But the principle of a balanced fleet with squadrons suited for a fleet-against-fleet war was dominant. Within the framework of existing or new limitations to be agreed upon for all powers, Raeder's aim was to construct the most formidable battleships possible. And after the conclusion of the naval agreement with Britain and preliminary work in 1935–6, two such battleships, the *Bismarck* and the *Tirpitz*, were commissioned and placed in service at the beginning of 1940 and in February 1941 respectively.

From this point of view two additional large ships built in the meantime, the *Scharnhorst* and the *Gneisenau*, were already obsolete even before they were completed. During the 1920s the navy had made great efforts abroad to keep abreast of developments in submarine construction, as it considered the U-boat to be the classic weapon of weaker naval powers. After 1933 sections of small U-boats were constructed in secret and then assembled after the unilateral discarding of limits on German naval construction in 1935. In view of the existing capacity for German armaments production, especially in shipyards, the naval agreement of 1935 created conditions for naval rearmament at the highest possible speed until 1942, but due to policy changes and delays this pace could not be maintained. Since only continental European powers were considered at that time to be potential military enemies, Raeder had difficulty preparing to pursue his long-term aims, in spite of the direct access to Hitler he achieved in 1933. In addition, there were Hitler's own preferences. Until 1935 he was reluctant to exceed the limits imposed on Germany naval armaments by the Treaty of Versailles, but then he began to press for the construction of the largest and most heavily armed ships possible, which the admirals considered senseless or which required time-consuming design work. Although they were aware of the provisional nature of the 'permanent' naval agreement, the navy essentially abided by its 35 per cent limit until 1937. Indeed, some ships were included in German naval planning only because 'free' tonnage was available in the relevant category. When, in mid-1937, the navy came to realize that Great Britain might oppose German expansion, it began drastically to revise its ship construction plans.

In addition to heavy artillery, the army was concerned above all with assessing the value of armoured units in future warfare. At approximately the same time as in France, Fritsch as well as Beck realized that armour, and indeed greater mechanization in general, could greatly increase not only the tactical but also the strategic striking power of an army. Planning for a defensive army was superseded by planning for an offensive one; and to obtain the necessary personnel for the future peacetime and wartime army, general conscription was extended to two years in 1936. At the same time the goal became to create a peacetime army of 36 infantry divisions and 7 additional divisions, including 3 armoured divisions, by the autumn of 1939. Including 21 militia divisions, a total of 102 divisions with 3.6 million men would be available for the wartime army as of 1940. That was far more than the imperial German army of 1914 had had and, in view of the starting-point of 100,000 men in 1933, it constituted a breathtaking expansion. With regard to personnel, the army (and the situation in the navy and the Luftwaffe was similar) spoke of 'the pressure of time', without admitting that this pressure resulted to a large extent from the aims and methods of Germany's own policies. At the same time, Major General Fromm of the General Army Office calculated the horrendous costs of maintaining supply and equipment stockpiles for the German army of the future and concluded: 'The rearmament period will have to be followed soon by actual use of the Wehrmacht or by a reduction of war readiness to moderate this burden.' It was necessary, he explained, to decide 'whether it is [our] firm intention to use the Wehrmacht at a certain, already determined time or not'.[6] He did not receive an answer, but the obvious economic consequences of the immense rearmament programme left only one clear conclusion for Germany's military leaders: there would be no choice but to go to war. This, moreover, had always been Hitler's intention.

THE WAR-ORIENTATED ECONOMY AND FOREIGN TRADE

After 1936 bottlenecks in the armaments programme became more frequent and increasingly affected the pace of rearmament. That had not been the case in 1933. Nevertheless, the slogan at the time, 'Everything for the Wehrmacht', could not be translated immediately into reality. To a large extent, German economic policy continued at first to follow traditional paths, and there was also the most serious domestic problem of unemployment. Average unemployment in Germany in 1932 was 29.9 per cent (in the United States it was 34 per cent; in Great Britain 22.1 per cent; the problem was not confined to Germany). The low point of the world economic depression had already been reached in the summer of 1932. But the number of unemployed in Germany was still 6 million in January 1933, the same level as a year earlier. Indeed, the unemployment problem had been essentially overcome by 1936; the average figure for 1937 was only 0.9 million. This amounted to full employment as it was defined at the time; in many sectors there was a considerable labour shortage. Job creation programmes using state funds were something new. They had been developed on a large scale under Schleicher, and could be carried out immediately after the cabinet of 'national concentration' assumed power. Hitler's demand in a cabinet meeting that every proposed measure should be examined to determine 'whether it is necessary from the point of view of re-establishing the ability of the German nation to defend itself' could not be realized in the first job creation programme, nor in the Reinhardt Programme drawn up in the spring of 1933.[7] Only after October of that year was rearmament actually given priority. At first, most money was invested in street and bridge construction, transportation and community projects, and in housing construction. But some of these measures had a significance for rearmament that was not clear in their details. Barracks construction, airfields, shipyard and harbour expansion, projects in which the military purpose was clear, easily fitted into the job creation programmes. Only by then had the actual rearmament plans been developed far enough. Nevertheless, the infrastructure and rearmament measures of 1933 did not anticipate the armaments boom that began in 1936 and that led to an even greater expansion of capacity.

An example of the uncertain relationships and effects between economic policies and armaments can be seen in the construction of motorways (*Autobahnen*), which was based on private preliminary work done during the Weimar Republic that had been called to Hitler's attention by the capable engineer Fritz Todt. On 23 September 1933 the Chancellor inaugurated the programme, on the Frankfurt to Heidelberg route, with the very effective propaganda gesture of digging the first spadeful. At the same time a call was issued for voluntary labour service. Contrary to legend, this measure was not intended primarily to serve military deployment, as was clearly evident in the predominantly north-south direction of the new routes, although the potential enemies were in the east and west. But the private motorization the motorways promoted did create important preconditions for the war. By the end of 1937, 2,000 kilometres of motorways had been built; by the end of 1940 the figure was 3,800 kilometres of 'roads of the Führer'. But at no time were more than 130,000 workers employed in motorway construction, which thus played no significant quantitative role in overcoming unemployment. Nevertheless, this propagandistic mobilization, which was declared to be a 'battle of labour', was effective in a mass psychological sense, and also had a positive effect on the economic situation by awakening hopes and expectations.

By the end of 1934, some 5 thousand million Reichsmarks in state funds for job creation had been appropriated, a sum that exceeded industrial investment more than threefold. Then, however, direct armaments expenditure exceeded all other factors.[8] According to later calculations, this factor amounted to between 45 and 82 thousand million Reichsmarks from 1933 to 1939. If one assumes the latter figure to be correct, direct expenditure rose from 700 million Reichsmarks in 1933 to 4.2 thousand million Reichsmarks in 1934, doubled again in 1936 to 10.3 thousand million Reichsmarks, and reached 32.3 thousand million Reichsmarks in 1939, almost double the figure for the previous year. The share of armaments expenditure in the gross national product rose from 1 per cent in 1933 to 23 per cent in 1939. The individual armed services were therefore able to draw on abundant resources for the time being. Unlike the Weimar period, when parliamentary control made extreme austerity necessary, in the midst of constantly expanding industrial capacity the military leaders, strongly encouraged at the beginning by the Chancellor, now ordered whatever they considered necessary. Finance for this programme was secured by the Reich Bank, whose president functioned as a complete economic dictator in his capacity as General Plenipotentiary for the War Economy after 1935, and whom the interested sectors of heavy industry readily followed. In fact, 'the printing presses were already being heavily used at the beginning of the armaments programme', as Schacht admitted in 1935, when four well-known armaments firms founded a bogus company under the name of Mefo. Mefo had a nominal capital of only 1 million Reichsmarks, on which bills guaranteed by the state could be drawn. Between 1934 and 1936 these bills secured almost half the relevant expenditure, which, however, still had an inevitable inflationary effect. As of spring 1938 they were replaced by Reich treasury warrants. Schacht saw the dangers of this ruinous financing and demanded as early as 1936 that it be stopped; but under the existing circumstances the alternative he offered of slowing the pace of rearmament had no chance of being accepted. In the final analysis he failed to understand the situation and the regime under which he had willingly assumed office. Of approximately 30 thousand million Reichsmarks in state expenditure in 1938 (35 per cent of the national income) only 17.7 thousand million Reichsmarks could be raised through taxes. This situation also constituted a time bomb, for only military conquests could compensate for the ruinous exploitation of the German national economy.

The policy directed towards war also affected various aspects of German foreign trade, but here the continuity from Weimar was, relatively speaking, most clear. Especially as a result of the world economic crisis, the buzz-word 'revision' acquired a new meaning that extended beyond the territory of Germany. In words such as 'Central Europe', 'single large economy', and 'Pan-Europe', business circles, governments, and intellectuals sought to propagate and realize a new course for German foreign-trade policy after the collapse of the liberal world economic system. Although it was in part directed towards Germany's western neighbours and Scandinavia, this policy had focused on south-east Europe, the Danube basin, and also the Baltic States since the beginning of the 1930s. The aim was to develop new international economic structures to Germany's advantage by promoting an exchange of raw materials from countries in those areas with industrial finished goods from Germany. Leading National Socialists, too, were attracted by this idea.

Such plans were often associated with the concept of autarchy, self-sufficiency within a closed economic area. The important question, however, was whether the policy would mean relatively restricted economic access towards foreign economic interests such as those of France or Britain, or whether it was intended as preparation for a war in which, with an eye to being able to supply only itself, an economic area dominated by Germany was to be uncoupled from all involvement in the world economy. Especially from the perspective of a war economy it was clear, however, that a lasting, blockade-proof German war effort would not be possible either in terms of the necessary raw materials or for a long period of time. It is important to distinguish clearly between these ideas of a single large economy, for which the term '*Lebensraum*' was occasionally used, and Hitler's particular idea of '*Lebensraum*' in the east, aimed at Soviet territory and bearing the clear stamp of his racial ideology. In Hitler's eyes, the former ideas of a large economic area and autarchy were a desirable first step to the conquest of real 'territory for natural expansion', which would then make possible long-term security for an autarchic Germany in relation to the other world powers.

Moreover, expanding German influence in south-east Europe offered immediate political advantages which were already recognized in Berlin in the early 1930s. Using economic leverage, it would be possible to undermine the political value of the loose alliance of beneficiaries of the Treaty of Versailles supported by France in that region. And this aim was indeed achieved by 1936, a policy supported by the elimination of the effects of the world depression as a result of the upswing in the German domestic economy. Nevertheless, it would be a mistake to speak of a uniform, consistent German policy in this region. Firstly, the differences in the interests of the individual states there were too great, and their conflicts, such as those between the countries which had been on winning and losing sides in the First World War, coupled with growing German influence placed Germany in the unpleasant role of an arbiter. Secondly, Hitler himself demanded consideration of Italian interests in the Balkans, and those interests were taken into account in Berlin until the war in Abyssinia. Moreover, German interests in the Balkans were extraordinarily varied and were often the source of friction between private enterprises, the Ministry of Economics, the Foreign Ministry, and individual emissaries such as Hermann Göring. And finally, especially in the agriculture sector, the capacity of the German economy to absorb imports was limited, which in turn adversely affected the export of German finished goods.

Trade ageements with Hungary and Yugoslavia marked the start of National Socialist policy in south-east Europe; and as early as the beginning of 1934 Hjalmar Schacht sought to systematize the German economic offensive under the name of the 'New Plan'. In view of Germany's shortage of foreign currency, priorities were determined for raw materials to be imported, especially for armaments. Each of the bilateral agreements was based on a clearing agreement, governing the reciprocal exchange of goods and the settlement of differences, with the aim of achieving a balanced exchange of goods on a barter basis. In this way, German trade with Latin America rose significantly, as did trade with Scandinavia, where the quantity of Swedish iron ore exported to Germany in particular increased fivefold between 1932 and 1936, and was indispensable for the German armaments programme. This trend has been correctly described as a development towards an 'informal empire' in south-east Europe,[9] in which closer ties were established with Yugoslavia and Hungary in particular (important suppliers of bauxite, an essential raw material for aluminium),[10] and in which Romania, with its oil fields, made a decisive contribution to German war preparations, delivering 187,000 tonnes in 1933 and 1,272,000 tonnes in 1939. Most economically dependent of all was Bulgaria, whose imports all came from Germany and two-thirds of whose exports were sent there. In general the German share of the imports of the countries of south-east Europe rose from 18.44 per cent in 1933 to 50.61 per cent in 1939; they received 15.35 per cent of Germany's exports in 1933 and 46.08 per cent in 1939. The corresponding percentages for the German economy were, of course, comparatively low, and Germany did not achieve a lasting increase in its imports from Europe as against those from countries overseas by 1938. In particular, the level of trade with the United States and also with Great Britain remained high. And in the course of economic appeasement these countries, in their economic relations with Germany, made clear the absurdity of the Germans' attempt to leave the international community.

A main reason for the continued orientation of the German economy towards the traditional industrial countries was that essential raw materials for armaments could not be obtained through clearing agreements, although armaments in particular were high on the shopping lists of some of Germany's trading partners and, in spite of Germany's own enormous armaments requirements, were also delivered in increasing quantities. The result was a shortage of raw materials for current armaments production at the end of 1935; supplies of some materials were sufficient for only 1 or 2 months. Plans to build up stocks, especially for the war, collapsed. In addition, Darré discovered that proper nutrition for the population was threatened by a 'gap in fats' (*Fettlücke*), which would have to be bridged by using foreign exchange reserves for imports. Schacht, however, refused to co-operate: 'As far as foreign exchange reserves are concerned, you can't demand the impossible. After all, I'm not a ducat machine'.[11] He was right; the foreign exchange reserves of the Reich Bank, which had amounted to 2,806,000,000 Reichsmarks in 1930, shrank so rapidly in the following years as a result of the economic crisis and expenditure on arms that on average only 164,700,000 Reichsmarks were available in 1934. And in the following years the figure sank well below 100 million Reichsmarks, a sum sufficient to cover import requirements for only a week. Only a slowing of the pace of rearmament could have brought real relief. The results of the 'export offensive', repeatedly proclaimed to be strengthening Germany's foreign exchange reserves, were disappointing. But in the spring of 1936 Hitler ensured that an additional 60 million Reichsmarks were made available for agricultural imports, so that in addition to 'guns' there would be enough 'butter', and possible social conflicts could be avoided.

THE FOUR YEAR PLAN OF 1936 AS ECONOMIC PREPARATION FOR WAR

In this situation, Hermann Göring persuaded Hitler to entrust him with the task of examining the situation for raw materials and foreign currency with a small staff at the beginning of 1936. But the liberal-conservative suggestions of experts such as Carl Goerdeler satisfied neither Göring nor Blomberg, and certainly not Hitler, who took the initiative in August 1936 and wrote a memorandum – something he did very rarely – for the two men containing his own suggestions.[12] He did not indicate a way out of the crisis, but simply described at length his basic idea of detaching Germany from the world economy in preparation for expansion through war. His memorandum ended with the unambiguous demand that the German economy and the Wehrmacht had to be ready for war in four years. In addition to appeals, Hitler offered a patchwork of emergency economic measures aiming at partial autarchy for the German armaments industry. Above all, these were intended to achieve self-sufficiency 'regardless of cost' and as soon as possible in fuels, synthetic rubber, and iron ore, as well as in industrial lubricants.

Such plans were not new. As early as December 1933, I.G. Farben, whose contacts with National Socialists in previous years had prepared the way, had signed a contract with the German government for the use of considerable state funds for promoting the otherwise unprofitable expansion of facilities to produce fuel from brown coal by gasoline synthesis. Substitutes for raw materials were used in the clothing industry among other sectors. Appeals to save raw materials and collect disused articles of all kinds mobilized the national community for a permanent effort by individual citizens. An aim of the New Plan was to direct the use of raw materials within Germany. Hermann Göring, who was named by Hitler as Plenipotentiary for the Four Year Plan, was able to take advantage of this opportunity. At first the plan itself amounted to little more than an intention to achieve autarchy, and it was proclaimed as such at the annual party rally of the NSDAP. But the Prussian Minister President immediately used his position as head of the state government to create a new agency consisting of representatives of industry, the ministerial bureaucracy (especially the Ministry of War), and the party, and was able to establish himself, to the exclusion of Schacht, as the highest, almost dictatorial authority in matters concerned with rearmament. He explained himself with the observation that 'we're already in the midst of a war; only the shooting hasn't started yet'.

The ambitious investment plans of the Four Year Plan rose rapidly from 3 thousand million Reichsmarks in August 1936 to 9.5 thousand million Reichsmarks by the end of 1937. Largely new production facilities, such as those for coal hydrogenation, had to be constructed, processes which had been rejected earlier by the participating industries as unprofitable. The steel industry remained uninterested in the exploitation of deposits of low-grade iron ore in Germany. In his memorandum, Hitler had already proclaimed: 'The nation does not exist for the economy or the leaders of the economy . . . but [their] exclusive task is to serve our nation in its struggle [with other nations] for survival.' and especially because of the iron ore problem he threatened the companies concerned that they would forfeit 'the right to continue existing as free enterprises'. The consequence was that the Plenipotentiary for the Four Year Plan, Göring, founded the Hermann Göring Works to mine the ore in the area of Salzgitter. Later, during the war, this enterprise spread throughout Europe by means of subsidiary branches. Only certain very specific parts of the economy profited from the Four Year Plan, but increasingly such companies belonged to I.G. Farben, whose representative, Carl Krauch, was actively involved in the Four Year Plan, and who worked out a new mineral-oil production plan for the war economy in 1937–8 which progressively transformed the previously comprehensive Four Year Plan into an I.G. Farben plan in that particular sector.

More precisely, the Four Year Plan came to consist of only partially co-ordinated sectors operating under intense pressure. In view of existing capacities, plans for these sectors were hardly realistic, and only half of them were realized by 1939. Nevertheless, the plan did achieve significant increases in the production of certain scarce raw materials which were to be indispensable for conducting a war. At the start of the war in 1939 Germany was still dependent on other countries for a third of its current raw materials requirements. And here, too, only the war was able to solve the problem as Hitler desired. In particular, 65 per cent of Germany's mineral oils and between 85 and 90 per cent of its rubber was still being imported in 1939.[13] With an eye to the possibilities of the projected single large economy, it was estimated that, in a war, considerable quantities of imports would no longer be necessary, including 46 per cent of iron ore imports, 85 per cent of copper imports, 85 per cent of lead imports, 91 per cent of zinc imports, 94 per cent of oil, and 96 per cent of rubber imports.

In view of the anticipated total war, the economics expert of the Wehrmacht, Colonel Georg Thomas, attempted not only to secure materials for the current diverse armaments programmes, but also to plan 'armaments [production] in depth', which was intended to force all important industries to provide for the standing equipment needs of the mass army, and which sought to achieve a long-term stockpiling at least as a stopgap measure. Although no fundamental decision was ever clearly taken against such logical and bureaucratic planning, the guideline had already been set in Hitler's directive in his memorandum of August 1936: 'War makes possible the mobilization of the last reserves of metals. For this is not an economic problem, but solely a question of will . . . And in any case, the quantities of materials required for a war are so large that there has never been real long-term stockpiling in the history of the world.'

THE POLICY OF EXPANSION: FROM SPAIN TO AUSTRIA

It is clear that German foreign policy was increasingly conducted from the standpoint of war-economy priorities after 1936. Every new foreign-policy commitment had a largely positive effect on this sector. Nevertheless, it would be a mistake to view the annexation of Austria or Czechoslovakia, the attack on Poland, and the resulting expansion of the War primarily from this perspective. This is also true of German involvement in the Spanish Civil War (1936–9). In August 1936 Hitler decided to give military support to General Franco, the leader of the *putsch* against the legitimate Spanish government, because he hoped a brief action would prevent what he considered an imminent Bolshevik encirclement of all of Western Europe. In France a left-wing Popular Front government was in power, and Hitler wrongly feared that Communists would take power in Spain. As Franco's forces did not, however, achieve a quick victory in the sanguinary civil war that so polarized America and Europe ideologically and emotionally as a result in particular of the presence of volunteers in Spain, additional factors came to play a role in Germany's involvement. Support for Franco made it possible to practise in secret the new co-operation between Germany and Italy. Spain also served as a test of German hopes for British co-operation under the slogan of anti-Bolshevism; in the final analysis the outcome was unsuccessful, since Britain refused to abandon her policy of non-intervention. Spain was also an opportunity to test parts of the army, navy and Luftwaffe under war conditions – such as the bombing of Guernica – but this also led to problems in the formation of new military units within Germany itself. Finally, by means of the founding of two German firms, Hisma and Rowak, which co-operated with Göring's Four Year Plan, Germany was able to take advantage of the Civil War to intensify economic ties with Spain, so that the German share of Spanish exports, in terms of value, rose from 13.1 per cent in 1935 to 40.7 per cent in 1938. In this respect iron-ore shipments from northern Spain were especially important, although under the conditions of the Civil War they declined as a percentage of total German imports.

Especially in the annexation of Austria, however, war economy considerations and Göring's urging played an important role. Germany's neighbour in the south-east possessed not only oil and iron ore but also had solid reserves of foreign currency in its national bank. Moreover, Austria suffered from continued relatively high unemployment, and had a significant number of skilled workers. After the Treaty of Versailles had forbidden Austrian unification with Germany in 1919, such a unification, with a country which had not belonged to the German Reich when it was founded in 1871, became one of the aims of German revisionism. In 1931 the Austro-German customs union, a clear step in the direction of unification and which was also intended to facilitate geographical access for Germany to south-east Europe, failed because of the objections of other states. But the National Socialists, and above all Hitler, who was born in Austria, were advocates of a 'greater Germany'; and from the very beginning they had a strong party organization in Austria. In 1933 they considered the unification of Austria and Germany to be only a variation of the domestic political process of bringing everything into line in Germany, somewhat on the model of what had been done in Bavaria. But such a revolutionary foreign policy which, moreover, made use of economic leverage, was incompatible with the moderate image German foreign policy sought to project at the time; in August 1933, the now-forbidden Austrian National Socialists, who had been pushing for revolutionary action in the country and from outside, were warned not to go too far. When the government of Engelbert Dollfuß became a corporative, one-party dictatorship and sought to move closer to Italy by adopting the Italian socio-political model, Austria's National Socialists, and the SA in particular, again pressed for immediate action. In a *putsch* on 25 July 1934, which they staged largely on their own initiative, they succeeded in murdering Dollfuß, but were defeated by the Austrian army. The deployment of Italian troops at the Brenner Pass deterred Hitler from further involvement. Thereafter he placed his hopes in a gradual development of National Socialism within Austria.

In a comprehensive Austro-German agreement of July 1936, Austria's sovereignty was expressly recognized, while her considerable economic dependence on Germany was also guaranteed. The 'Austro-fascist' government of Kurt von Schuschnigg committed itself to entrust members of the 'national opposition' with political responsibility. On 5 November 1937 Hitler announced to his Foreign Minister and the heads of the Wehrmacht his intention to move against Austria and Czechoslovakia soon, without wanting to provoke a major war, as a solution to the problems of Germany's war-orientated economy. The opportunity for such action was provided by Schuschnigg's desperate effort to secure his regime and Austria's independence by holding a referendum after National Socialist attempts to blackmail him. On 12 and 13 March 1938, after fictitious calls for help, the Wehrmacht marched into Austria. Under the influence of the enthusiastic response of a large part of the Austrian population, the inclusion of Austria in the so-called Great German Reich was proclaimed. Measures to persecute opponents of the National Socialist regime, and to give it control over all aspects of life and society in the country, which had taken years in Germany, were carried out within a few months in Austria. And on 10 April 1938 Austria's unification with Germany was sanctioned by 99 per cent of those who voted in a plebiscite, a result that marked a new high point of Hitler's popularity and revived his spirits after the nadir of the Blomberg-Fritsch crisis. To many Germans – and not only National Socialists – it seemed that the mistaken trend begun in 1866 with the exclusion of Austria from Germany had now been reversed. In view of the fact that this violation of international law seemed to reflect the will of the German people, the Western European Powers reacted only with weak protests. In 1936 an axis between Berlin and Rome had been proclaimed with great fanfare; in Spain it had passed an additional test.

With a firm hold on all aspects of the political preparations for war, Hitler now showed his determination to continue his series of surprise moves without interruption. He hoped for as long as possible to avoid provoking the active resistance of the western democracies, which he increasingly viewed as incapable of action, by making apparently moderate demands on behalf of ethnic German minorities in other countries, which in each case could be presented as his final wishes for revision. Indeed, Great Britain, with France increasingly in her wake, continued her appeasement policy until 1939. Through economic concessions and colonial offers Neville Chamberlain's government sought to bind Germany's great-power ambitions, which Chamberlain recognized as legitimate in themselves, into a new general European peace settlement. But the other side of this willingness to accommodate German ambitions was the increasing weight of British rearmament, which was intended to make clear to the aggressors the absurdity of a major war under twentieth-century conditions.

These methods were also typical of British policy in the Far East, where Japan's waging an undeclared war it could not win in China since 1937 had already opened the Second World War in that region. In some respects, the United States took over traditional British roles in East Asia as early as 1938–9. But concrete negotiations on a British general settlement or on Hitler's wish for a worldwide alliance to permit the realization of his plans for aggression never took place, in spite of many signals from both sides. The basic aims of the two countries were too well known, although the depth of their differences was not completely understood. After 1937 it became increasingly clear to Hitler that his aim of conquering territory for natural expansion (*Lebensraum*) could only be achieved against British opposition, and that a strategic window of opportunity would only remain open for a brief period (until about 1940) before possible or certain British intervention. In that period his goal had to be to defeat France at the very least and, if no other solution were possible, to keep Britain from interfering on the European continent by military means. At the same time, he sought to eliminate enemies individually and thus to expand his geostrategic and economic base for as long as possible.

THE WAY TO WAR

From a military point of view the position of Czechoslovakia, whose Czech part was almost surrounded by the Great German Reich, was completely untenable after March 1938. Czechoslovakia was a well-armed, industrialized country and had been formally allied with France and the Soviet Union since 1935; but Hitler used as a lever against it the approximately three million Germans who, in addition to the dominant groups of Czechs and Slovaks, constituted the third strongest ethnic group throughout Czechoslovakia, concentrated especially in the frontier areas of the Sudetenland. The originally pluralistic Sudeten German Homeland Front, which in 1935 turned into the Sudeten German Party under Konrad Henlein, became increasingly radicalized along National Socialist lines and was instructed, in accordance with Hitler's wishes, to constantly raise its demands, beginning with cultural autonomy, so that the government of Eduard Beneš would not be able to fulfil them. But, as Hitler informed the leaders of the Wehrmacht on 30 May 1938, it was his 'irrevocable decision' to destroy Czechoslovakia as a state. These very questions of nationality, however, also offered the Western Powers, especially Britain, an opportunity for mediation to reconcile the legitimate rights of the Sudeten Germans with the continued existence of the Czechoslovak state. Germany did not have military deployment plans even to deal with a two-front war in the event of an intervention by the Western Powers, quite apart from the fact that German military experts did not see any prospect of victory in such a war.

In the summer of 1938 a group opposed to Hitler's plans began to form around the Chief of the General Staff, Beck, and the State Secretary in the Foreign Ministry, von Weizsäcker. This group, however, sought to prevent not a military attack on the Czechoslovak republic, but the outbreak of a major war in Europe. While Beck, in numerous memoranda, demanded a general political right to be heard in vital questions of national concern, and in the end gave up his struggle and resigned, the diplomat wanted to achieve a 'chemical' dissolution of Czechoslovakia beneath the threshold of the feared major war. Between 15 and 29–30 September 1938, in dramatic negotiations with Hitler, who was determined to wage a regional war, the British Prime Minister Chamberlain with the assistance of the French Prime Minister, Edouard Daladier, and Mussolini in Munich, finally succeeded in reaching an agreement among a concert of the four West European powers on the cession of the Sudetenland to Germany, which Hitler had demanded in the form of an ultimatum. The Czechoslovak government was forced to accept this death sentence for the independence of its state, the status of a satellite of Germany, and territorial claims by Hungary and Poland.

In Hitler's view the divergence between internationally justifiable German revision demands and the desired deployment area for a European war was still too great, even after the Munich Agreement. He was disappointed, and ordered plans to begin immediately for the military occupation of the rest of Czechoslovakia. On his orders, the preparation by propaganda of the German population, which on the whole had shown itself concerned about the risk of war, was also intensified. After threats in the form of an ultimatum to Czechoslovakia, the Wehrmacht occupied Prague in a surprise move on 15 March 1939. The western part of Czechoslovakia became the Protectorate of Bohemia and Moravia, and was annexed by Germany; the eastern part proclaimed itself independent as the state of Slovakia, and became a German satellite. In the wake of this event, the Germans also occupied the Memel Land, which had been annexed by Lithuania in 1923. An act of naked aggression, the extinction of the remnant of Czechoslovakia caused the European Western Powers to shift to a policy of determined resistance to further Nazi expansion, without, however, completely excluding the possibility of a negotiated solution. Among other measures, the British introduced general conscription.

Already in mid-1938, with an eye on Great Britain, Hitler had permitted the navy to accelerate U-boat construction, and had ordered a more rapid completion of important parts of the 35 per cent fleet by 1940; after that date it would be able to deter Britain from intervening on the European continent. Moreover, the navy developed a long-term plan extending to the mid-1940s centred around battleships and new kinds of armoured cruisers for a war against British naval forces and trade in the North Sea and the Atlantic. Hitler, however, insisted on the construction of a fleet centred around large battleships that would be available in 1944 at the earliest. While he prepared for a series of isolated campaigns as a precondition for a war to conquer *Lebensraum*, his plans for naval armaments pointed to a later phase involving a conflict for world domination. In the same direction, intensive planning was undertaken for colonial conquests in Africa. After the summer of 1938 large quantities of steel and cement which could have been used for armaments programmes were continually required for the West Wall fortifications, which were of limited military value but intended to have a politically deterrent effect on Belgium and France, and Göring announced a new five-fold increase in the size of the Luftwaffe in November 1938; and because of this the armaments bottlenecks became more acute. In addition to the struggle among all consuming industries demanding greater quantities of raw materials, increasing competition developed for workers in armaments concerns. To meet this problem more than a million people were conscripted for essential jobs. It was clear to all informed people that all these programmes amounted to an attempt to square a circle, which would place excessive demands on available resources and lead inevitably to social unrest in the long term. War, which had always been Hitler's aim, now received a new significance as an instrument of social integration. With an effect on the corresponding allocation of resources in the summer of 1939, the navy, however, was given priority for its large-ship construction programme (called the 'Z-Plan') by a Führer order in January of that year, another indication of Hitler's long-term aims.

In the spring of 1939 the British and French governments attempted to contain further German expansion. Poland and Romania received guarantees of independence, and negotiations on a mutual-assistance pact were begun with the Soviet Union, but were conducted only hesitantly because of concern about Bolshevik expansionism. Indeed, Poland was the next object of German aggression and, unlike Czechoslovakia, a consensus prevailed among German leaders on this question. In the winter of 1938–9, German-Polish negotiations to achieve an alliance for expansion and conquest eastward, which were intended to make Poland a junior partner in a future war in the east and which would also have given Germany the option of fighting a preceding, separate war in the west, were not successful. The Wehrmacht immediately drafted a deployment plan for early autumn on the basis of those from the previous year under the code name 'Case White'. Using a tactic similar to that practised against Czechoslovakia in 1938, Germany now deliberately escalated the problems of the German minority in Poland and played up the question of the free city of Danzig, now governed by National Socialists but still under a commissioner of the League of Nations.

For its part, Japan was involved in a military conflict with the Soviet Union along the Mongolian-Manchurian frontier and therefore shied away from closer ties with Germany, which might have had a deterrent effect on Britain and France. And the 'Pact of Steel' which Mussolini concluded with Hitler on 22 May 1939 did not correspond to any actual readiness on Italy's part to go to war. However, the German dictator did succeed in gaining strategic cover for his next act of expansion by signing a non-aggression pact with the Soviet Union on 23 August 1939.

Even in the published part of the pact his intention to attack Poland was clear. Indeed, in the preceding years the Soviet Union under Joseph Stalin had not succeeded in convincing the Western Powers that it should be accepted as a serious partner in containing Nazi aggression within the framework of collective security. It had been excluded in a humiliating fashion from the Munich Agreement, and thus had not had to prove its professed readiness to help Czechoslovakia. A pact with his ideological mortal enemy at least gave Stalin a period of security against an attack in the west and permitted the Soviet Union to continue its own rearmament, which had been proceeding at top speed during the 1930s. Moreover, under the existing circumstances an alliance with Nazi Germany was a desirable arrangement for a war that Stalin considered inevitable: the 'imperialist' powers would first weaken each other, which in turn would improve the position of the Soviet Union. In a secret supplementary agreement to the non-aggression pact, Germany was to be granted Lithuania and the part of Poland west of the Vistula in the event of a future war, while the Soviet Union was to receive Finland, Latvia, the eastern part of Poland, and Bessarabia. In their negotiations in Moscow, the

Western Powers for various reasons could never even consider such concessions. Hitler had taken a completely different route, and his aims were on the
whole quite different, but in his pact with Stalin he had realized the aims
advocated by Neurath and Bülow with regard to Poland in 1933.

Nevertheless, Hitler's and Ribbentrop's great trump to deter the Western
Powers did not succeed. After the German attack on Poland had been
postponed to test the effect of Hitler's pact with Stalin on the British and
French governments, German troops marched into Poland on 1 September
1939. As he had done in Munich in 1938, Mussolini attempted to mediate a
settlement, but this time he failed. On 3 September 1939, Britain and France
declared war on Germany. Hitler had accepted the risk of a war, which now
began as the Second World War in Europe; although the Wehrmacht was by
no means prepared for a war in the west, and likewise Britain and France did
not consider themselves sufficiently prepared to be able to give immediate
help to Poland.

|4|

The Führer State

FORMAL POWER AND THE READINESS TO BELIEVE

Neither the rise to power of the NSDAP as a radical protest party nor the 12-year history of Germany under National Socialism would have been conceivable without Adolf Hitler. At first he seemed to be mainly interested in acquiring posts of office and expanding his authority; but in the NSDAP he was and remained the Führer, not simply the party chairman, but an authority figure with unlimited powers. Of course this was also true of the party organizations, especially the paramilitary ones. Hitler was also the supreme commander of the SA after 1931, although this title did not acquire any real importance. More important was the SA and the SS's personal loyalty towards him, expressed, after 1931, in the phrase 'SS man, your honour is loyalty'. This assumed an absolute readiness to subordinate oneself to the will of the Führer. In the cabinet, the Chancellor was the first among equals. But as early as the spring of 1933 this situation had changed: 'There is no more voting; the Führer decides [everything]'.[1] Over the years the number of cabinet meetings declined steadily, with the last one taking place on 9 December 1937; although the cabinet was never formally abolished. After August 1934 Hitler also took over the office of Reich President and officially used the title of Führer and Reich Chancellor. This signified more than a mere combining of party and state offices, for it gave him an additional claim to personalized authority in the state. It was typical of the new situation that the Wehrmacht no longer took an oath to defend the constitution and pledged loyalty to the Reich President, but instead swore unconditional obedience to Hitler personally. Likewise, ministers no longer took their oath of office to the law and the constitution, but swore personal loyalty and obedience to 'the Führer of the German Reich and nation, Adolf

Hitler'. Soon Hitler was only spoken of officially as 'the Führer'; his title of Reich Chancellor faded into the background. Most important in regard to the military establishment, whose leaders set standards for the German armed forces, was Hitler's decision in February 1938 to undertake direct personal command of the Wehrmacht. He was thus able to issue direct orders to the military, whereas in his previous position as supreme commander he had exercised his authority through the Minister of War. On 19 December 1941 he placed himself at the head of the German Army. This step was the result of a temporary crisis, but it completed symbolically what had become increasingly commonplace: Hitler's intervention in military matters, down to the lowest level of command.

The Enabling Law had already transferred legislative powers to the government of the Reich, which was now able to make laws by decree, without parliament. After the mid-1930s it was accepted as a matter of course that Hitler himself had the power to make laws. This comprehensive authority was expressed in numerous Führer laws, decrees, ordinances, and, in military matters, orders. The countersigning of laws, intended to indicate the political responsibility of the minister concerned, became a mere gesture and occasionally was not even formally obtained before his name appeared with that of Hitler under a law. Increasingly this procedure signified only the attempt of the state bureaucracy to maintain a semblance of consistency and unity in the regulations and procedures concerning lawmaking. Hitler claimed dictatorial executive powers as of 1933, and as a lawmaker at the latest 2 years later. In his speech of 13 July 1934, after the murders of the SA leaders, he also claimed to be the supreme judge of Germany. The logical conclusion of this development was presented by Göring in a 'Resolution of the Great German Reichstag' of 26 July 1942:

> Without being bound by existing legal norms, the Führer, as leader of the nation, supreme commander of the Wehrmacht, head of the government and supreme executive, as the highest judge, and as leader of the party, must, therefore, always be in a position if necessary to compel any German to do his duty and, if he neglects his duty, to punish him suitably, after careful consideration, without regard to so-called well-established rights.[2]

This was a general statement of dictatorial powers unique in German history, of power over life and death, and it was meant literally. In reality, Hitler had long exercised such authority. Definitions of responsibilities and legal limitations provide only a superficial outline of his powers. He himself regarded jurists and thus all juristic limitations with abiding contempt, so that all such measures constituted nothing more than retroactive legal descriptions and frameworks for claims to an extra-legal freedom of action. More accurately, the nature of the powers Hitler ordered, expressly confirmed in legal form, and the time at which he did so were indications of his wishes and intentions at a given moment, and not of a respect for clear constitutional and administrative procedures.

More important was the readiness with which this development was accepted in German society and the willingness of many Germans to place their faith in a single individual. We have already seen how this was true of members of the NSDAP before 1933; now, in the established National Socialist state, the same tendency spread to the great majority of Germans. For one thing, there was a pre-democratic, often even anti-democratic longing to overcome the adversarial nature of politics by vesting all authority in a Führer. German society had long been pluralistic, but many Germans did not want to accept the fact that this inevitably led to political conflicts and confrontation. Inadequate development of parliamentary institutions in Imperial Germany, and the lack of a readiness to accept responsibility among the parties of Weimar, were symptoms of the tensions in the political system and social developments whose resolution, typically, many Germans did not wish to achieve through an improvement of the parliamentary democratic system. Instead, they wanted to discard it entirely. The election of Hindenburg as Reich President in 1925, and the feeling of fatherly security which radiated from his person, provided social unity in this situation; but, with increasing age, his ability to fulfil that function declined. And his presidency did not offer any prospects for the future.

Adolf Hitler's concept of political leadership was entirely different. We have already pointed out the religious aspects of the cult centred around and in Hitler as an individual. A fundamental confidence was placed in his ability to solve everyday problems. Germans wanted to see the unity and solidarity of the national community restored in his will; and in doing so, they were only too ready to overlook the terror and the ostracizing of certain groups and individuals. Unlike the redemption offered by religious traditions, however, the quasi-salvation offered to Germans by National Socialism was to be of this world, would take place in history, and would be achieved by German policies. Indeed, history was given its meaning and purpose in German greatness and power, in which individual Germans would be able to participate. To realize this aim, all Germans had to subordinate themselves to the authority of the Führer, even to the point of sacrificing their own lives. 'You are nothing; your nation is everything' was one of the slogans expressing this idea. There is no doubt that there was a close relationship between the nation of the German people and their Führer, Adolf Hitler. 'The Führer is the party and the party is the Führer. Just as I feel myself only to be part of the party, the party feels itself only to be a part of me,' Hitler proclaimed in Nuremberg in 1935.[3] A year later he returned to the subject of this almost mystical unity: 'It is a miracle of our time that you found me, that you found me among so many millions. And that I found you, that is Germany's good fortune.'

One can explain these affinities as resulting from Hitler's individual traumas and loss-anxieties, which in many respects reflected the collective reaction of all Germans to the First World War. Such interpretations have a certain internal plausibility, but they cannot be proved by using available historical sources. They do, however, make understandable the importance of the emotional quality of the Hitler factor for the political integration of Nazi Germany.

The painter Emil Nolde had declared his loyalty to National Socialism as early as 1920, and therefore could not understand why his pictures were declared to be 'decadent art' and why he was forbidden to paint. Ludwig Mies van der Rohe, one of the pioneers of modern architecture, at first attempted to continue working and contributing to the Führer state even after the prohibition of the Bauhaus school; only then was he driven to emigrate. Other members of that movement wanted to preserve a 'German Bauhaus', and some of them were able to continue their work and received public commissions from the National Socialist state. Especially intellectuals, inspired by the feeling of a fresh beginning, became zealous champions of the new way of thinking. The philosopher Martin Heidegger understood the Führer principle as the realization of Plato's idea of the rule of philosopher kings, and hoped to be able himself, from his position as rector of the University of Freiburg, to reorganize German universities according to that principle. Gottfried Benn, a medical doctor and poet, saw in the 'total state' the intention to achieve a complete identity of individuality and community:

> [The idea of the] Führer is not the quintessence of power; it is not at all conceived as a principle of terror, but is considered the highest spiritual principle. [The idea of the] Führer is the creative element. It encompasses the responsibility, the danger and the decision, and also the completely irrational factor of the historical will, which becomes visible only through him. . . . In our case the people have delivered themselves to this Führer.[4]

In Cologne the respected Germanist Ernst Bertram proclaimed, with reference to Hölderlin and Goethe, 'We have been permitted to experience what too many had forgotten or believed that they could deride: that in a people who have not been abandoned by the spirit of history a great danger will call forth a great salvation, and a great saviour.' In May 1933, with a scarcely concealed anti-Bolshevism, he celebrated the 'second great Battle of Tannenberg against Asia' in the 'wondrous capacity for self-rejuvenation of the peoples with a truly Germanic spirit'. In their own specialized fields other scientists, jurists, educators, historians, and philosophers followed these examples. Although this effusive tone was dominant only in that atmosphere of dramatic new beginning which characterized the formative phase of the National Socialist regime, it never completely disappeared, and continued, on various occasions and for various reasons, in the following years.

Above all, the faith in the Führer affected all classes: students, lawyers and doctors, farmers and industrial workers, artisans and white-collar workers. Hitler became the point of reference and focus of personal loyalty in the integration of German society; and of course, some aspects of this development also had a political content. Many Germans later mentioned the fascination that Hitler exerted over them, in personal conversations with members of the Nazi leadership, in the mass experience of political rallies and marches. Conversely, those who later described in detail how the Führer had not exercised any irresistible emotional power over them were surprised to find that their experience was not typical.

THE GERMAN PUBLIC AND
THE FÜHRER CULT

If people believed in such a charismatic personality, as many Germans and even some non-Germans clearly did in Hitler, it is difficult to discern what appealed to the genuine emotional needs of his followers, and what was caused merely by manipulation. In any case, their predispositions were aroused, reinforced, and maintained through periods of political discontent and crises by a multifarious, differentiated propaganda. Hitler was also a media product, part of a phenomenon that involved the penetration, to a much greater extent than ever before, of state-controlled propaganda into the daily lives of individual citizens. Hitler's speeches were broadcast by radio, a medium which only few could afford at first. But after 1933 a simple, cheap 'people's receiver' (*Volksempfänger*), which could receive only one broadcasting station, was produced in huge quantities. Even before the war, annual production exceeded 1 million.[5] In 1935, 7 million such receivers were registered; in 1943 the figure was 16 million. 'The Führer Speaks' was the title of an oil painting showing, in an almost iconic style, a farming family listening intently while gathered around a 'people's receiver'. 'All Germany Listens to the Führer' was the title of a poster of 1933 in which, similar to the Kaaba in Mecca, such a receiver towered above a vast crowd of people. Plans were made to add a visual element to German broadcasting propaganda through television, which had been tested at the Olympic Games in Berlin in 1936 on a small scale; but its introduction did not take place because of the war. The weekly newsreel in the cinemas, which had been a popular feature since the beginning of the 1930s, brought Hitler's face as well as his voice close to the people, thus providing a collective experience before the feature film. Hitler as a speaker, with his ecstatic, electrifying gestures, was one of the main subjects. In 1937, Hermann Hoyer entitled a picture he presented at the Great Art Exhibition, 'In the Beginning Was the Word'. It showed Hitler making a speech in a back room in the early 1920s. The religious reference was obvious. Thousands, even hundreds of thousands were able to experience Hitler's presence personally at mass events such as Harvest Festival Day (*Erntedanktag*) on the Bückelberg, or the annual NSDAP party rally in Nuremberg. At such events society was constituted symbolically in its orientation towards a revival experience through the medium of Hitler's speech; in terms of their intended aim, such events were manifestations of a constantly repeated miracle of Pentecost.

The omnipresence of pictures of the head of state, from offices to postage stamps, was a tradition. But when Hitler appeared as a hero hewn out of stone, and occasionally on the motion-picture screen as a hero among heroes or, as in the works of Fritz Erler, in the form of a larger-than-life stone hero armed with an eagle and sword, his much more far-reaching, almost religious claim to leadership was suggested. On the other hand, Hitler was also intended to be a 'leader you can touch', who concerned himself with the cares and needs of ordinary people. And it was on the basis of this propaganda-induced tension that the Führer myth developed. Cigarette packets contained coupons for a total of 200 photos which made up an album called *Adolf Hitler*, published in an edition of 100,000 copies in 1936.[6] Even children could build up a complete collection of 'Führer' pictures. For the de luxe collector's album, leading National Socialists composed texts of praise that had as their common theme the bonds between Hitler and the most varied social classes. Pictures of him in seemingly relaxed everyday life were placed next to those of jubilant, massed, or deeply moved people. On the first page was a dedicatory quote from Göring:

> My Führer, we are not able to express our thanks in words. Nor are we able to show our loyalty and affection for you in words. Our entire gratitude, love for, and trust in you, my Führer, is shining upon you today from hundreds of thousands of eyes. Today the entire nation, the entire people feels strong and happy, because in you not only the Führer but also the saviour of the nation has appeared.

Each chapter showed Hitler with members of various social groups, from German workers to artists, young people, and members of the Wehrmacht. In the foreword Goebbels declared his faith in propaganda as an art:

> National Socialism and its most important representatives not only have a natural gift for this art; in constant work and contact with the people they have learned and applied it while progressively refining it to the highest level.

By praising Hitler here and everywhere else as the 'great teacher', Goebbels combined a kernel of objective truth with an exaggerated estimation of the importance of the area for which his Ministry of Popular Enlightenment and Propaganda was responsible.

The veneration of Hitler is all the more notable if one considers the real Adolf Hitler. Whenever he did not appear in a party or Wehrmacht uniform (and after 1939 he appeared only in such uniforms) he was by no means impressive. In speeches his voice sounded hoarse; his agitated pathos was precisely calculated, as were his often abrupt gestures, which he practised before a mirror. In daily life he was quite different from his public persona, often proceeding in a disorderly fashion. He liked to travel, frequently by aeroplane, often by car. 'Everywhere in the country farmers left their machines standing, women waved; it was a triumphal journey,' his travelling companion reported, thus underlining the fact that Hitler's popularity went beyond staged mass meetings.[7] He was inclined to continue his earlier Bohemian lifestyle as far as possible, and to live withdrawn from the public eye. He liked to spend his time with informal groups of old party comrades or adjutants, or with certain artists. His working day did not proceed according to any set plan. In the evening he frequently watched feature films in private until late at night and began his work again around noon the following day. Above all, he increasingly made access to himself a matter of personal affection or aversion. He was often absent from Berlin for weeks, devoting his attention to architectural plans or music. After 1935 he spent much time in his house on the Obersalzberg near Berchtesgaden; several of his vassals (Göring, Speer, and Bormann) were permitted to build houses nearby.

In spite of telephone communications, Hitler's governance of Germany lacked any real continuity. He usually expressed his will as Führer spontaneously and irregularly. He followed matters which interested him in detail, but put off dealing with other, important questions, or did not concern himself with them at all. This was primarily a matter of his personal style, but it was also a consciously applied method of rule. Not taking decisions also has certain consequences. During the war, Hitler spent much time at various Führer headquarters, which was intended to emphasize his role as a soldier. This resulted in a further reduction of the number of people with whom he dealt directly and restricted his access to information even more. Even ministers no longer had direct access to the 'Führer'. The discrepancy between the Hitler who was adored with religious fervour and the real person can only be explained by the eagerness to believe, by the will to venerate, which was shared by many Germans as well as by others.

Especially because the feeling of a new beginning in the first months did not last, and dissatisfaction with National Socialist policies – whether with the persecution of the churches, the availability of material goods, or with the sight and experience of the violent ostracizing and persecution of certain groups, and of the war itself – the Hitler factor was essential to the survival of the National Socialist regime. It united large parts of society and held the Germans together. Only in 1941, and especially in 1943, were there serious declines in Hitler's popularity. He also remained popular because important parts of the National Socialist system of rule, individuals as well as structures, were rejected or viewed critically by large parts of the population. But this faith in Hitler was not self-perpetuating. In spite of all the dynamism he and his regime created and repeatedly unleashed, it required political successes and aims, whose implications or alternatives were not always completely clear to those whom they were intended to impress. 'Silent night, holy night / all is calm, one is keeping watch / Adolf Hitler guides Germany's fate / Leads us to greatness, to fame and to good fortune / Gives us Germans power again.'[8] This revision of a Christmas carol did not become generally popular, but it was meant to be taken seriously, and it shows the goal for which all energies were to be mobilized: power. 'Today Germany hears us, tomorrow the world,' Germans sang to marching music; and they often shifted the stress and changed the word for 'hear' (*hören*) to 'belong to' (*gehören*).

THE 'LITTLE FÜHRERS'

If a charismatic leader was guiding the country, the Führer principle also applied elsewhere in the state. Borrowed from military principles, it meant the subordination of the individual to the authority of the Führer or leader, who then assumed responsibility for all orders. Decisions based on expressions of popular will from below were thus frowned upon in principle. It was inevitable that a large number of little and very little 'Führers' should shoot up like mushrooms. This was, for example, true of NSDAP functionaries. On paper the party was thoroughly and tightly organized. From the Reich leaders as the central office, the hierarchy extended down to Gau, district, and local group leaders, and to cell and block leaders. But most important of all were the Gau leaders, and occasionally the district and local group leaders. They were often 'old fighters' from the 1920s who stayed in their positions until the end. The party, which was relatively young at all levels of the hierarchy, inevitably grew older. In 1933 the Gau leaders were, on average, 40 years old; by 1944 their average age was 48.[9] They headed the Gaus of the party, which usually followed the lines of Reichstag election districts. But, like little rulers, the Gau leaders often tried to expand their domains. In fact, all they recognized was a personal allegiance to Hitler; they basked in his reflected glory and even attempted to imitate his gestures. Occasionally these provincial potentates were inclined to close off their Gaus from the outside world and, as it were, return to a feudal system in the twentieth century. But they were not completely successful in such efforts.

All the groups of functionaries mentioned above were 'political leaders' and, according to the rule that 'the party commands the state', they had to issue orders, realize their wishes, and expand their own power bases in order to strengthen their prestige. They reviewed party paramilitary formations, performed ceremonial functions, made plans, and distributed sinecures. As a rule they were not from the fringes of society, nor were they uprooted *Freikorps* fighters, although such persons could be found in their ranks. Rather, whether they were social climbers or persons who had suffered a decline in their social position, they owed their careers to the party, and that remained the decisive factor in their loyalties. Ideologically there were some differences among them: in their more or less rabid anti-Semitism or anti-

Bolshevism, and in their more or less intensely held views of a uniform, 'socialist', national community. After 1933–4 they often found no outlet for their dynamism as subordinates; they had to look for new fields of activity. Terror against and intimidation of enemies whom they were able to create and define themselves, such as the churches or the Jews, represented one possibility. Social or charitable activities were another. Above all, they sought to keep the rest of the population in line, and especially to induce them to make public professions of political faith in Adolf Hitler. But in the Gau leaders' own lives the level of commitment often declined.

When these functionaries wore their uniforms on official occasions it was obvious that they were doing well, and that all their activity for the party had not reduced their waistlines. The hierarchy of full-time functionaries extended downward to the level of the district leaders (*Kreisleiter*). As early as 1935 there were 25,000 of them in the National Socialist bureaucracies. In 1937 the total figure was 700,000; during the war it rose to 2 million at the level of block leader or above. Block leaders were each responsible for several housing blocks in the cities. They checked the hanging-out of flags or air-raid equipment in the attics, and were noted for their self-importance, which was not always well-received by those whom they supervised. Party functionaries often led a life of luxury; talk of the corruption, drunkenness, and violence of these 'golden pheasants' was widespread. Their informal network was considered a means of avoiding work and responsibility, especially during the war, when their inflated apparatus was reduced only slightly. The contrast between the appeals of the party for saving and selfless sacrifice for the national community and the contempt for such appeals obvious in the lifestyles of the functionaries embittered the average German. Undoubtedly the lower functionaries had no charisma and were unpopular. But they formed the foil for the popularity of the Führer. 'If the Führer knew that' soon became a common phrase of daily life when improprieties concerning party bosses became known. It was for this reason especially that Hitler was removed from and raised above everyday concerns and was thus able to preserve his function of uniting German society. And in principle the Führer did know everything, whether it involved the bottlenecks in the economy or that he let the lower functionaries do what they liked. Among other things, he let them use terror. In his remoteness and asceticism, which supposedly served only the nation as a whole, he alone retained his credibility; while in the everyday reality of Nazi Germany the exact opposite could be observed. As a police report noted:

> Many people are of the opinion that in the selection of lower-ranking leaders too little weight is placed on their private lives. Party comrades, namely heads of offices, who spend a lot of time in pubs, do not meet their obligations or do not take adequate care of their families, offer black [i.e. Catholic] circles a welcome opportunity to criticize the whole [National Socialist] movement.[10] ... The people place their

hopes in a strong leader and expect from him deliverance and security. They gladly obey him. On the other hand, the little incongruities caused by petty or mistaken measures of organs at lower levels tend to dampen the enthusiastic acceptance of the new state in broad segments of the population.

Because of the distinction between the Führer, who was honoured almost as a religious figure, and the clearly imperfect 'little Führers', there were considerable differences among the Gau leaders themselves.[11] Pathological cases, such as Julius Streicher in Franconia, who distinguished himself primarily by his obsessive, prurient anti-Semitism and occasionally went too far even for Hitler in his incendiary paper *Der Stürmer*, were rare. For Joseph Goebbels, who was the Gau leader of Berlin, that position was only part of his power-base. On the other hand, Bernhard Rust, Gau leader in Hanover, had little say in what happened there, for he functioned primarily as the Reich Minister of Culture, which itself was not a strong power-base. Many Gau leaders derived their power from the accumulation of additional offices. Combining the offices of Gau leader and governor (*Reichsstatthalter*), or in Prussia *Oberpräsidenten*, the highest provincial administrative officials, and in Bavaria *Regierungspräsidenten* ('Government Presidents') became frequent. Such a combination of party and state offices usually strengthened the position of functionaries as independent princes; they were often able to evade their formal subordination to Minister of the Interior Frick because of their party functions, even when their state office was more important. This combination of regional state and party office was not the rule. Above all, the boundaries of their areas were not congruent, and during the entire National Socialist period the situation did not change, in spite of the reform planned by Frick. Hitler was simply not interested in the question.

For example, Joseph Bürckel, originally the Gau leader of the Bavarian Rhine Palatinate, first became State Commissar and not Government President there. When the Saar again became part of Germany and he began to reorganize his Gau on the party level into the Saar Palatinate in 1936, he needed an additional 4 years to bring the state administration under his control, but even then he was still unable to eliminate all remnants of Bavarian authority; one reason for the frequently continuing dualism of state and party was that state offices, too, were occupied by party members, especially as the NSDAP was also the state party as of the end of 1933. In this case, Bürckel found himself in conflict with Wagner, the Bavarian Minister of the Interior (who was also Gau leader of Munich) and his Minister President, Siebert; both of these men were veteran National Socialists. And claiming, for example, that the party was responsible for leadership and the state for administration, the former for dynamic change and the latter for continuity, only served to paper over conflicts. At any rate, the clear authority of party organs to issue orders to the state administration was not established, and Frick himself fought doggedly but unsuccessfully for a clear order of appeal in the machinery of the centralized state. But this problem could only be solved on a case-by-case basis, which usually meant through contacts and negotiations between individuals. Chief burgomasters (*Oberbürgermeister*) and district leaders, local group leaders and mayors, government presidents and Gau leaders developed their own individual working relationships with each other which extended from close co-operation without friction to intense hostility in which the men involved were not even on speaking terms; and this was to remain a characteristic feature of the system.

COMPETITION AND RIVALRY
WITHIN THE NSDAP

In 1937 more than four-fifths of all civil servants in Prussia, and more than two-thirds in the other parts of Germany, belonged to the Nazi Party. A considerable number in both groups had joined the party only in 1933. Rivalries between state and party authorities thus usually involved party members on both sides, showing how limited was the dualism between state and party as an instrument to explain such conflicts. Obstinate or convinced National Socialists were inclined to place most value on ideological loyalty and their personal positions as leaders, which they often emphasized by wearing their uniform; then on heightened control, supervision and terror; and later on holding out to the bitter end. Moderate or 'reasonable' National Socialists tended to conform rigidly but superficially to accepted norms of behaviour, but sought to retain objective, technical factors and bureaucratic rationality as criteria in decision making. The entire spectrum of behaviour was to be found in the state as well as the party hierarchy. In addition to these two hierarchies, and the frequent personal union of state and party offices in them, as we shall see later, more and more organizations and authorities developed that did not clearly belong in one area or the other.

The party itself was a tightly structured hierarchy only on paper. This was true even at the top. Contrary to all National Socialist ideological principles, under Hitler, who based his power on the Chancellery of the Führer (as of 1941 the Party Chancellery), bureaucratic structures developed which had a tendency to strengthen their positions. The 'Brown House' in Munich remained the central party office. The initially important liaison office in Berlin soon lost most of its influence. Rudolf Hess was named Deputy of the Führer in the Bavarian capital, and as early as 1936 he presided over more than 3,000 employees there. Although he became a Reich Minister at the same time in 1933, he never achieved an importance commensurate with his title. The strong position of Hess's predecessor, Gregor Strasser, made it especially advisable in Hitler's eyes to have a loyal vassal completely dependent on his favour in Munich. Although he did possess a certain rhetorical talent, Hess, a former student of the geopolitician Karl Haushofer, was able only occasionally in relations with state authorities to present himself as a spokesman for the entire party. Within the party itself he did not have such a role, for he was, in June 1936, only one of sixteen Reich leaders (*Reichsleiter*) in the party, who for their part were responsible for certain areas ('Reich offices' or *Reichsämter*). He hardly had anything to say to the outwardly unimpressive but influential party treasurer, Franz Xaver Schwarz. With Robert Ley, the Reich Organization Leader, he was involved in bitter struggles. Ley increasingly developed his power base in the German Labour Front (*Deutsche Arbeitsfront*). It was hardly conceivable that the Reich Propaganda Leader Goebbels, the Reich Press Chief, or the head of the Foreign Policy Office of the party (*Aussenpolitisches Amt*) would accept orders from Hess.

Attempts to control the nominally subordinate Gau leaders from the central office of the party were equally unsuccessful. To be sure, some Reich leaders created their own party and bureaucratic hierarchies extending down to the district and local level when that was in keeping with their areas of authority. Such hierarchies were subordinate to the respective regional NSDAP authorities, but loyalty conflicts with the Reich leader were frequent. All these offices functioned under the collective designation of 'political organizations'; their functionaries were called 'political leaders' (*Politische Leiter*)

The situation was made more complicated by the fact that there also existed party organizations and associated formations. The first group included primarily the SA, the SS, the National Socialist Motor Vehicle Corps (*NS-Kraftfahrkorps* or NSKK), the Hitler Youth, the National Socialist German Student Union, and the National Socialist Women's Organization (*NS-Frauenschaft*). The second group extended from the German Labour Front to the National Socialist Welfare Agency (*NS-Volkswohlfahrt*) and the National Socialist teachers', civil servants', and jurists' federations. Thus Baldur von Schirach as Reich Youth Leader or Heinrich Himmler as the Reich Leader SS had considerably more power over their organizations, and therefore in the state as a whole, than did Gertrud Scholtz-Klink in the Women's Organization or Adolf Hühnlein of the Motor Vehicle Corps. But all of them considered themselves to be 'Führers' although they had occasion to realize such claims only in rather ludicrous and trivial ways. While the Nazi Party was omnipresent in the political life of the country, it was at the same time, on the whole, a rather formless organization. There was no established decision-making process in the party. In the first years after 1933 it seemed that the Reich governors and the Gau leaders might become a directing body; but their assemblies later served only as sounding-boards for Hitler's speeches, just as their occasional meetings with the 'Führer', especially on 9 November every year, remained informal and mostly non-political in the narrower sense of that term. The party was simply not a uniform and unified body. As in the state apparatus, shared decision-making in the cabinet fell into disuse while the accumulation by individuals of personal power, which could only be maintained for certain periods of time became increasingly important.

This uncontrolled growth of the various changing concentrations of power renders futile any attempt to illustrate the structures of the National Socialist regime in diagram form: at best, such efforts only provide approximations and snapshots of the regime at a given point in time. And this situation accurately reflected Hitler's intentions; for all legally unambiguous, established decision-making processes were contrary to his view of the importance of dynamism in politics. He was more interested in the social Darwinist ability of individuals to assert themselves and carry out extraordinary plans and projects in accordance with his wishes. It was thus typical of him often to give relatively young men special assignments to solve problems requiring expert knowledge, and to vest them with extensive special powers. A given task was to have priority above all other established authorities. Such tasks were usually connected with important political decisions which Hitler had to take; and he thus ensured that their completion would receive priority and would be executed outside the traditional bureaucratic approach. It was therefore, as a rule, not dynamism in itself but rather the fulfilment of assigned tasks requiring a goal-orientated display of activity which led to individual concentrations of power. Not only the slogan 'Make Way for the Able!' (*Freie Bahn dem Tüchtigen*) was the guiding rule; individuals also gained significant positions of power as a result of the dissolution of traditional mechanisms of control. Indeed, there was even a tendency in this way to dissolve the traditional concept of the modern state as a whole.

FUNCTIONAL POWER: TODT AND SPEER

The case of Fritz Todt provides an example of how power and authority were often accumulated in National Socialist Germany.[12] Todt combined expert technical and technocratic competence with National Socialist, ethnocentric attitudes. Only at first glance does this constitute a strange combination of rational planning and irrational, emotional longings; it was actually typical of a large number of people in his profession in Nazi Germany.

Todt was a civil engineer. He had joined the Nazi Party in 1922, when he founded a local party group. Until 1933 he devoted his time primarily to his profession and only occasionally took part in SA marches. In December 1932, while serving as an adviser to Gottfried Feder in the Office for Economic Technology and Job Creation of the NSDAP (*Amt für Wirtschaftstechnik und Arbeitsbeschaffung der NSDAP*), Todt produced a memorandum in which he argued that unemployment could be eliminated by a programme of large-scale road construction. Hitler heard of the memorandum and combined plans for motorways (*Autobahnen*) developed elsewhere with Todt's ideas. The fact that the 'Company Reich Autobahn', which was established by virtue of a special law, was initially under the Reich Railways (*Reichsbahn*) soon became as unimportant as its later position as a high Reich agency, for Todt became general inspector of the German road system, a position to which he devoted himself with great energy. As we have already seen, Autobahn construction did not contribute significantly to reducing unemployment, but Todt was able to employ a quarter of a million men by 1936. His people were soon busy building Autobahns, usually with the enthusiasm of artists and landscapers, in all parts of the Reich.

In the Sudeten Crisis in 1938, the German plan was to use any means to deter France from intervening to stop the German aggression. As the rapid construction of a line of fixed fortifications in the west was too much for the military planning staffs responsible, Todt was given a second great task in May 1938: to build the so-called West Wall. This was a system of bunkers and anti-tank obstacles, and consumed a large part of German steel and cement production urgently needed for other parts of the armaments programme. At times the project employed 430,000 people, from persons in the German Labour Service to skilled workers, some of whom were conscripted by decree for labour service. They worked up to 13 hours a day, and were referred to for the first time by Hitler as the Todt Organization (OT). Large parts of the construction industry were occupied with this task until the start of the war.

From a military point of view, the entire project was of very doubtful value, but it did underline the importance placed on the ability to accomplish the seemingly impossible through sheer determination and energy in Nazi Germany. When at the same time the navy was supposed to expand rapidly, but the shipyards were already operating at the limits of their capacity or were unable to increase it fast enough in spite of all the funds and materials made available to them, Hitler wistfully expressed his wish for a 'man like Todt'.

But it was the experience of the first war months which resulted in Todt's also being made responsible for armaments production. As early as the end of 1938, Hermann Göring had attempted to draw Todt into the bureaucracy of the Four Year Plan as 'plenipotentiary' for the organization of the construction industry in areas under his authority. In March 1940, when bottlenecks developed in preparations for the war in Western Europe, Todt was given special authority as Reich Minister for Armaments and Munitions for those areas of the economy. It was now a matter not only of concentrating raw materials, labour, and people, but also of co-ordinating parts of private industry, a task which Todt fulfilled with considerable success for individual types of armaments. With all his technocratic achievements in increasing production, Todt was more than merely a gifted organizer without ideological background: and he attempted to organize engineers and technicians in keeping with his understanding of National Socialism. In competition with similar efforts by Gottfried Feder, on Todt's advice the

National Socialist Union of German Technology (*Nationalsozialistischer Bund Deutscher Technik*) was founded as a national professional organization in 1934. Todt himself became the head of the Society of German Engineers in 1938, but this did not take in even half of all German engineers. In addition, therefore, Todt took over the Main Office for Technology (*Hauptamt für Technik*) of the NSDAP and several positions in the German Labour Front. In July 1941 he was given his last office, that of General Inspector for Water and Energy. But before he was able to make any decisive changes in that sector, where bottlenecks were becoming increasingly frequent, he was killed in an aeroplane crash on 8 February 1942.

Todt's successor in all the positions he had occupied was Albert Speer, who had a similar career. As a young architect, born in 1905, Speer had attracted Hitler's attention early with decorative commissions and remodelling projects. In 1937, as General Inspector of Construction for the Capital of the Reich, he was put in charge of a project especially close to Hitler's heart which, in its basic tendency, was soon extended to include most large German cities. After the start of the war, a part of Speer's now very extensive bureaucratic apparatus was placed in the service of the war effort, taking on the organization, for example, of transport tasks. After Todt's death, Speer expanded his authority in the war economy more and more. In addition to his other offices, he was named Reich Minister for Armaments and War Production in September 1943. His all-encompassing Ministry was given the task of co-ordinating and directing most areas of German war production, and was responsible for the related programmes of all three service branches. His influence extended to distant parts of German-occupied Europe, especially in the west. The Todt Organization, the only National Socialist organization except the Hitler Youth that ever bore the name of a living political figure, also became a Europe-wide apparatus with 70,000 employees, from the Atlantic Wall in France, to road construction in Lapland, to the Soviet Union and Turkey.

Several things become clear when we consider the careers of Todt and Speer. Both men built their careers on authority they had received from Hitler. Todt did not belong to the smaller circle around the Führer; Speer believed for a time that, as an architectural adviser, he had become almost a personal friend of the dictator. Special commissions for activities connected with a number of related projects were often carried out within differing legal frameworks. Here the framework and foundation of the necessary authority consisted primarily of positions of state. For such special projects the title of Minister signified no more than an increase in the power of the individual concerned, who then still had to overcome the resistance of the established ministries normally given such tasks. Overcoming such resistance did not deprive those ministries of their traditional functions and authority; they continued to exist, so to speak, as empty shells. Most important were the authority, dynamism, and aggressiveness with which a plenipotentiary overcame the opposition of the existing, and thus apparently rigid and bureaucratic institutions. In addition to the markedly youthful gestures of men such as Speer, a policy of threats and intimidation was also needed, together with a knowledge of and readiness to use terror and the doctrine of the master race, a readiness to stop at nothing if that were necessary to achieve one's own goals. State and party authorities penetrated and complemented each other. In the case of Todt and Speer, their authority and influence in the party at least guaranteed that no-one else there would begin to develop his own plans and policies. In such concentrations of power not only the dividing lines between the state and the party were blurred, but those separating the state and industry were also affected. Although the role of the state in determining production goals was not limited to the war years, during that period it became especially prominent, allowing one to use the term 'command economy'. But already under Todt, and then in the extensive system created by Speer, leaders in the economy and industrialists accepted responsibility for co-ordinating tasks that otherwise would have been performed by the state bureaucracy.

Special tasks and orders directly from the Führer were in conflict not only with traditional administrative forms and practices, but often also with each other. As early as 1938 a bitter dispute developed between Todt's West Wall construction projects and Speer's remodelling measures for German cities. And grants of sweeping powers concerned only with results and not with the methods used also became more frequent for other tasks. Examined more closely, the resulting situation appears as a chaotic free-for-all which often led to personal hostility and compensation negotiations as between feudal lords. A jungle of conflicts of authority developed; bureaucratic rationality, in which decisions were taken in accordance with set procedures, was ignored and fell into disuse. Tendencies towards similar developments can undoubtedly be found in other regimes, but in National Socialist Germany they became the established practice. The setting of aims replaced a weighing of the means available to realize them. In 1938, Göring characterized this situation: if one took the present level of performance and use of capacity as 100, Hitler demanded performance at the level of 300, which in itself was impossible. In retrospect it was later clear that a level of 300 had indeed not been achieved, but, to continue this illustration, in an astonishingly short time, a level of 150 had been reached, which was sufficient to keep things going.[13] The consequence of this was a feverish activity and dynamism on one hand, together with idling and paralysis in other areas, and a new bureaucratization of the co-ordination of organizations among themselves and in the new special administrative organs. This beginning of the dissolution of previous state structures continued to function throughout the 12 years of National Socialist rule and, despite outward appearances, it led to a high degree of psychological and material mobilization which made it possible to wage a world war for 6 years.

THE PROPAGANDA CHIEF: JOSEPH GOEBBELS

Joseph Goebbels was the complete party functionary. He owed his rise as Nazi Gau leader of Berlin (1926–45) above all to the mass success of the public events he staged and to the aggressive journalism of his party newspaper, *Der Angriff* (The Attack). In the party he secured his position with such additional posts as that of Reich Propaganda Leader. The mass events he staged, especially the assemblies in the Berlin Sport Palace, were essential components of a specific form of the conquest and maintenance of power. Although, as a skilled media expert, he was indispensable for the National Socialist movement, after 30 January 1933 he had to wait for several uneasy weeks until a ministry was created for him. That shows how insecure he considered his role to be, although the delay was probably due primarily to the fact that Hitler needed time to make the radical agitator palatable to his conservative coalition partners. Then, however, Goebbels began with great energy to expand the Ministry of Popular Enlightenment and Propaganda; in 1937 it already employed 1,000 people. As many of them were very young and had little previous training, this situation was often incompatible with the traditional civil-service hierarchy.

Goebbels based his seemingly comprehensive combination of state and party office on his Ministry. But he did not receive a monopoly in the area of public media and publishing; in the party leadership Reich Press Chief Dietrich developed a strong position, and the party publisher, Max Amann, retained his authority. Nor did Goebbels have sole authority in determining what was considered news and what the press should publish. Like National Socialist authorities, traditional Ministries such as the Foreign Ministry and the Ministry of Defence also claimed a right to release information as they saw fit. The manipulation of the controlled media was usually done by means of Reich press conferences, at which individual media organs were given different topics for editorial comment in order to create an illusion of pluralism.

Goebbels was able to realize only the beginnings of his most ambitious plans for a comprehensive national educational and cultural programme. This was not only because there was a (relatively weak) Reich Minister of Culture, but also because Goebbels' main rival in this area was Alfred Rosenberg who, as a Reich leader, occupied the position of a chief ideologue and 'representative of the Führer for the schooling and education of the entire national movement'. In general Rosenberg, whose pseudo-philosophical approach was even made fun of by many National Socialists, was no match for 'little Doctor' Goebbels. But Rosenberg's many-faceted activities extended from genealogical research to the Nordic Society and, by 1940, he was beginning to construct a university-level 'Higher School' of the Nazi Party at Chiemsee. It was decisive that, as early as the end of 1933, Goebbels was able to push through his project for a Reich Chamber of

Culture (*Reichskulturkammer*), whose chairman he became, against similar ideas advanced by Rosenberg. The vain attempt by Robert Ley, with whom Goebbels at first allied himself, to take all 'workers of the brain and the fist', including artists, under his wing in the German Labour Front did not change this situation.

In the Reich Chamber of Culture, a Reich sub-chamber for each area was created, from graphic arts to literature, film, music (with Richard Strauss as president), the press (with Max Amann as president and Otto Dietrich in the Presidential Council), and radio. These sub-chambers thus represented a corporative organization, and they attempted to define a German, Aryan, or National Socialist concept of culture and to suppress other views by exclusion, which was one factor that often led to the emigration of the people affected. In addition to his activities as a Minister, Goebbels liked to assume the role of censor and adviser, in films, say. And he enjoyed being honoured in the company of film stars and entertainers; in this respect he was similar to Hitler. His main activity consisted of staging spectacular, memorable events, and it covered a broad spectrum: the Day of Potsdam, book burning (May 1933), the Olympic Games of 1936 in Berlin, Mussolini's state visit to Germany in 1937, the persecution of the Jews in the pogrom night of 1938, (*Kristallnacht*), and his publicly broadcast speeches, like that on total war in 1943. Although Hitler associated privately with the Goebbels family, Goebbels was among those initiated into his political plans only in the pre-war years. During the war, as can be seen in Goebbels's very informative diaries – themselves a mixture of self-persuasion and self-promotion – he was no longer kept informed of the latest developments. As impressive as his power and real influence were, they both show the permanent struggle he was engaged in with other institutions, a struggle in which at least the leadership of the German youth organizations must also be included.

NATIONAL SOCIALIST MASS ORGANIZATIONS: THE WORKERS AND THE RURAL POPULATION

Whereas Goebbels was in the spotlight of public notoriety in particular because of his efforts to manipulate public opinion, the heads of the highly regimented mass organizations attracted less attention. Robert Ley, who had a doctorate in chemistry, built his career as Gau leader of the Rhineland and then as Reich Organization Leader (*Reichorganisationsleiter*) of the Nazi Party.[14] Occupied with the *Gleichschaltung* of the free trade unions and then with reducing the power of the NSBO, he used the latter assignment to improvise the development of the German Labour Front (*Deutsche Arbeitsfront* or DAF), ideologically intended as a peaceful union of employees and employers. The DAF embodied the desired national community in the economy. By the beginning of the war, at least in part as the result of some pressure, 90 per cent of all 25.3 million German workers and other employees were DAF members. Its total membership contributions were three times the figure for the Nazi Party; in the end, it was also paying 44,500 full-time employees. Of course it was not a traditional organization for defending the interests of employees, but Ley's ambitions grew to fit the size of his organization, and he soon claimed more and more authority in the formulation of economic and social policy. In this respect, however, he failed because of the resistance of other National Socialist organizations as well as the Labour, Economics and Finance Ministers and, not least, the Four Year Plan and the Wehrmacht. In spite of price and wage freezes, especially in the armaments industry, the DAF pushed through wage increases in the pre-war years. Moreover, it developed comprehensive social services for employees at work and in their free time. This extended from better lighting of workplaces to break-rooms and canteens in factories as a result of the efforts of the office 'Beautification of the Work Place' – in which Speer initially played an important part – to competition for the title of 'National Socialist Model Company' and to the Reich Vocational Competition, in which points were awarded in nineteen fields for professional performance, ideological reliability, and athletic ability. In 1939, some 3.5 million people were engaged in such DAF activities, and this continued during the war. The 'Strength through Joy' (*Kraft durch Freude*) organization of the DAF, which sponsored leisure-time activities for German employees, was one of the few areas in which Italian fascism served as a model. It became the most popular institution of the regime. A cruise fleet brought simple workers to Norwegian fjords, Naples, or Madeira, although cruises to these destinations represented only a small fraction of the total. The construction of a beach resort for 20,000 people on Rügen, theatre and other quite popular, non-political events, and housing construction were some of the incentives for DAF members to support Ley and the regime. Everyone could save for their own automobile and thus could hope for the realization of a piece of 'people's socialism'. The 'Strength through Joy' automobile became the 'people's car' (*Volkswagen*); but, in the event, the savings were used to pay for armaments during the war. The DAF-owned book and press concern had few points of friction with Goebbels. During the war the DAF concentrated on the psychological mobilization of labour for the war effort, but also on the welfare of the troops. As Reich Housing Commissar after November 1940, Ley sought to build a strong position in competition with Speer's urban-planning ambitions. At first his aim was the rebuilding of German cities after the expected final victory, but this was increasingly replaced by emergency measures during the war.

In view of the priority given to sound training, which was essential for rapid rearmament, Ley soon encountered difficulties with the organization of skilled workmen. And in spite of continuing struggles over the years, he did not achieve any lasting success among agricultural workers. The radical 'blood-and-soil' ideologue Walter Darré, who had a B.Sc. in agronomy – among his works were 'The Pig as the Criterion for Nordic People and Semites' in his book _Nation and Race_ (1926)[15] – already in 1933 united in his own person the authority of the party leader of the agricultural policy apparatus, the Reich Food Minister, and the Reich Farmer Leader at the head of the farmers' organizations, all of which had been subjected to _Gleichschaltung_. On paper this was an impressive concentration of power, but the party apparatus declined in this sector and was almost entirely absorbed into the regional organizations of the Reich Food Estate (_Reichsnährstand_), the state or the district farmer leaders, although these organizations generally did not lose their traditional character as an agrarian lobby. For example, in East Prussia the state farm leader was able to fight against the party organization because of its 'Bolshevik' aims and methods, while the Gau leader (Koch) accused him of 'agrarian reaction'. It should be noted that in reality the influence of the big landowners east of the Elbe was not an issue here, for that was eliminated as a political factor during the National Socialist period. But on the whole, Darré's aims were realized only incompletely. After a starting period, the Reich Food Estate included approximately 17 million people in an outwardly corporative organization. It became increasingly an organizational support structure for the Reich Agriculture Minister. Basing his policies on the primary assumption of the unity of the community of the individual farm, which included self-sufficient farmers as well as agricultural workers, Darré also organized the processing and distribution of agricultural products in the Reich Food Estate. In addition to the often folkloristic interest in the social welfare of the agricultural population – where the DAF offered a very different programme – Darré was concerned, in the final analysis, with ensuring the food supply for the entire population, and that plan had its limitations.

Darré himself was one of the few National Socialists who clearly failed to achieve his aims, and this was due to his personal qualities as well as to his task. For within the framework of the preparations for war he was supposed to ensure self-sufficiency in foodstuffs; agricultural autarchy was the goal. This task itself could hardly be fulfilled and, if at all, it could only be through appropriately organized, large-scale agricultural concerns and not by bureaucratic regulations for the cultivation of individual products contrary to elementary principles of business management. But for Darré, more than for some other National Socialists, keeping the farmers on the soil (_Schollenpflichtigkeit_) was important and was, in fact, the foundation and source of strength for an ethnic-racial renewal. Moreover, several ecological insights could also be combined with such views and realized, at least in their initial phases. The Reich Hereditary Farm Law (_Reichserbhofgesetz_) of 1933 was intended to restructure agriculture in the mid-term against the development of large as well as undersized farms by means of regulations concerning farm size, inheritance, and limitations on freedom of movement. But already in 1936 it was clear that Darré had failed because of the priority given to war preparations and autarchy. Herbert Backe, his State Secretary, who thought primarily in technocratic terms, essentially took over the Reich Food Estate, integrated it into the Four Year Plan, and replaced Darré there and as Minister of Agriculture in 1942. In August 1944, the Reich Food Estate still had 10,000 civil servants and 20,000 employees.

GÖRING'S PERSONAL EMPIRE

While Ley and Darré built their empires by taking care of or organizing sectors of German society, Hermann Göring based his power on a number of different activities and related offices, many of which resulted from his role as the second man in the National Socialist hierarchy.[16] The highly decorated fighter pilot of the First World War was one of the most important contacts for the National Socialist party with circles of the wealthy middle class and the nobility before 1933, including the exiled former Kaiser. It was therefore no accident that Göring took over the highest state office yet held by a National Socialist, that of President of the Reichstag, in August 1932. Strengthened in his position by a secret law already decreed by Hitler in 1934, he remained the dictator's official successor until the last days of the Third Reich; but when the regime was still in its death throes he was expelled from all offices by Hitler. Göring soon filled his lack of specific role as minister without portfolio with his dream job, directing the secret build-up of German air power as Reich Minister of Aviation and, after 1 March 1935, as official Commander-in-Chief of the Luftwaffe. But on the whole it signified a setback for his immense power, and not only from a military point of view, that he did not become Blomberg's successor as head of the Wehrmacht in 1938, but had to be satisfied with the title of Field Marshal. That, like the even higher rank of Reich Marshal, which he received in 1940, was only an honorary position, a military rank especially created for him, appealing to his fondness for pomp and show.

Outwardly Göring pushed forward the build-up of the Luftwaffe forcefully, and he probably took the important decisions regarding armaments for the new service branch. But in that area, as elsewhere, he left the real work to competent co-workers, often friends from the First World War. To a greater extent than was usual for someone in a leading position, he delegated responsibility to his subordinates, which in turn resulted in strong personal rivalries. This was an indication of a tendency that later became especially pronounced in other areas, such as in the activities of Todt and Speer: individual sectors were taken over by new leaders, who became independent of their previous superior, and the sectors for which they were responsible often slipped out of his control. Thus materials programmes for certain branches of the armaments industry, or technical tasks for which certain individuals were responsible then developed their own momentum, and could be separated out in this way from organizations or structures that were becoming increasingly bureaucratic. The Four Year Plan of 1936 was an excellent example. Göring, who had little knowledge of economics but who had already taken over a limited task in that area as Commissar for Raw Materials and Foreign Exchange, recruited co-workers from other agencies for the individual departments of his new office. These new people, such as Backe, who continued in the Food Ministry (*Ernährungsministerium*), retained their former functions. Wilhelm Keppler, who took over another department, had already established contacts between the Nazi Party and the business world by 1932–3, but received only a relatively low position with Göring and, probably for that reason, soon left to concentrate his attention primarily on policy towards Austria with success and forcefulness. With both men one has the impression that they were interested in mutual advantage, as was also the case with the Gau leader Wagner in the Four Year Plan. For jobs in the new Plan, leading officials were attracted from the Ministry of Labour. The Office for German Raw and Processed Materials (*Amt für deutsche Roh- und Werkstoffe*) under Colonel Löb, who came from the Ministry of Aviation and brought other officers with him, acquired a decisive role just because it was essentially concerned with the production of substitute materials for immediate war preparations. And Subsection III of that office was under I. G. Farben director Carl Krauch, who was only one of several industrial executives from the private sector in the Four Year Plan. The Plan dissolved into its individual projects. Because of its significance for the war, the War Economy New Production Plan of 1938 soon became the Krauch or I. G. Farben plan.

Attempts after 1939 to make the Four Year Plan into a war-economy command centre failed. But in 1942, Speer himself found it advisable to signal his readiness to co-operate with the still-powerful Göring by taking over the office of 'Central Planning' in the Four Year Plan.

Göring included the economy in his empire rather late. As mentioned above, he was active in foreign policy in specific questions, but often in an uncoordinated way. He travelled to Italy, Yugoslavia, Hungary and Poland, took an interest in Britain and occasionally conducted negotiations on his own authority that complemented, or contradicted, the line set by the Foreign Ministry. But among Göring's first tasks in 1933 as temporary Prussian Interior Minister, and then as temporary Prussian Minister President, were the *Gleichschaltung* and expansion of the police and terror apparatus. After 1934 he increasingly delegated his direct authority in this sector. In spite of the *Gleichschaltung* of the German states, his position in the formerly largest German state and, above all, his title of 'Prussian Minister President' became the most important part of his power. He even tended to drop the modifier 'Prussian' and functioned as 'the Minister President', thus at least suggesting that he had overcome the dualism between the 'Reich' and Prussia which had been fashionable in Imperial Germany.

And he had many other offices. His position as Chairman of the Ministerial Council for National Defence (*Ministerrat für die Reichsverteidigung*) did not give him any great authority, but as the Chief Hunter of the Reich (*Reichsjägermeister*) he had real influence on agricultural and forestry policies. It was decisive that, whether due to his mentality or caused by illness, Göring's power suffered a progressive decline during the war. But even his obvious failures, like that in air defence, did not affect the outwardly jovial man's comparatively great popularity.

HIMMLER, THE SS, AND TERROR

We must not overlook, however, the contribution of Göring and other functionaries to the terror and persecution practised by the Nazi regime. The embodiment of this side of Nazi Germany was Heinrich Himmler.[17] Here we shall outline only the basic pattern of his rise to power. Along with Hitler, Göring, and Goebbels, he was the best-known National Socialist. By profession a trained agriculturalist, Himmler made his career as head of the SS (*Schutzstaffel*). After he became Reich Leader SS in 1929, he headed a paramilitary formation distinguished by a strong élite consciousness of being the real core troop of the National Socialist movement. At first, the SS became Hitler's bodyguard and also assumed the task of providing protection and order for Nazi assemblies. In spite of its rapid growth after 1929, from approximately 280 men to more than 52,000 by 1932, the SS quickly established and maintained a sense of its own separate identity, an identity which was strengthened by many specific rituals internal to the organization. In 1933, it numbered more than 200,000 members. Again, in March 1933, Hitler selected a core troop of the SS, the *Leibstandarte*, which in the end became an armoured division in the war. Until the murder of the SA leaders in June and July 1934 the SS and its members, organized into armed 'political readiness squads,' were formally under the SA; only then did they become independent. It was not important that the SS was an organization of the Nazi Party. One did not have to join the party to be an SS man. The terror in the streets, which the SS at first practised together with the SA as auxiliary police, and in the 'wild', or unauthorized, concentration camps which were also established by other party authorities, only formed the initial base for Himmler's rise. Later, the foundation of his power was in his control of the regular police, especially the political police, which already existed in many German cities.

The political police in Berlin co-ordinated related activities on a national level. Now new institutions were created and old ones expanded. In the *Gleichschaltung* of Bavaria, Himmler was given a relatively minor position. But only a few weeks later the entire Bavarian political police were placed under his authority. He directed a special department in the Ministry of the

Interior and, together with his closest vassal, Reinhard Heydrich, he single-mindedly began to create a Reich police for political purposes. In this way, within the framework of each *Gleichschaltung*, Himmler was given command of the political police in each German state one after the other by the beginning of 1934, with the exceptions of Prussia and Schaumburg-Lippe. In Prussia, however, he encountered initial resistance from Göring, who placed the dependable senior government executive, Rudolf Diels, in charge of the Secret State Police Office (*Geheimes Staatspolizeiamt*); Kurt Daluege, a member of the SS, became a general of the police and, in spite of his SS background, occasionally employed forceful methods to beat back Heydrich's attempts to gain control of the political police in Prussia. Only later, in 1934, did Göring gradually entrust tasks to Heydrich as his nominal deputy, who in fact had full powers as Inspector of the Secret State Police. Heydrich became the head of that office, and brought into it the espionage apparatus of the SS, the Security Service (*Sicherheitsdienst* or SD), which he had built up since 1931.

In 1936, Himmler was appointed Reich Leader SS (*Reichsführer SS* or RFSS) and Chief of the German Police in the Reich Ministry of the Interior. The fact that he was technically subordinate to Frick was unimportant. This appointment not only signified the personal union of a party and a state office but also strengthened the already-existing tendency to merge the police and the terror organizations. In addition, as a reward for the participation of his organization in the murders of June 1934, the Wehrmacht conceded to Himmler the authority to establish military formations, the SS Special Service Troops (*SS-Verfügungstruppe* or VT). These SS VTs, which grew to the strength of a division by the start of the war, retained their ideological, élite self-image. Moreover, in the event of domestic unrest, the General SS was also to be permitted to conscript recruits at the expense of the Wehrmacht. After 1936 the units guarding the outer boundaries of the concentration camps were called SS Death's Head Formations (*SS-Totenkopfverbände* or SS-TV) and they also had a strong military element. SS officers were called *Führer* and were all trained militarily for the General SS, the police, and the Special Service Troops in officers' schools (*Junkerschulen*). Himmler once explained his guiding principles in this regard:

> I complete the number of police, as far as possible, with men leaving the Special Service Troops and the Death's Head Formations; I complete the police officer corps using SS officers who come from the two officers' schools Tölz and Brunswick via the Special Service Troops and the police.

Thus he encountered no difficulties in creating a (predominantly) military force, the Waffen SS, from these formations at the start of the war.

The police had now been standardized on a national level. From the order police to the criminal police and the Gestapo, propagandists in the General SS, concentration camp guards, and espionage and sabotage specialists only seemed to form an unconnected jumble of functions. The SS as a whole was held together by its mentality of an élite order which Himmler promoted and sought to realize with great energy and persistence; it was an élite consciousness based completely on racial ideas of Germanic superiority. Its far-reaching intentions for the future and the breeding of a new master race were evident in its standards of physical appearance, its requirements of genealogical certificates for its members, and its regulations concerning marriage and having children. Himmler's foreign-policy ambitions were evident in the interest the SS took in the welfare of Germans abroad and in the activities of the SD in other countries. In the economy, the activities of the SS were at first confined to its own porcelain factory for the production of lanterns for the celebration of the winter solstice, or to the takeover of a mineral water bottling company such as Apollinaris, in order to promote abstinence from alcohol. But as early as 1938–9 the idea occurred to the SS leaders of establishing their own enterprises not only to supply the concentration camps, but also to exploit the labour of the prisoners themselves. Even so, this idea was realized on a large scale only during the war. By 1939, Himmler had taken the first step in the direction of competition with the Wehrmacht. Internal security, however, understood in the specifically terrorist National Socialist sense of that term, was already in the hands of the Reich Leader SS.

'POLYOCRACY' AND THE NATIONAL COMMUNITY

Such policy monopolies in certain areas were rare in the National Socialist system. Usually there were rivalries which were decided in free competition between bureaucratic institutions and persons. In various areas of foreign policy a dozen such rivals were active, and this did not change significantly after the National Socialist Joachim von Ribbentrop took over the Foreign Ministry in 1938. Baldur von Schirach was the Reich Youth Leader, but the party organization he headed, the Hitler Youth, never became the only organization in Nazi Germany concerned with young people, although membership in it, as in the Union of German Girls, was made compulsory in 1939. Other National Socialist institutions sought to develop their own strategies for maintaining their influence over the younger generation.

Many party figures also had their own intelligence services and propaganda institutions. In the area of economic policy the number of competitors was also large. Several of these 'empires' were systematically expanded during the whole National Socialist period; others lost their functions during those 12 years. Traditional institutions such as ministries were occasionally left standing as empty shells, but were restored to new importance when the need arose. 'General disunity. Ley is arguing with Kerrl' (who was among other things Reich Minister of Church Affairs). 'Rust is against Rosenberg etc. And this in the midst of a war, and all of them claim to be doing what the Führer wants', Goebbels noted in his diary at the beginning of 1940.[18] Personal animosities became fundamental questions of power that could have an important influence on policy. These constant conflicts can be described as a 'polyocracy' (*Polykratie*), a multicentric system that consisted of an unstable, constantly shifting balance of power among the competing Nazi leaders, and it was one of the most important features of National Socialist rule. But the term 'polyocracy' here must not be confused with two things: on one hand, with democratic pluralism, in which, in addition to informal methods, primarily institutionalized decision-making procedures are used; on the other hand with the existence of a number of equally powerful, independent persons or groups. In Nazi Germany there were indeed various opinions about the proper course to be taken in different areas of policy, but Hitler's decision remained all-important. 'Polyocracy' did not represent an alternative to his dictatorship. As the above quote indicates, his wishes regarding different options did indeed vary. The result was that he wanted to take as few decisions as possible, as Göring once apologetically acknowledged in 1938. Increasingly Hitler demanded prior agreement among the rivals, which, as it were, he only wanted to ratify. It can be shown that he was occasionally incapable of or unwilling to take a decision; he then rejected an unpleasant weighing of options and indulged in long-winded speeches, in which he declared the solution of the problems under consideration to be a mere act of will. His speech of 5 November 1937, as recorded in Hoßbach's notes, is only one excellent example of this tendency. But it was the competition among his underlings that constituted the main condition for his own dictatorship, which he maintained until the end of the National Socialist period. 'Polyocracy' is thus a misleading description of the National Socialist system only if it is used to imply that Hitler's dictatorial position, which on the whole continued to determine the basic orientation of that system, was not the decisive factor. Double and multiple responsibilities and offices were more than an instrument of rule; in many cases they developed independently of any specific decisions taken by Hitler. The many middle-level and little 'Führers' who attempted to expand their own areas of authority in a social Darwinist struggle for personal power were typical of the regime down to and especially including the lowest levels.

After 1933 there were no more hard or direct confrontations with Hitler in committees or the cabinet. In informal situations he showed himself open to arguments that differed from his own views, but in questions involving the basic orientation of the system towards war and annihilation he remained the most fanatical advocate of the most radical course. For example, at the end of August 1939 when Göring warned him about the risk of a great war, at the beginning of 1942 when Todt allegedly sought to induce him to admit defeat in the World War, and in March 1945 when Speer wanted to prevail upon him to surrender before Germany was completely destroyed, this would have represented, in Hitler's view, only defeatism and he responded with at least a temporary withdrawal of his favour. This was certainly not an organized decision-making process.

THE MATRIX OF TOTALITARIAN IMAGERY: PUBLIC SPACE, THE NATIONAL SOCIALIST YEAR, AND THE GENERATIONAL CYCLE

Thus the circle closes: Hitler's position within the system was based not least on the faith of others in him as the Führer. As that faith had its limits, not only among the victims of National Socialism, the claim that Germany was one national community was not completely accepted. But in the stereotyped phrases of Nazi propaganda the Führer and the nation constituted a unity, and this was expressed in many ways. The organization of public space, the calendar of events and celebrations during the year, and the teaching that every German was simply a biological link in a long succession of generations reflected the claim to totalitarian inclusiveness.

The motorways (*Autobahnen*), the 'roads of the Führer', have already been mentioned. After the First World War, city and housing construction had not kept pace with the needs of an industrial society, and it largely came to a standstill in the world economic crisis. In spite of their claims and proclaimed intention to give priority to social policy, the National Socialists energetically promoted only one partial aspect of such a policy: the remodelling of city centres using monumental architecture.[19] In Berlin, Hitler, who himself would have liked to have become an architect, soon ignored existing authorities and simply began, with a staff sworn to carry out his plans, to construct monumental buildings in the centre of the city. For Hitler, Berlin had remained a city of Hohenzollern palaces. But he was interested in creating the capital, to be named Germania, of a future world empire. The centre of that capital would be the intersection of two gigantic streets in a north–south and an east–west direction, with imposing buildings for ministries and other state and party agencies. The intersection would be dominated by an enormous triumphal arch twice as high as the Arc de Triomphe in Paris. In the north of a bend formed by the Spree a domed hall with space for 180,000 people was planned, whose volume was to have been seventeen times that of Saint Peter's Cathedral in Rome. In Munich, at the Königsplatz, the National Socialists were able to realize their first plans as early as 1933–4. The main features of their plans for Munich involved the construction in Pasing of a gigantic new railway station, whose domed hall would have a diameter of 285 metres, and the building of an impressive boulevard where the tracks of the previous station had been. The old main railway station was to be replaced by a monument to the 'Movement' reminiscent of the Washington Monument, but with a height of 189 metres, crowned by an eagle with outspread wings. In the western part of Hamburg, Germany's largest port, a gigantic bridge was planned over the Elbe; to the east of it, in Altona, a Gau forum was to rise along the river with a party tower block of 250 metres and a public hall for 50,000 people. Similarly, in Linz on the Danube a great bridge over the river, construction projects along its south bank and, at right angles to them, a square for public functions surrounded by large buildings were planned. In Nuremberg, the area outside the city used for the annual Reich party rallies was expanded beyond the size required for its existing functions. A stadium for 400,000 people and the Luitpold Arena with an assembly area for 200,000 people were intended to provide a quite different setting for future party rallies than had the previous assembly area at the Zeppelin Field. In 1940 these five cities were politically canonized as 'Führer cities'. Partly through Hitler himself and partly through party functionaries this building frenzy spread to all large German cities, which could be declared 'renewal cities' on the basis of a law as of 1937. In 1941 there were at least forty-one such projects, most of them with a Gau forum of the party, a march-up area, and/or a broad street with correspondingly prestigious buildings, often intended for cultural institutions. In addition, planned towns were built in connection with armaments production, such as Wolfsburg (the city of the 'Strength through Joy' car), and Salzgitter (built for the smelting of domestic iron ore).

Very few of these projects were completed during the war, but many were started and, from 1937 onwards, their number increased: entire old city centres were ruthlessly gutted, torn down, levelled. In view of the general housing shortage, this did not strengthen social cohesion. At the same time, by order of the Führer, thousands of millions of Reichsmarks were diverted from rearmament, which in itself had priority. For Hitler, this urban redevelopment was actually intended for the next thousand years: 'Therefore, we deliberately exempt from criticism . . . the work to be performed for this purpose in coming years, and submit it to the judgement of the generations that will come after us' (1937). In this sense the plans presented to the public were intended to strengthen the German people's national self-confidence 'to satisfy legitimate requirements for their existence . . . by all [necessary] means' (1939). This was to be done primarily through armaments, which were used to prepare for war. But that was to remain a secret. The buildings were the visble part of the same process. They would not be constructed because of 'megalomania', but 'for the coldly calculated reason that only such imposing works can give a people the self-confidence . . . that their nation is the equal of any other, even America'. It was an urban architecture intended to promote the development of a mentality among the German population which would prepare them for future world domination, and was often not even functional. In spatial form, from the parade streets to the great halls and arenas, individual Germans would be made clearly aware of their absolute subordination to uniform thinking and acting, and also of their chance to participate in later national greatness. In many respects this reflected adolescent fantasies of omnipotence that had been raised, as it were, to the level of a state doctrine and which now were to be acted out.

Of course not every Gau leader who wanted to erect his own Gau forum with party buildings did so with the primary intention of promoting German world domination. Rather, Gau leaders were mainly interested in their own provincial prestige. And this occasionally made them objects of scorn even within their own ranks, as when the Gau leader of Mecklenburg, Schwede-Coburg, expressed his concern that the 'great ideas' were 'often misunderstood by the smallest "Führers and Artists" in pocket editions'. But the high costs in the present created a framework for a rite which was to be fully developed only in a vision of the future. This became clear above all at the party rallies held annually in Nuremberg under various titles ('Will', 'Freedom', 'Honour', 'Work', 'Greater Germany') until 1938. For 1939 a rally under the title 'Peace' was planned, and probably for the following year one with the title 'Victory'. At the rallies a different National Socialist formation marched up every day, from the Labour Service to the Hitler Youth and the SA. And the armed forces, too, participated. The formations were drawn up, roll-calls were taken in military style, parades were held, and flags were dedicated. But Hitler himself was always the centre of attention around which the activities of the formations were organized. He appeared at every assembly and made a speech or brief address, which was then declared to be a definitive guide for the future. And the rallies and military roll-calls were not limited to September in Nuremberg; there was an abundance of such events at other times and places in Nazi Germany.

The entire year was marked by new holidays which in many respects competed with, but were not able to replace, those of the Church year. Himmler, Darré, and Rosenberg all had the intention of presenting themselves as founders of a neo-heathen religion; but they were able to do this at most within their own spheres of activity. Official celebrations continued to be characterized to a considerable degree by the use of cultic elements of the most varied origins in addition to those of the Christian churches, all of them presented in such a way as to suggest, as it were, an inner salvation through the Führer. The National Socialist year began with the celebration of the 'Seizure of Power' (*Machtergreifung*) on 30 January, and continued in March with 'Hero Remembrance Day' (*Heldengedenktag*). This was followed by Hitler's birthday on 20 April, the Day of Labour (*Tag der Arbeit*) on 1 May, and Mothers' Day and the summer solstice in June. The festival of thanks for the harvest (*Erntedankfest*) on the Bückeberg near Hameln at the beginning of October became a kind of agricultural annual party rally of the NSDAP. In addition to the party rally in Nuremberg in the autumn, the festival of 9 November commemorating the failed *putsch* of 1923, itself an attempt to blot out the disgrace of the revolution of 1918, was the high point of the National Socialist year. What had not succeeded in 1923 seemed to have been realized with the establishment of National Socialist power and was repeated annually for that reason. Moreover, there were a number of less important memorial days that gave the year additional structure. In a decentralized fashion as well as at certain locations, people were constantly mobilized and admonished to participate in public acts. After a few years the impression was so widespread that life was becoming a permanent celebration that Goebbels thought it necessary to take corrective measures, especially as the numerous festivals and memorial events were economically unproductive and costly in view of the self-appointed task of rearmament.

> Then there will be a new German youth, and we shall train them from a very early age for this new state . . . These young people will learn nothing but to think German and act German. And when these boys and girls join our organizations at the age of 10 and for the first time in their lives get a breath of fresh air there and feel, then 4 years later they'll come to the Hitler Youth. And there we'll keep them another 4 years. And then we certainly won't put them back in the hands of those who trained people to be members of our old classes and social groups. Instead, we'll take them right into the party and into the Labour Front, into the SA or the SS, into the National Socialist Motor Vehicle Driver Corps [*Nationalsozialistisches Kraftfahrkorps* or NSKK], etc. And if they've been there for 2 or $1\frac{1}{2}$ years and still haven't quite become National Socialists, then they'll be sent to do labour service and trained hard for another 6 or 7 months under one symbol, the German spade. And whatever may be left here and there of class consciousness or conceit after 6 or 7 months will be sent to the Wehrmacht for further treatment for 2 years. And when they return after 2, 3 or 4 years, we'll take them immediately into the SA or the SS, so that they can't possibly backslide. And they will never be free their whole life long.

This claim, frightening by traditional standards of civil freedom, was announced by Hitler to the applause of his listeners in 1938.[20] Such totalitarian inclusiveness was not only meant politically but also extended to areas not directly related to politics. It encompassed social tasks, especially for girls and women, from the Union of German Girls (*Bund Deutscher Mädel* or BDM) to the Winter Relief Organization (*Winterhilfswerk*), from collecting money and useful articles, to knitting and tinkering. Integration in National Socialist organizations weakened traditional social influences.

The efforts to establish a totalitarian state were never completely successful. Many of the appeals directed especially at German youth were narrow, specifically Nazi forms of ideas which had originated in youth organizations before the First World War. But it was several years before all other organizations could be eliminated. Youthfulness and physical conditioning, above all in sports, but also through physical labour, were among the aims that helped make the word 'intellectuality' a disparaging term and caused the quality itself to be ridiculed. But in many respects the kindergartens of the National Socialist Public Welfare (*NS-Volkswohlfahrt* or NSV) were built upon the foundation of beginnings of pedagogical reforms in the 1920s, and had to compete with church establishments until 1940–1. In addition to the schools, the Hitler Youth and the Union of German Girls played important roles in the rearing of young people through youth centres and hostels, scouting games, and other leisure-time activities. These organizations competed both with parents and with schools, where more or less convinced National Socialists clashed with traditional teachers and with the content of their teaching. Because the schools could not be changed quickly enough, élite National Socialist schools were established. These were the National Political Education Institutes (*Nationalpolitische Erziehungsanstalten* or Napolas) under the direction of the SS, and the Adolf Hitler Schools of the NSDAP; both types were boarding schools that tried to attract pupils from a relatively broad social spectrum. For the subsequent education of select pupils there were the so-called Order Castles (*Ordensburgen*), which were located in scenic areas and established a new curriculum for the further ideological training of future party functionaries. It is doubtful whether, apart from the SA and the SS, these institutions were able to exercise as strong an influence in forming the consciousness of their pupils as Hitler claimed in his speech. It must be emphasized, however, that the Wehrmacht was legitimately incorporated into the National Socialist educational system, as it had been quick to revise its training guidelines to make them compatible with a fanatical National Socialism.

In this multi-dimensional matrix of National Socialist public space, the party year, and the biological-generational chain, one parameter had a decisive role: military orientation, subordination, and obedience to superiors, any superior and especially to Hitler personally. In its unconditionality this expressly included the readiness to give one's life for the national community when ordered to do so, especially in war.[21] The visible side of this was, of course, the active fighter, the soldier prepared to die. Of a total of 134 state funerals held in Germany between 1888 and 1989, seventy took place in the National Socialist period. Here the after-effects became evident of the deaths of millions of soldiers in the First World War, which in the 1920s had led to unprecedented efforts to bestow meaning on that catastrophe, and not only in Germany: the dead were declared to be, and then transfigured as, heroes who were to be emulated. Monuments were only one of the more conspicuous manifestations of this tendency. And among the German monuments, the Tannenberg Memorial in East Prussia, which provided the backdrop for the funeral of Hindenburg in 1934, was the most notable example. The cult of the dead was omnipresent, and previously canonized heroes were joined by specifically National Socialist martyrs. Even in the Weimar period a large monument was dedicated in Düsseldorf to Albert Schlageter, who had been shot for sabotage by the French during the occupation of the Ruhr in 1923. Horst Wessel was an SA man honoured because of his death after a fight with the members of the Communist Party in 1930; the song named after him became a second national anthem of the National Socialist state. Then there was Herbert Norkus, a member of the Hitler Youth who died in a similar brawl in 1932. The martyr cult with honours for the dead played a role in numerous National Socialist ceremonies, but nowhere more importantly than on 9 November, when the march of 1923 to the Feldherrnhalle in Munich was symbolically repeated and the National Socialists who had died then were, so to speak, resurrected when during the subsequent roll-call their names were called out individually over their coffins and the crowd responded by loudly shouting: 'Here!'. Radio coverage of the march was reminiscent of Christian religious processions with individual stations of the cross. The conclusion of the ceremony caused spectators and participants to think of resurrection and even salvation. Here, as elsewhere, the message was clear: only in a new, and as it were an expiatory war could fulfilment be found. Every training camp of the Hitler Youth had as its motto, 'We have been born to die for Germany.'[22] Everything was directed towards this aim, although such emotional conditioning to be heroes who could only reach their goal through death was incompatible with the official peace propaganda of the regime before September 1939, which itself was conducted with an eye to international opinion.

The test for the success of this indoctrination was the concrete danger of war. When a European war seemed imminent in the Sudeten crisis of September 1938, the German people showed themselves dismayed and displayed no readiness, not to mention enthusiasm, to go to war. In a secret speech to the press on 10 November 1938, Hitler was forced to take this reaction into account when he admitted how regrettable it had been that 'circumstances' had forced him to 'mouth a pacifist line' for years.[23] But it was not possible to create enthusiasm for a war. When the policy of extreme risk actually did unleash a war, in September 1939, the prevalent mood in Germany was one of anxiety; there was no war euphoria such as had marked the outbreak of hostilities in 1914. The memory of what a major war in the twentieth century could and would inevitably mean was still too strong. To die a hero had not become the joyfully accepted life's goal of most Germans. Interestingly enough, during the Second World War, which constantly provided new opportunities for funeral ceremonies for men who had died for Germany, the propaganda glorifying precisely that supposedly highest aim in life was reduced. Reality overtook myth. The experience of suffering caused by the deaths of millions of soldiers in the war made such heroic pathos appear increasingly hollow.

|5|

The War

It was only the European war which began in September 1939. In East Asia the Japanese had already been fighting for 2 years in China, but 2 more years passed before both wars fused to become a world war in the true sense of the phrase. Moreover, military operations were only one small element of this, as mobilization had been proceeding in Germany for years. One spoke of a 'war economy in peacetime', with all the social consequences that implied. This war differed in many respects from traditional conflicts in Europe, in which the aim had always been to subdue an enemy politically by killing his soldiers and breaking his resistance. 'This war is not the second world war', Hermann Göring proclaimed in 1942 to the thunderous applause of a selected public in the Berlin Sports Palace.[1] 'This war is the great race war. Whether here the Teuton and Aryan will stand or the Jew will rule the world, that is what it is about in the final analysis and that is why we are fighting out there.'

The war fought by the National Socialists with German military power thus constituted a single event at home and abroad. It was fought against a perceived universal enemy, and was aimed at a racial reordering of Europe and at racial annihilation. The fact that in October 1939 Hitler signed the order for a programme of euthanasia, the killing of people who were, by National Socialist standards, ill, and backdated it to 1 September of that year was another reflection of the ideological nature of the war. Likewise, Hitler later claimed repeatedly that in his speech of 1 September 1939 he had 'prophesied' that a new world war started by 'finance Jewry' would not result in a 'Bolshevisation of the world and the victory of the Jewish race in Europe', which in his view the Jews were obviously planning.[2] Rather, it would mean 'the annihilation of the Jewish race in Europe'. In fact, these words had been spoken earlier, in his speech to the Reichstag on 30 January 1939. Clearly, whether deliberately for political reasons or as the result of a slip, Hitler shifted the start of the process of annihilation, which had long been in progress in Germany itself, to the day on which the guns had begun to fire. Enemies within Germany and those in German-occupied areas were placed in a single category. More accurately, when German soldiers (and occasionally Germany's allies) occupied an area, this offered the opportunity to extend to it the ideological war being waged within Germany, and to continue that war in a much more radical fashion. Occupation policy did have its own function as part of the military conduct of the war, especially in Western Europe, but it was also pursued as an instrument to achieve and consolidate lasting German dominance on the European continent.

To provide a better overview, different categories that represented a single whole in the eyes of Hitler and his followers are presented separately here. The victories and the defeats of the German armed forces formed the framework that was shaped for varying periods of time by German rule in Europe.

MILITARY BATTLES AND POLITICAL ALLIANCES

The European War

From a German perspective the war began with the wrong fronts. Germany was almost allied with its ideological mortal enemy, the Soviet Union, but was at war with Hitler's preferred partner, Great Britain, and also with France. German propaganda was able to reverse its orientation without any particular difficulties, but of course Hitler did not forget his basic convictions and long-term goals. Uneasiness about the war was widespread in the German population and elsewhere. As in 1914, it would now have to be fought on several fronts at the same time. Hitler's hope that he would be able to continue fighting separate wars against isolated individual enemies such as, in this case Poland, had proved to be unfounded. But at first it did not seem that way. To oppose the German deployment of 1.5 million men in the east, the Poles had an almost equal number of soldiers, but they were hopelessly inferior to the largely motorized and mechanized German troops. In spite of stubborn resistance, the fighting power of the Polish forces was essentially broken within 3 weeks. After heavy German air attacks, Warsaw surrendered on 27 September. By 7 October, fighting had ceased. German losses were 11,000 men; 70,000 Poles died on their western front. But an additional 50,000 died fighting the Red Army, which at the urging of Germany had marched into eastern Poland on 17 September, in part into areas previously conquered by the Wehrmacht. In Brest-Litovsk, German and Soviet troops paraded together on 22 September. The Polish government fled into exile; hundreds of thousands of Polish soldiers reached other countries.

Ribbentrop flew to Moscow a second time and signed a German-Soviet frontier and friendship treaty on 28 September.[3] In that document the phrase 'disintegration of the former Polish state' was used, the new frontiers were 'definitively' agreed upon, and 'any interference by third powers in this settlement' was rejected. In comparison with the August agreement, significant changes were made in the frontiers of Eastern Europe. The Soviet Union renounced its territorial claims extending to Warsaw and accepted a frontier along the Bug River 100 miles further east which generally followed the line projected by the British Foreign Minister, Lord Curzon, in 1919. In exchange it received Lithuania as part of its sphere of interest. The eastern areas of Poland, where more than 5 million Polish-speaking people lived, were incorporated into the neighbouring Soviet republics. In October 1939 the three Baltic States were forced to accept Soviet military bases on their territory and alliances with the Soviet Union. When Finland refused to do likewise, it was attacked, stood its ground surprisingly well against large Soviet forces, and had to accept a peace treaty in March 1940 in which it only surrendered several small pieces of territory. Strengthened by a mutually advantageous exchange of goods, Germany and the Soviet Union had become temporary accomplices; their pact had been sealed by blood. On 6 October, Hitler offered peace to the Western Powers, Britain and France, on the basis of the newly created status quo. Molotov seconded the proposal, but Britain and France rejected it.

But why did the Western Powers not attack immediately to gain a quick victory? At the beginning of September the Germans were able to deploy at most only half as many divisions in the west as the French, and those divisions were poorly equipped and trained. Of course the French government did not believe Hitler's professed desire for peace; but they were rather deterred from acting by the largely unfinished West Wall and by their own over-estimation of German military strength in the west. The mentality of the French population and the doctrine of French military leaders were both orientated towards defence. By October the British were able to move only four divisions to the Continent; by May 1940, the figure was fifteen. On the whole, the French hoped to be able to hold out in their defensive positions for several years and to count on help from outside, not least from the United States. In the meantime Britain and France wanted to weaken Germany by indirect means. As early as April 1939, the British and French general staffs had agreed to subdue Italy first in the event of a war in order to be able to attack the stronger enemy much later; but initially Italy did not even participate in the war. Then they drafted plans to weaken the Soviet Union first, whether in the north, through Scandinavia or in the Caucasus by bombing the Soviet oil fields there, fields which were, after all, also supplying Germany. Initially, the first plan also served to support Finland, and planning for it then continued until May 1940, even after Finland had accepted a peace treaty with the Soviet Union. At the same time, the second plan acquired greater importance. A year later, in 1941, the British government again considered such an operation, but it was rendered irrelevant by the German attack on the Soviet Union. In short, because of the image they had developed of Germany since 1871 and their subjective estimate of the level of German armaments, the French did not believe that they were in a position to attack Germany in autumn 1939, although their chances of success would probably have been good and, until their final defeat, the Poles urgently demanded the relief such an operation would have provided. The French confined themselves to reconnaissance penetrations and minor air attacks.

After his surprisingly quick victory over Poland, Hitler immediately focused his energies on an attack in the west. Combat units were transferred to the western front as rapidly as possible. On 22 October, 12 November was set as the date for the attack on France; but this was subsequently postponed. The reasons for Hitler's haste were clear. In spite of high material losses suffered in the Poland campaign, he could not wait for long, as he feared that 'it is more probable that time is the ally of the Western Powers', among other reasons because of the possible future policies of the Soviet Union and the United States.[4] Victory in the war on several fronts was not expected as a result of a successful, isolated blitzkrieg, and it remained uncertain whether and how the Western Powers could be beaten. Moreover, it was becoming clear that, taken worldwide, a consolidation of Germany's expanded sphere of influence would have to be defended against the interests of other powers. Weighing the risks and chances would perhaps have caused other political leaders to modify their plans, but for Hitler there was only the way forward. The United States was still neutral, but President Franklin D. Roosevelt was clearly on the side of the democracies, although for domestic political reasons he was not able to support them actively for the time being. From the standpoint of Soviet power politics as well as Communist ideology it was rather improbable that Stalin would accept an unlimited increase in German power during the war. With regard to Hitler's all-or-nothing programme, conservatives in Germany were rather sceptical. Peace feelers were extended to London; military opposition to the way the war in Poland had been conducted and against the coming war in the west was expressed sporadically. On the whole, the sceptical, worried general mood in Germany was a cause for concern, for the constellation of the First World War seemed to be repeating itself, and that meant a long period of trench warfare with heavy casualties. The issuing of the German order to attack in the west was postponed a total of twenty-nine times for reasons ranging from poor weather to disclosure of deployment plans. Moreover, the operations plan was modified in decisive respects. Instead of directing the main thrust of the attack across flat country through The Netherlands and Belgium, as had been done a generation earlier, General von Manstein suggested trying a much more risky direct breakthrough via the Ardennes. Against the opposition of the general staff, Hitler agreed to this idea, and the success of the operation formed the foundation of his reputation as a great strategist, which shaped his self-confidence and actions thereafter.

In the meantime, however, the German navy was promoting another aim: that of the invasion of Scandinavia. For years, the German navy had been demanding a gateway from the North Sea to the open Atlantic. The ability to import Swedish iron ore in winter was of great importance for future German armaments production. When British moves towards a landing in Norway became known, at first mainly to support Finland, German plans had already been made. Beginning on 9 April 1940, German forces occupied the neutral state of Norway and then Denmark, as a second objective, almost in passing. With support from the Luftwaffe, the navy deployed all available forces and suffered heavy losses. Denmark surrendered without a fight, but in central and northern Norway resistance continued, with British support, until 10 June, when the Germans were able to consolidate their hold on the country. From that point on, 300,000 German soldiers were engaged in Scandinavia. Even before operations in Norway had been concluded, the attack in the west began on 10 May 1940. In the meantime increased production had eliminated the most potentially dangerous deficiencies in German armaments. The Wehrmacht began the attack with 141 divisions, on paper slightly fewer than the 144 available to the French, British, Belgians, and Dutch. German planning disregarded the neutrality of the smaller states from the very beginning. Due to the technical superiority of the armoured formations and the Luftwaffe, the risky German campaign plan succeeded. Holland surrendered after 4 days, on 14 May. The Belgians followed on 28 May after suffering approximately 10,000 military dead, not least as a result of the bombing of cities. The German troops broke through the Ardennes and pushed on quickly to the Channel coast. Between 27 May and 4 June, a total of 231,000 British and 139,000 French soldiers, without their heavy equipment, reached Britain via Dunkirk and thus laid the foundation for future British resistance.

In the second phase of the campaign, the Germans pushed on primarily from northern France towards the south. There they also quickly broke through French lines. In this hopeless situation, the government of Paul Reynaud, which had been in office since March, resigned on 16 June. Marshal Pétain, the hero of the First World War and Reynaud's successor, requested an armistice, which Hitler ordered signed on 22 June and which was to go into effect on 25 June. The signing took place in the railway carriage in which the Germans had completed their *de facto* capitulation in 1918, thus erasing symbolically the disgrace of the German defeat in the First World War. But this had always been only an interim goal for Hitler. Earlier, the Italians had entered the war, as it were at the last moment, and had advanced with little success to the edge of the Alps. In this way they won a right to pursue their limited great-power ambitions in future negotiations. In accordance with the armistice agreement, France retained some of its independence with its governments under Pétain in Vichy, as they were able to base their power on the French fleet and colonial empire. A small strip of French territory was occupied by Italy; Paris and the rest of northern France, including the coastal areas to the Spanish frontier, were occupied by the Germans. For many Germans the war seemed to be over. And losses had been relatively light: 27,000 dead Germans but three times as many French.

Germany was in its most powerful position since 1871. The trauma of the battles and losses of the First World War seemed to have been overcome. From the North Cape to Sicily, from Brest to Brest-Litovsk, there were only allies and countries under German domination. Only a few European states preserved their neutrality; in the centre only Sweden and Switzerland were able to maintain such a position until the end of the war. Various groups in Germany produced a great number of plans for a peacetime order in Europe. A German hegemony in Europe seemed within reach. On the day the armistice with France was signed, Hitler himself ordered the monumental reconstruction of Berlin, which had been interrupted when war broke out, to be resumed as the 'most important contribution to the definitive securing of our victory'.[5] The popularity of the regime and of Hitler himself reached new heights. On 19 July, Hitler made a new 'peace speech', in which he also offered the British a place in the new Europe. In his view they did not need to keep fighting. For Britain was now the only power still at war with Germany, and this situation did not change for another year. To be sure, a war cabinet under Winston Churchill had been formed in London on 10 May, and there was strong desire in Britain for a settlement, but the new Prime Minister clearly showed that he intended to continue the war by bombarding the French fleet in the Algerian port of Mers-el-Kebir on 3 July. In addition to the remaining British forces and those of the Commonwealth, the decisive factor in the position of the British government was its expectation of material help from the United States, which, after brief American hesitation because of uncertainty with regard to future British policies, was resumed in increased volume. Although Hitler still hoped the British would realize they could continue to exist as a junior partner in an alliance of world historical importance, especially as German forces outside Europe were not sufficient to compel them to accept such a relationship – he placed his faith in their 'Aryan racial core as a power to maintain order, e.g. in Asia' – plans were now pushed forward to force Britain to her knees by military means. In the existing situation, the German navy was given the main role, and it primarily urged variations of a (German) peripheral strategy. Raeder wanted to shift the main focus of the German conduct of the war to the Mediterranean to sever the enemy's sea links there and to lay the foundation for a naval war against Britain from North Africa to Scandinavia. On the other hand, Karl Dönitz, the commander of the U-boats, urged an intensification of the Battle of the Atlantic, already begun in 1939 because of Britain's dependence on vital imports. He expected to achieve an early victory by shifting German armaments production as a whole to focusing on U-boats fit for service in the Atlantic. Both strategies were pursued, but neither received the demanded priority.

In contrast to these long-term strategies, it was generally agreed that the British could be defeated quickly only by a landing on their island itself. But

that presented difficulties. It began with intensive bombing of British armaments factories and cities, especially London, in order to create the
conditions for a later landing. But the Luftwaffe was not adequate for this
task, either numerically or in terms of the kinds of aircraft it had. In the final
analysis, the Battle of Britain in August–September 1940, which was played
up in the propaganda of both participants, was a defeat for the Germans. In
those 2 months they lost 1,244 aircraft, the British 723. At the same time it
became clear that the enemy's production capacity in this sector had been
seriously underestimated. The date for the invasion was repeatedly moved
back, in the end to 1941. And by then other questions about the further
conduct of the war were more pressing. Thus Britain could not be defeated at
sea or in the air, nor could she be forced to accept a political surrender. But
in Hitler's view this was not the main problem. There were still possible
political alliances directed against Britain that were intended to consolidate
Germany's sphere of political influence and power in Europe. For example,
Germany attempted to draw Franco's Spain and Vichy France into its war
coalition. These efforts failed because neither those countries' own interests
nor their conflicting war aims could be resolved; both Italy and Spain were
interested in acquiring parts of France's North African colonial possessions.
In spite of Hitler's personal efforts to persuade Pétain and Franco, Vichy
France and Spain refrained, at first for the time being and then, in fact,
permanently, from entering the war. As a non-belligerent, Spain declared its
benevolent neutrality towards the Axis powers, but it also maintained good
relations with the United States, while Vichy France was able to preserve its
limited independence even though large parts of its territory were occupied
by Germany.

The Way to a World War

The signing of the Tripartite Pact between Germany, Italy, and Japan on 27
September 1940 showed that the global dimension of the war, and especially
the future role of the United States, was becoming increasingly important. In
this way, differences between Germany and Japan resulting from the
German-Soviet Non-Aggression Pact of 1939, which was incompatible with
the Anti-Comintern Pact of 1936, were bridged over. But, contrary to the
propagandistic display at its signing, the Tripartite Pact remained largely an
empty political gesture. In German eyes, the new alliance was intended as a
demonstrative gesture by the expansionist powers, at least to keep the United
States from becoming more involved in the war; but in the end it achieved the
exact opposite. This development took place within the framework of efforts
by Foreign Minister von Ribbentrop to create a 'continental bloc', which
included attempts to persuade the Soviet Union to join the Tripartite Pact. In
Ribbentrop's plans (and those of the German navy), the sea powers (Great
Britain and the United States) appeared as Germany's main enemies; for him

anti-Bolshevism was not a decisive factor. Even Hitler permitted occasional exploratory efforts. When the Soviet people's commissar Molotov visited Berlin on 12 and 13 November 1940, it was proposed to him that if the Soviet Union directed its future expansion in Asia southward, its interests and those of Germany would not conflict. Molotov, for his part, responded by making considerable and unacceptable territorial demands that extended all the way to western Europe.

Hitler expected a war with the United States in the mid-term for world domination, in which the role to be assigned to Great Britain remained open for a long time; and this can be seen in the shifting of German armaments production to concentration on the navy and the Luftwaffe for several months in July 1940. But this did not mean that Hitler now placed his hopes in a lasting alliance with the Soviet Union against the naval powers of Britain and the United States. The German leaders did calmly accept the fact that in the wake of the German military victories in western Europe the Soviet Union now completely annexed the areas to which it was entitled under the non-aggression pact of August 1939: after political blackmail and a social-revolutionary transformation, the three Baltic states were declared constituent republics of the Soviet Union, as was Bessarabia. At the time, this action violated British and American ideas of the right of self-determination more than it gave rise to German fears about future Soviet attacks. However, the Germans did begin to provide Finland with military equipment in order to strengthen it against new Soviet pressure, and they also intervened diplomatically to prevent a further Soviet advance in Romania, which, because of its oil deliveries, was vital for the German war effort. But Hitler's main interest was focused in a different direction, on the war he had really always wanted. Just as he had demanded a blitzkrieg against France imme-diately after the victory over Poland, after the German victory over France in 1940, when he still expected or at least hoped that Britain would accept German dominance on the Continent, he began to consider an attack on the Soviet Union. In July 1940, he accepted the argument that because of the limitations of the armaments industry such plans could be realized only in the coming spring. After planning had continued in various military staffs for several months, at first without great energy, the directive for Operation Barbarossa, in which Hitler ordered his generals to 'be prepared to defeat the Soviet Union in a quick campaign as of 15 May 1941', was issued on 18 December 1940.[6] This expectation, namely that the military strength of Germany's strongest remaining enemy on the Continent could be broken within a few weeks, was shared by leading German military men. And it was also a view widely held in other countries after Stalin's purges of the late 1930s. The previous course of the war for both powers, together with a strong anti-Bolshevism, strengthened that conviction: in such a racially and politically 'inferior' system as the Soviet Union was considered to be, no sustained resistance was to be expected. Since Great Britain refused to become a part of Germany's sphere of influence, contrary to Hitler's real wishes, the war in the east acquired a function in the continuing war in the west. As Hitler frequently argued, in discussions with his military leaders, the British would give in more quickly if the Soviet Union, their last potential ally on the Continent (*Festlanddegen*), were eliminated. Likewise, a German victory over the Soviet Union would greatly strengthen the position of Japan, which would then be able to push forward more rapidly with its own expansion. And that would in turn produce increased friction with the interests of the United States and deter it from intervening in Europe.[7]

It would be a mistake to consider this rather mechanistic geopolitical argument to be Hitler's main motive. The indirect effect on Britain of a German victory in the east was, rather, an auxiliary argument, and failed to convince such competent people as General of the Artillery Franz Halder, Chief of the General Staff, and State Secretary von Weizsäcker of the Foreign Ministry. In the final analysis, Hitler's main concern was to solve permanently the 'territory (*Lebensraum*) problem' as National Socialists saw it. Hitler had not abandoned this objective in spite of all the political and economic advantages for Germany of the pact with the Soviet Union. Thus in March 1941, the police and the SS, leaders of industry, and the Wehrmacht intensified their planning for a war in which, to an unprecedented degree, plunder and annihilation were prepared as part of the military operations. This was done before the fighting started and initially had nothing to do with the Soviet conduct of the war.

But without initial German involvement, and even contrary to Hitler's plans, the war spread to the Balkans before the attack on the Soviet Union had even begun. Italy's participation in the war against France had brought it few political gains. Hopes of additional acquisitions following a settlement with Britain proved to be unfounded; Mussolini's idea of making the Mediterranean an Italian domain and thus gaining a link with Italy's colonial empire in East Africa had suffered a setback. But he needed successes. Military thrusts from Libya against the British in Egypt bogged down, and so he hoped to win new prestige through a war against Greece from Albania, 'parallel' to that of Germany, which he started on 28 October 1940. Because of Mussolini's modest aims in comparison to Hitler's, the defeats suffered by the allegedly 8 million mobilized Italians were all the more humiliating, and the Greeks soon launched a counter-attack. To prevent their only real alliance partner from being driven out of the war, but also to prevent a British advance in the Balkans, the Germans not only came to Italy's assistance but were soon taking the initiative, although efforts were made to take Italian prestige into consideration.

In December 1940, Mussolini urgently requested German help. In February 1941, a German Africa Corps under General Erwin Rommel was sent to Libya and fought its way almost to the Egyptian frontier by mid-April, but the feasible aim of weakening the British position in the Near East by supporting national revolutionary movements among the Arabs was not given priority. The German involvement in the Balkans became even more important. Originally, the Germans planned only an attack on northern Greece from Bulgaria, but then they had to expand their plans. Yugoslavia sought to preserve its neutrality against pressure from Germany, Russia, and Britain, and in doing so (like the Greeks, who were supported by Britain) became the victim of a German attack on 6 April 1940, which was immediately supported by Italy and Hungary on the Adriatic coast. This Balkan campaign ended with a new German 'lightning victory'. It was concluded, at the end of May 1941, against stubborn British resistance, with the capture of Crete in a large-scale airborne operation that cost more German casualties than the preceding land war.

The end of Italy's 'parallel war' meant that the conflict between Britain and Germany had now spread to the Mediterranean. Germany (and Italy) carried out a provisional settlement of political and territorial questions in the Balkans, without taking into consideration the interests of the Soviet Union. But this was of no significance for the German attack plans, which were already completed. Only the attack on the Soviet Union was postponed for a good month. In accordance with the economic agreement with Germany of January 1941 and because of concern about German intentions, the Soviet Union did increase its deliveries of raw materials to Germany and continued them until the last moment. Stalin refused to take seriously several warnings about German plans to attack; the largest part of his troops was still stationed near the frontier.

On 22 June 1941 the Germans attacked on a broad front: and the decisive phase of the world war had begun, in two respects. Most important was the race and ideological war of annihilation against 'Bolshevism' as a movement of 'asocial criminals', as Hitler described it to leading officers on 30 March 1941. We shall return to this aspect of the war later. But, nevertheless, the war against the Soviet Union was planned as a new blitzkrieg, and was intended to bring about a collapse of not only the military but also the political and social organization of the enemy within a few months. In spite of this careless, not to say reckless planning, which contradicted traditional military principles, the Germans deployed all available troops for the attack and left no adequate reserves to deal with possible reverses. Although Hitler did not place any value on allies in this campaign, he did permit Finland and Romania, which had both suffered as a result of his non-aggression pact with the Soviet Union, to participate immediately. But Hungary also joined the campaign in order not to be at a disadvantage against its rival, Romania. Later, other states in Germany's sphere of direct or indirect influence joined, some by sending regular troops, others through volunteers. This permitted German propaganda to play up the war as a 'European crusade against Bolshevism'. In addition to this motive, political considerations of having a voice in a future German-dominated Europe also played an important role.

The German attack was carried out by approximately three-quarters of the combat units of the German army, over 3 million soldiers, and two-thirds of the Luftwaffe. On the Soviet side there were fewer soldiers – considerable forces had been deployed in East Asia and the Caucasus respectively against possible attacks by Japan and Britain – but in aircraft and tanks the Soviet Union enjoyed a clear qualitative superiority. Nevertheless, at first the German war plan was largely successful. Large parts of the Soviet air force were destroyed; German troops advanced rapidly eastward. Hundreds of thousands of Soviet prisoners were taken in each of a quick series of encirclement battles. Chief of the General Staff Halder considered the 'campaign in Russia' to have been won 'within 14 days' (3 July 1941).[8] Shortly thereafter the main emphasis in German armaments production was again shifted to the navy and the Luftwaffe. While the highest-ranking German officers advocated a quick drive by the Army Group Centre towards Moscow, as the transportation and political heart of the Soviet regime, Hitler wanted the main weight of the attack to be in the north (blocking Soviet links to the Baltic) and primarily in the direction of the Caucasus (oil, coal, iron ore) for political and economic reasons. On 21 August 1941, he prevailed.

But even earlier it had become clear that this time a lightning victory (*Blitzsieg*) could not be expected. In spite of high losses, the Soviet enemy was able to mobilize material and personnel reserves, and its system did not collapse. The German advance slowed. When the attack towards Moscow was finally launched at the beginning of October, it quickly became bogged down. While the German public was being told that victory had already been achieved, the start of the autumn rains, the resulting mud, and later frost caused the advance to grind to a halt a short distance from Moscow. Attempts to resume the offensive in spite of these obstacles failed. Further territorial gains, especially on the southern front, did not prevent the Red Army from launching a counter-attack in the Moscow region. The rapid German advance earlier, and the shortage of supplies, meant that now the German forces were at the end of their strength. Approximately a quarter of their men were not fit for action; over 170,000 had been killed. Another force of comparable quality could not be created. The Wehrmacht had very probably lost the war, and not only because of its heavy casualties. Hitler occasionally understood this, but the German population could not. The absence of a 'final victory' meant, however, that for the first time doubt began to spread about the 'genius' of the 'Führer' and his ability as a strategist and commander.

And the world political role of the United States as the decisive power in future had become even more important. A lightning victory in the east in 1941 was necessary to secure the entire Eurasian area for the Tripartite powers against possible American and British attacks. Plans were also made to secure the Atlantic coasts against landings by capturing Gibraltar and north-west Africa. German troops were to advance in several spearheads into the Near East via Egypt, the Balkans, and the Caucasus, expel the British, and threaten India from Afghanistan. But an efficient division of tasks with Japan (as earlier with Italy, which at first was not even informed of the date of the attack on the Soviet Union in June 1941) could not be achieved. Although it had been informed in general terms about German intentions, Japan achieved a détente in its relations with the Soviet Union through a non-aggression pact in April 1941. On 14 July 1941, when Hitler believed that Germany had defeated the Soviet Union alone, he offered the Japanese ambassador in Berlin a truly global alliance in order to 'annihilate' the United States together; as he admitted, this was a 'hard' task in the life of their nations.[9] But in view of the slower German advance in the area of Smolensk, and their own country's lack of raw materials, the Japanese leaders decided not to attack the Soviet Union in the east and instead devoted their attention to a southward expansion in the direction of French, Dutch, and British possessions with their vital natural resources, a course that would inevitably lead to a collision with the United States. In July, Japan occupied the southern part of Indochina. In the end the parallel negotiations with the United States produced no positive results. But a total American embargo of oil and other products confronted the Japanese government with the choice of either completely abandoning their plan for a 'Greater South-East Asia Co-Prosperity Sphere' dominated by Japan, or seizing the initiative and resorting to war. They decided to attack and, in the last weeks, to eliminate the threat of an American flank attack from the Philippines by destroying the American fleet at Pearl Harbor. This attack, on 7 December 1941, was successful, with the result that both countries entered the war. Four days later Germany (and Italy) declared war on the United States, although under the circumstances this was not required by the Tripartite Pact. The war had now become a world war.

Germany's Repulse and Defeat by the Anti-Hitler Coalition

What caused the German dictator to declare war on the strongest naval power in the world at the very moment that his land war against the Soviet Union had led to a Soviet counter-offensive? There was no doubt that, on the whole, the United States would increasingly support Britain. But President Roosevelt's hands were tied by the neutrality laws of the 1930s, which were intended to prevent a new American involvement in a war like that of the First World War. While preserving a formal neutrality, Roosevelt succeeded step by step in increasing economically, and thus politically, his commitment in Europe (and Asia). The 'cash and carry' export of war materials permitted since November 1939 benefited only Britain and France. On 19 July 1940, after the German victory in the west, the American Congress decided to build a two-ocean navy that would be equally strong in the Atlantic and the Pacific within 6 years. Moreover, as Roosevelt put it on 29 December 1940, the United States became an 'arsenal of democracy'. As early as 1940, it sold a large part of its aircraft production to Great Britain and turned over destroyers to the British for anti-submarine warfare in exchange for British colonial bases. It was clear that the United States would in any case prevent the victory of the states whose expansion was directed against free trade and democratic political institutions as Americans understood those terms. On 11 March 1941 Congress passed the Lend-Lease Act, not to prepare for, but to avoid a military intervention, which permitted the supplying of all states with war material as the President saw fit. In addition to Britain, the Soviet Union was soon to benefit from this law. In the second half of 1941, the United States occupied Iceland and extended its security zone to include the greater part of the North Atlantic (July), gave its navy a shoot-on-sight order against German ships in that zone (September), began to share with the British the results of its communications intelligence, and finally, as the British had already done, introduced the convoy system. The joint declaration by Roosevelt and Churchill in the Atlantic Charter of 14 August 1941 regarding a future democratic and liberal, capitalistic world order showed that the United States was prepared to accept the challenge of the expansionist powers in Europe and East Asia.

The German decision to declare war on the United States had already been taken before Pearl Harbour; and, contrary to Hitler's usual practice, it was proclaimed in a formal declaration of war in accordance with international law, which was probably due primarily to the fact that Germany was not in a position to mount a surprise attack against its new enemy in the war. Hitler himself admitted that he did not know yet how to defeat the Americans. Ostensibly he was therefore mainly concerned with being able to respond to what he considered American provocations with equal freedom of action in a war which, *de facto*, already existed. On a somewhat deeper level, Hitler probably expected that Japan would prove to be the weaker contender in the Pacific war. He hoped that a German declaration of war would force the United States and Great Britain to spread their available forces over two oceans. But this decision, too, showed the increasingly desperate situation in which Hitler now found himself in spite of all his conquests.

In view of American production capacity, however, a division of American forces in the two main theatres of the war was of only limited significance. In December 1941 the Tripartite countries signed an agreement not to conclude a separate peace, which, however, they did not abide by in 1945. They also agreed to a separation of their respective zones of operation at 70 degrees east longitude, in the western Indian Ocean. But this did not lead to agreements on joint operations. The military means and successes of the Axis powers and Japan were not sufficient to form the basis for a common war strategy. The only concrete result of the agreement was economic co-operation, maintained with difficulty by sea links, which was especially important for Germany (for rubber, among other things). Above all, Hitler's attitude towards his Japanese ally remained ambivalent because of his race prejudices; on 7 February 1942, for example, in a small circle he expressed his regret that the British would lose Singapore. Attempts to foment revolutions in the respective spheres of interest claimed by the other pact partners, such as the Arab countries or India, were not based on close consultation. Moreover, for Japan it was extremely important that the British and the Americans should remain the only common enemies. For this reason the Japanese-Soviet neutrality treaty remained in effect until after the German surrender in 1945. But the danger of a Japanese attack from China still tied down some Soviet troops in eastern Siberia. Thus to a large extent the Germans and the Japanese fought parallel wars. And in spite of impressive Japanese successes in South-East Asia and the Pacific in the first months of 1942, the Battle of Midway in June of that year was the turning-point of the war there. Nevertheless, contrary to its proclaimed 'Europe first' strategy, the United States concentrated a large part of its resources in the East Asian theatre until the spring of 1943.

This was one of the reasons why the second front in western Europe, urgently demanded by the Soviet Union in its battle for survival, was slow to materialize. Basically, Stalin's Soviet Union held its own after the initial German attack without foreign help; a formal alliance with Great Britain was concluded only in May 1942. Deliveries of war materials from the United States and Great Britain first began to play a significant role in 1942. Precisely because of the successful Soviet defence against the Germans, the main German offensive in 1942 began on the southern sector of the front, after numerous indecisive battles, only at the end of June that year. At first the offensive gained ground rapidly, but it could not reach its two main objectives, the Caucasus on one hand and Stalingrad on the Volga on the other, at the same time, as well as threatening the Turkish or the Iranian frontier or even the British position in the Near East. After mid-November 1942, Soviet forces launched a counter-attack and forced the surrender of the German 6th Army, which had been encircled at Stalingrad with over 200,000 men, at the beginning of February 1943. This was the first time the Germans had suffered such a defeat in the Second World War, and it had happened in spite of all heroic, morale-boosting slogans. It caused a profound change of mood among the German population. Optimistic expectations of victory, and confidence in Hitler and the regime on which they were based, had been shattered. Stalingrad made obvious to the entire world the change in the course of the war, which had actually taken place more than a year earlier, in November and December 1941.

While German surface ships, on the whole, were not very effective against enemy warships or trade, as was evident in the sinking in May 1941 of the modern battleship *Bismarck*, which had been commissioned only a short time earlier, the U-boats were considerably more successful in their war against enemy shipping. In 1940 and 1941 they sank over 4 million gross registered tonnes of enemy shipping each year, and in 1942 over 8 million gross registered tonnes, a figure that exceeded by far the tonnage of new cargo built by the enemy in the same period. But in May 1943, already affected by successes of Allied communications intelligence, the German U-boat war under Admiral Karl Dönitz largely collapsed and did not recover during the rest of the war. As a substitute for an early direct deployment of their troops on the Continent demanded by Stalin, the British (and later the Americans) expanded their air war to include area bombing of German cities after March 1942, which, however, did not decisively affect the morale of the German population or the German war economy.

In North Africa, too, the German advance was halted at El Alamein in Egypt. In November 1942 the British began their counter-attack. And by May 1943 the German troops in North Africa had been pushed back to Tunisia, where they were forced to surrender. More important were the landings of American and British troops at several places in Morocco and Algeria; the Allied strategy was to force a dispersion of the German forces by attacking the periphery of German-controlled Europe, without, however, losing sight of the aim of an Allied invasion of the Continent itself. The first expression of common aims of the unsteady coalition between the Soviet Union and the British and Americans was the vague phrase 'unconditional surrender' in their Casablanca Declaration of 24 January 1943. But now they had seized the initiative on all fronts. While the Germans had been able to begin and conclude individual campaigns with victories and occupation before June 1941, that situation had changed as early as 1942. The usual distinction between the combat zone and pacified rear areas disappeared not only in the Soviet Union; in other parts of occupied Europe, too, the Allied military successes encouraged resistance. Increasingly, German troops were transferred from relatively peaceful locations to others according to operational requirements, as the strength of the Wehrmacht, which in 1943 and 1944 was slightly under 9.5 million men, could not be increased. The number of German soldiers killed each year rose from 160,000 in 1940–1 to figures between 485,000 and 573,000 in each of the following 3 years. Thus the 'total war' that Goebbels proclaimed in a speech to a mass audience and broadcast by radio on 18 February 1943 had long been a reality for most Germans: the economic efforts at home to support the war were as important as the fighting on the battlefields. Civilians and soldiers were equally threatened by death. The slogan was proclaimed at a time when the will of the population to continue the war was threatening to fail and had to be mobilized anew. Similarly, the catchphrase 'Fortress Europe' was used by the Germans to gain support of other peoples for the defence of supposedly common interests; but in view of the German system of exploitation and oppression this effort received only a very limited response. The 'fortress' also had the disadvantage of being without a roof, as Allied air superiority clearly demonstrated.

For the German conduct of the war after Stalingrad and until June 1944 the most important battles continued to take place on the territory of the Soviet Union. There the Germans undertook counter-thrusts near Kharkov and then north of that city near Kursk. But they were able to achieve only limited gains, and after 17 July 1943 the Soviet military began to launch offensives aimed at liberating large areas from German occupation; by the beginning of January 1944 they had already reached formerly Polish territory. The siege of Leningrad, begun in autumn 1941 with the aim of levelling the city, was breached by the establishment of a land bridge at the beginning of 1943. Only in the spring of 1944 did the Germans abandon the effort. In spite of promises to the Soviet Union, a large-scale Allied landing in Europe did not take place in 1943. In addition to strategic political considerations (until 1943 the possibility of letting the Soviet Union continue to fight the land war in Europe alone), the Allies took the view that an operation on such an unprecedented scale simply could not be permitted to fail, and they needed time to be sure of success. For a time, the Americans and the British considered a landing in the Balkans, continued their advance from North Africa via Tunisia to Sicily (10 July 1943) and then landed in southern Italy (3–9 September 1943). Between these two events Mussolini was deposed by the King of Italy, the Fascist Grand Council, and the Italian military, and was imprisoned. On 8 September his successor, Marshal Badoglio, negotiated an armistice with the Allies. This act of Italian *raison d'état* had been expected by the German government, but they were nevertheless indignant about the Italians' alleged 'betrayal' and treated them thenceforth as enemies. The establishment in northern Italy of an almost puppet regime under Mussolini, who had been liberated from imprisonment, did not change anything in this regard. In France and the parts of the Balkans remaining under their domination the Germans extended their control to areas previously occupied by the Italians. Beginning in May 1944, the German forces in Italy were pushed back northward.

The decisive British-American landing which Hitler had long expected to be carried out in Norway, and for which the construction of the Atlantic Wall represented more of an act of propaganda than a real obstacle, took place on 6 June 1944 in Normandy. In spite of the utmost efforts by the inadequate German defensive forces, more than 1.5 million Allied soldiers had landed by the end of July 1944. At the same time, the Allies broke through German defensive positions. American and French troops gained a foothold in southern France; the British occupied Brussels. Paris was liberated intact by the Allies on 25 August 1944. On 23 October 1944, Aachen became the first German city to be conquered. With the last great German offensive, which began in the Ardennes on 16 December 1944, Hitler hoped to achieve not only a military but also a political and psychological breakthrough and to split the enemy coalition as a whole. But after only a week the failure of the offensive was obvious.

In March and April 1944, Soviet troops resumed their advance in the Ukraine, captured the Crimean Peninsula after the middle of May, and, on the third anniversary of the initial German attack on 22 June 1941, began a large-scale offensive in the central sector of the eastern front. The German forces there were decisively defeated and were able to mount only limited resistance to further attacks. In contrast to the peaceful entry of General de Gaulle and the Americans into Paris, the Polish Home Army organized an uprising from 2 August to 2 October 1944 to liberate the Polish capital, Warsaw. The uprising was, however, put down by the Germans, while the Red Army stopped its advance on the other side of the Vistula. Warsaw was totally destroyed. From Finland to Bulgaria, in their own national interest Germany's allies attempted to withdraw as soon as possible from their unequal partnership by signing armistices with the Soviets or even changing sides. Soviet troops and those of the Western Allies reached German territory at almost the same time, but the Soviets were stopped temporarily in the northern part of East Prussia. In mid-January 1945, the offensive in the west and the Soviet attacks in the east resumed. Millions of Germans in the east fled by land or, with the help of the German navy, across the Baltic to the west.

The simultaneous attacks in the west and east were a coincidence and not the result of military planning. Since the Moscow foreign ministers' conference (from 19 to 30 October 1943) and the meeting of the Big Three (Roosevelt, Churchill, and Stalin) in Tehran (from 28 November to 1 December 1943) and in Yalta (from 4 to 11 February 1945), the Western Allies and the Soviet Union had been attempting to co-ordinate their short-term military planning and their long-term peace aims, especially with regard to Germany. The American and British governments had long remained undecided as to how a peaceful and democratic Germany could be created in the post-war period: by reducing the size of the country, breaking it up, and placing it under strict supervision, which could lead to a rebirth of revanchism, or by making possible reconstruction through the preservation of German unity and the granting of sovereignty. In the view of the victors, however, given the continuity of German traditions or even because of the German 'national character', the latter approach could also lead to an undesirable aggressive reaction. The Big Three were in agreement on the need to re-establish Austria as an independent state and to shift Poland's frontiers westward, as far, say, as the Oder river. The Soviet Union would retain the areas it had occupied in 1939 as well as the area around Königsberg. The rest of Germany was to be divided into independent states and would be required to compensate other countries for damages suffered under German occupation. No attempt was made to reach agreement on details. And none was achieved, as the four victors – after Yalta, France was also included – after March 1945, shortly before their military victory, abandoned their plans to divide Germany and decided, on 6 June 1945, to keep the country united and to retain the highest authority there themselves for the time being.

This joint responsibility for Germany was a result of the agreements of 1944. An advisory commission created by the Moscow foreign ministers' conference envisaged a division of Germany into three (later four) zones for the occupation and the period immediately thereafter, as it were for military tactical reasons, and on 12 September 1944 this plan was signed in the form of a zone protocol. A special area, Greater Berlin, constituted an exception;

a second, Allied protocol of 14 November 1944 divided the western zones between Britain and the United States and created the Allied Control Council as a joint decision-making body. In Yalta it had been agreed that France would receive an occupation zone to be taken from the British and American zones. In view of these agreements, there could be no race among the Allies to occupy Germany. Instead military logic was the dominant factor. On 25 April 1945, American and Soviet troops met at Torgau on the Elbe and thus split the area still defended by German troops. After Hitler's suicide on 30 April 1945, Dönitz took over the functions of his office. He was unable to arrange a partial surrender to the Western Powers. A total capitulation was signed in the French town of Reims on 7 May 1945 and repeated in Berlin-Karlshorst on 9 May. On that day, German troops still occupied bases in Norway and on the French Atlantic coast, parts of Kurland, Crete, and some small parts of northern Germany together with larger areas in the south, from Saxony to Croatia.

The National Socialist regime had proved to be incapable of making peace. Tactical peace feelers extended since 1943 had only been intended to split the Allied coalition. In the final months of the regime they were renewed unsuccessfully by such leading National Socialists as Himmler, Ribbentrop, and Göring. This was due not to the demand by the Allies for unconditional surrender (which did, however, create problems for opposition groups in Germany), but rather to the revelations of the nature and extent of the policy of annihilation pursued by the Germans in many areas they had occupied, especially in Eastern Europe. This policy was also reflected in Hitler's slogans intended to boost morale, and in the motto 'Victory or Destruction'. When Hitler himself realized the inevitability of his defeat, he saw the reasons for it only in the weakness of the German people, whom he was prepared to sacrifice without hesitation, declaring 'The future belongs exclusively to the stronger peoples from the east'; while in his will of 29 April 1945 he advised the Germans to abide by the race laws and to conquer *Lebensraum* in the east in future.[10] Hitler's refusal to face reality, together with his dogmatism, determined German policies until the end of the war.

THE 'OSTRACIZING' OF ENEMIES: PERSECUTION AND EXPULSION

The war that began in 1939 was fought to enlarge the German sphere of influence, to conquer new economic resources for long-term German exploitation, and to solve the current armaments crisis. And with the attack on Poland it already had the character of a war of enslavement and annihilation fought according to racial criteria. This was only an extension abroad, to an increasingly large part of Europe, of what had been taking place in Germany since 1933: the struggle of the German national community (*Volksge-meinschaft*), defined in racial-ethnic terms, against 'the others', its enemies. For Hitler this elimination of enemies had the character of a military conflict from the very beginning, although its specific forms were not determined in advance, were formed in an *ad hoc*, experimental way, and, because of domestic political and international considerations, did not always begin in a way which led to fatal consequences. It would be an exaggeration to describe the persecution that began in 1933 as a kind of one-sided war, but the continuity from this to the actual war, in the persons, institutions, and intentions involved, is clear.

The Basic Characteristics of the Policy of 'Ostracization'

The process of ostracization, the exclusion of persons considered to be unfit to belong to the German national community, began with the persecution of political 'enemies' in the narrow sense of the word: Communists and Social Democrats. But its victims soon included Liberals, Christians, and con-servatives. Discrimination against Jews began immediately; then came the Gypsies; and the term 'criminal offender' was expanded to include new concepts, especially 'professional' or 'habitual criminals'. Later, homo-sexuals, the mentally ill, the handicapped, and the infirm were threatened by ostracization. During the war, large parts of the Slavic nations were affected, as were other peoples, ethnic groups, and individuals who did not accept German domination, deserted, or took up resistance as 'Maquis' or parti-sans. Every expansion of the area under German domination increased the possibility that people belonging to these groups there would be directly threatened, persecuted, or murdered; but whether or not this actually hap-pened was often a question of expediency and of taking into account the particular governments of the area (where they still existed). The political stability of German domination was an important factor in this; but in individual countries there were also people and groups with their own reasons for practising persecution and discrimination. For them, German policy against the Jews offered a desirable and rare opportunity for fruitful co-operation. In many respects German rule was a hothouse that permitted and encouraged the extermination of enemies on an otherwise inconceivable scale. Social, political, and economic tensions in Germany and then in large parts of Europe erupted against groups or people considered to be racial or political enemies, and those who vented their anger and frustration in such a way made themselves accomplices with the Nazis. Nevertheless, the real initiative and will lay with the National Socialists, who distinguished them-selves by adding a new quantitative and qualitative dimension to the meaning of murder. The murder of the European Jews exceeded anything that had gone before. In many respects, it was at the same time the culmination of the war and of its brutality.

Ostracization often began on a very modest scale. Verbal attacks on political opponents, who became enemies, was merely a more aggressive form of previous practice. But discrimination, especially against Jews as 'parasites', 'vermin', or 'bloodsuckers', represented an attempt to ostracize the victims from human society. Intimidation through more or less spontaneous use of violence, for example in brawls, was a continuation of what had happened frequently in the Weimar Republic; but the difference now was that one side was soon defenceless, while the other enjoyed the toleration or even support of the state power apparatus. Deaths as a result of political violence were also not new; but legally sanctioned discrimination was another matter. It was a result both of the sweeping powers granted by the emergency laws and decrees, and of deliberate, precisely formulated restrictions with exact descriptions of how far freedom of activity or movement was permitted, together with an equally detailed list of penalties for transgressing these restrictions. During the National Socialist period almost 2,000 regulations and laws were issued directly or indirectly against Jews. And in this area, too, much had been prepared before 1933 and only needed to be published in an intensified or modified form. Often it was based on allegedly 'scientific' knowledge, which was then illustrated and popularized for a wider audience. This extended to comic strips intended to show that 'inheriting physical and mental weaknesses' would lead to a 90 per cent 'inferior' population within 300 years.[11] Measures to create not only a new human being but also a new social order were declared to be an unavoidable necessity.

Potentially, ostracization could take place everywhere. The mechanisms of the process extended even into private lives; but it was carried out mainly in public and professional areas. Traditional places of confinement and segregation were used: jail cells, prisons, homes, and hospitals, all of which were penetrated by and subordinated to the instrument of despotism which the state had become. And ostracization was practised most consistently in the concentration camps. These underwent an especially profound change when they ceased to be improvised institutions, intended to relieve the overcrowded prisons and to terrorize certain persons and groups and deprive them of their rights, and became a central institution of the state. At first, most concentration camps were created arbitrarily by SA and SS units and other party organizations and offices; then they multiplied to become a system extending throughout Germany and, in the end, across Europe. They served the most varied purposes: in the beginning they were institutions for what might be called National Socialist re-socialization; but then naked terror pushed other considerations aside. Forced labour to the point of overwork and death, depersonalization, and finally killing were the oft-proclaimed, or, at the least, immanent functions of the camps. The final number of victims of another kind of policy, that of a deliberately created scarcity of resources, was even greater. This policy led to hunger, thirst, freezing, and illness, and thus just as surely to death, as did direct physical violence. In many cases, such scarcity was a deliberate policy, planned at the highest level. It sometimes arose as a result of the war, or of emergency situations and sudden, unexpected difficulties which affected members of the German 'national community' and its allies. But usually it was an expression of intent or enormous indifference that excluded, from the very beginning, protective measures and care for rejected and outcast people.

At first the executors of the policy of persecution were the members of the NSDAP and its organizations, who retained a dominant role in this area beyond the period of the consolidation of power in Germany. The ability to ostracize other people was often an essential part of their own identity, and even more, of the cohesion of their own group within the 'movement': the persecution and even murder of enemies, often spontaneous but increasingly premeditated and planned, served to bond their group and promoted their awareness of their own higher rank, of what they were indoctrinated to view as their historic mission. State institutions and, in particular, the Ministry of Justice and the Ministry of the Interior, were usually responsible for legal matters, for bureaucracy and administration. All government departments were involved in ostracization; for example, almost all of them had their own 'expert for Jewish affairs' by 1938. The differences between the more spontaneous, arbitrary forms of persecution practised by party organizations and the deliberate, methodical procedures of state authorities do show tensions, friction, different approaches, and occasionally a divergence of opinion as to their goals. But these distinctions became blurred not only because of the increasing interpenetration between the party and state, the *Gleichschaltung* of the public institutions and private organizations, and the creation of such separate entities as the German Labour Front and the Todt Organization. More important was the fact that the classic executive instrument of the state – the police – was combined with the SS under Heinrich Himmler. As of 1936, the Reich Leader SS (*Reichsführer SS*) was also the head of the German police. Not only did he single-mindedly expand the concentration-camp system into the core of the persecution and then the annihilation apparatus, but he also extended the activities of his empire, a symbol of the National Socialist state, into such areas as the economy, the military, and ethnic policy, with the consistent purpose of carrying out a social transformation.

But its constant growth and expansion into ever more sectors in territory under German control did not give the SS a monopoly on ostracization and extermination in Europe. All agencies, especially in the economy, and indeed the majority of Germans, were directly or indirectly involved. This was especially true of the policy of restricting resources, which led to mass deaths, especially in the occupied areas of Eastern Europe, and which was usually not based on any purposeful planning of an overall strategy. In the chaos and confusion often found in the areas immediately behind the eastern front (the army rear areas and army group rear areas), millions of Germans, especially soldiers, were confronted with the policy of annihilation. In spite of the general readiness to participate in or at least not oppose this policy, individuals occasionally attempted, even within the persecution apparatus itself, to relieve the plight of some of the victims, at least to the extent that it would not result in their deaths, especially as killing such people was normally not the task of soldiers or guard units.

The ostracization itself was openly and loudly proclaimed from the very beginning. Its fatal consequences were usually only implied metaphorically, leaving the perpetrators some latitude for interpretation. Between knowing, half knowing, and not knowing at all there was a grey zone of looking away and denial that manifested itself in ambiguous language which often served to disguise what exactly happened in radical annihilation. 'Protective custody' (*Schutzhaft*) was the term normally used by the police to describe a procedure to protect endangered people who could not otherwise be helped, but beginning in 1933 it served as a pretext for the arbitrary arrests of people who were in any case victims of ostracization. And the terms 'concentration camp' and 'final solution', along with many others, originally had and continued to retain for many people quite innocent connotations corresponding to their dictionary meaning. But for others, the perpetrators, they served from the start to conceal persecution and annihilation.

In discussing the perpetrators, persecutors, and occupiers, the perspective of the victims is especially important. This was the central dividing line of their experience. Only in this role did the outcasts form a single group; they became victims as a result of the views and actions of the perpetrators. Among themselves the groups mentioned were as varied as were their societies. For example, the definition of the terms 'Jew' or 'asocial' (*asozial*) grouped people together as victims who otherwise had nothing to do with each other. Moreover, this changed social relations among the outcasts. Wherever possible, they became closer, sometimes in accordance with the wishes of the persecutors, to moderate by co-operation the effects of the complete arbitrariness to which the victims were subjected and to prevent their situation from deteriorating. Nevertheless, the lines between victims and perpetrators were not always clear or permanent: it was possible to be both at the same time or successively. It did happen occasionally that functionaries of the regime were forced by their superiors to act brutally to make them compromise themselves. More frequently, however, the victims, such as politicians or public employees in occupied countries, were forced to organize more efficiently groups to which they themselves belonged, in order to facilitate the work of the perpetrators. The Jewish elders (*Judenälteste*) in the ghettos were the most obvious example, as they had to establish an orderly framework for the plundering and exploitation and finally for the deportation and murder of the ghetto residents. In the concentration camps, prisoners as functionaries of the prisoner self-administration had to or were permitted to assist the perpetrators. The 'Kapos', concentration-camp prisoners who were often hardened criminals in civilian life, were especially notorious and became effective perpetrators themselves. This classic method of indirect rule placed many in a hopeless, tragic situation: victims were forced to become part of the system of German rule and even of the murder apparatus. They sometimes did so in the hope of being able both to moderate the arbitrariness to which they and others were subject and to survive. In many cases such hopes proved to be illusory.

The Victims: Jews, Communists, and Social Democrats

The experience of being a victim was imposed from outside. It was always individual, even when the social group to which the person concerned belonged was occasionally able to provide moral support, especially at the beginning. Some victims resisted and rebelled, but more typical was the attempt to preserve a minimum area of freedom or privacy by adjusting to the new situation. Beyond a certain point in their oppression, victims became similar: fear, hunger, and direct torture often led to depersonalization, in which the people affected cared for nothing any more beyond the immediate necessities of life and survival. This was a development which was usefully exploited for German propaganda purposes to exhibit 'sub-humans'. Even when it was not irreversible, as murder (whether through physical violence, technology, hunger, or illness) clearly was, it signified the social death of the victims preceding their physical death.

As mentioned above, persecution began with the Communists and the Social Democrats. In many respects the revolutionary impetus and demand for change of the SA and the SS was vented on them spontaneously and displayed the entire scale of terror from intimidation to murder. In the course of 1933, the SPD and the trade unions began to focus increasingly on maintaining their organizations or establishing forms of co-operation outside existing political structures. The exile organization of the SPD (Sopade), at first in Prague and then London, came to consider the collection and exchange of information in the Reich to be its central task for the time being. The Communists, directed from Moscow, still considered themselves to be part of the Comintern. At first they made much greater efforts than the SPD not only to maintain their mass organization as a whole, but also to promote the revolt which was still expected against National Socialist rule through limited, demonstrative acts of resistance. Believing that the Hitler regime would soon collapse, the KPD continued its attacks on the SPD until the introduction of the Popular Front in 1935, its rigid position possibly reflecting the deliberate intention of Moscow. Accordingly the Communists were subjected to even more severe persecution. By the end of 1934 approximately

2,000 of them had been killed.[12] By 1945, according to their own figures, 20,000 had died. Some 60,000 Communists were arrested in 1933 and 1934, and another 15,000 in 1935. After 1935 the working-class and workers' movements (the SPD and KPD) were forced to resort primarily to clandestine action.

Hatred of Jews *per se* is at least as old as the Christian religion. The persecution of the alleged 'people who murdered Christ' historically formed the rationale for a special role of the Christian churches in society throughout Europe, which sought to preserve their religious identity by emphasizing the role of Jews as an enemy. In the second half of the nineteenth century the religiously motivated ostracization of Jews was reinforced by a growing national consciousness in many European countries, and finally by pseudo-scientific teachings about race. Parallel to these developments came the emancipation of the Jews in many European countries, which promoted their complete integration into civil society. By 1933 in Germany it had reached a comparatively advanced stage, a main objective being the providing of legal safeguards for Jews by the state. But it was still easier for Jews to accelerate this process by converting to Christianity, which often did not prevent them from maintaining their Jewish cultural identity, than by expressly affirming their Jewish faith. Fed by various conflicts in German society, anti-Semitism grew into a mass phenomenon during the First World War and the Weimar Republic. In particular, the influx of Jews from East European countries gave strong impetus for a new, legal ostracization of Jews. In the new national states of Eastern Europe, the Jews were persecuted much more severely than they had been in the earlier supra-national empires. Often Jewish immigrants from the east were poor, and for that reason alone were easily distinguished from the rest of the population.

More important, however, was the fact that political mass movements in Germany, among which the NSDAP became the largest and most influential, adopted anti-Semitism as a central cohesive element in their programmes. A latent anti-Semitism had long been present in a large part of the German middle class, where the view was widely held that there were too many Jewish lawyers or doctors, although many people who shared such opinions had no qualms about entrusting their own legal affairs or health to a competent specialist who happened to be Jewish. But the mass of the population was indifferent to the matter. In 1933, approximately half a million people in Germany belonged to Jewish congregations; most of them lived in cities, a third in Berlin alone. Because of their above-average level of education, as well as in medicine and law they were also especially numerous in banking, trade, the arts, and among intellectuals. Moreover, Jews in the country typically earned their living as traders in livestock. But, on the whole, the professional and social differences between German Jews were almost as great and varied as those in the rest of German society.

Acts of anti-Semitic violence began to increase immediately after 30 January 1933 and became even worse after the election in March. In part they were spontaneous, and served to strengthen the internal cohesion of and to increase support for the NSDAP: 'Hit the Jew wherever you find him!'; and in part they were staged, and played down as expressions of 'justified popular anger'. This already marked the beginning of deliberate re-interpretation by the state of positive action as simple reaction. On Hitler's instructions, Goebbels channelled this development into a 3-day boycott of Jewish businesses on 1 April 1933, and described it as a 'defensive struggle' against the 'world enemy'.[13] But for foreign-policy and economic reasons it was broken off after only a day. At almost the same time, on 7 April, a law concerning the professional civil service was enacted, in accordance with which 'civil servants of non-Aryan descent are to be retired'. For the time being there were exceptions. But this marked the beginning, in complete agreement with the National Socialists' conservative coalition partners, of the elimination of the rights of German Jews. Step by step the emancipation of the Jews in Germany was reversed. Not only were appropriate legal clauses introduced, as in the civil-service law, but from universities to professional organizations, and even for the self-employed, licensing was required. Together with the terror in the streets, this formed a consistent policy and increased the psychological pressure on Jews. Many other citizens conformed to the new situation opportunistically, finding it no longer useful to maintain previously cultivated private or public relations with Jews. Looking away, and hypocrisy in discrimination, were the dominant forms of behaviour.

But, beyond the Nazi party itself, persecution of the Jews did not prove to be a very effective means to unite the country behind the regime. On 17 September 1933, at the initiative of the best-known German Jewish scholar, Leo Baeck, German Jews, who did not constitute a uniform political or social group, merged their various organizations to form the Reich Organization of German Jews (*Reichsvertretung der deutschen Juden*) in order better to defend their rights. Very different views were represented among German Jews. Very few welcomed the supposed new beginning under National Socialism, or considered spontaneous acts of persecution to be only a temporary phenomenon. Their reactions ranged from silence to indignation and resignation; some began only then to think of themselves primarily as Jews. Only a few realized that there was no longer any place for Jews in Germany. The possibility of the mass murder of Jews probably did not occur even to them; but 37,000 German Jews emigrated in 1933 alone. In the following years, when the direct terror abated for a time, some considered returning to Germany. But that hope was illusory. In addition to the informal ostracization, formal legal measures were introduced. There had already been public campaigns against 'race treason' (*Rassenverrat*), but in the 'Law for the Protection of German Blood and German Honour' and the Reich Citizen Law (*Reichsbürgergesetz*) – these were the Nuremberg Laws of 15 September 1935 – the 'clear separation of Germans and Jews necessitated by their blood' was given a pseudo-scientific, legalistic basis by providing a definition which included being from one-quarter to one-half Jewish. Marriage of non-Jews to the victims of such discrimination was made punishable by law, and finally Jews as mere 'nationals' (*Staatsangehörige*) were given an inferior legal status compared with 'Reich citizens' (*Reichsbürger*). Numerous regulations for carrying out the Nuremberg race laws were based on this distinction, including the requirement that the passport of a Jew be stamped with a 'J' and the decree that, in addition to their family names, Jews always had to use the additional first names 'Sarah' or 'Israel'. Both of these requirements were introduced in 1938.

The pressure also increased from another side: the looting of Jewish assets, which was conducted with particular intensity after 1936 to finance rearmament and obtain foreign exchange, made the expulsion of the Jews a profitable business. They fled without possessions; although emigration was officially promoted, they were permitted to take little with them. Many Jewish firms, especially small ones, closed. Of 50,000 small Jewish businesses in Germany in 1933, only 9,000 still existed in July 1938.[14] Of the total of twice as many Jewish firms, two-thirds closed in the same period. Many were 'Aryanized'. In 1938 this policy acquired a new quality in the November pogrom, soon referred to as 'the night of broken glass' (*Reichskristallnacht*). This event had been preceded by the expulsion of 17,000 Jews of Polish nationality to the east as part of the policy of making Germany 'free of Jews'. As the Polish government refused to accept them, these Jews remained in a no man's land between Germany and Poland. The reaction of the son of one of the families affected, who fatally shot a German diplomat in Paris, suited the National Socialists perfectly. There had been local pogroms in the years before 1938, and synagogues had also been destroyed. In agreement with Hitler, Goebbels exploited the opportunity to unleash an unprecedented persecution of Jews all over Germany, to which he attempted to give the appearance of spontaneity. It was carried out by non-local SA men out of uniform, who destroyed or set fire to 1,000 Jewish businesses and almost 200 synagogues. Many people witnessed this outbreak of barbarism silently and uneasily. Some helped Jews secretly; others began to think critically about the National Socialist system. Especially in other countries, indignation towards the Nazi regime reached new heights, which clearly showed even the rulers of the Third Reich the folly of proceeding against their intended victims in such a public fashion. Approximately 100 people were killed in the pogrom, and some 25,000 taken to concentration camps, of whom many were later released so that they could emigrate. Jewish property in Germany had suffered considerable damage. The payments from insurance companies were seized by the state and, in an exhibition of perverse logic, German Jews were held collectively responsible for the shooting in Paris and the damage to property, and were required to pay a sum of a thousand million Reichsmarks as punishment. Financing rearmament as well as increasing the pressure on Jews to emigrate were equally important factors in the enactment of this measure.

By the beginning of 1938 approximately one-third of German Jews had already emigrated, most of them to neighbouring countries in Europe, but also to Palestine (made possible by co-operation between German agencies and Zionist organizations) or to North America. By the start of the war, another 120,000 had left Germany, often destitute and robbed of their funds by the state, and in many cases blackmailed into making 'voluntary' contributions to obtain exit papers. As early as 1938, state authorities began to register the assets of German Jews. With the founding of the 'Reich Organization of Jews in Germany' (*Reichsvereinigung der Juden in Deutschland*) on 7 July 1939 the 'Jewish guarantee organization' Hitler had been considering for years became a real institution. It was responsible not only for the contributions of its members, but also had the task of organizing their lives within the increasingly severe restrictions and the prohibition of most forms of gainful employment. There were still 200,000 Jews living within the German frontiers as they existed prior to March 1938.

Fanatical, racially ideological single-mindedness, cautious tactical conformism, terror and the preservation of legal forms, economic bottlenecks, and the need to strengthen the cohesion of the National Socialist movement had created this situation. There was still no talk of mass killing. The main current objective was still to force Jews to emigrate by depriving them of their rights and plundering their assets. Most German Jews came to understand this monstrous process only slowly; in the short term, pogroms were as much a factor in forcing them to emigrate as were Hitler's public, but variously interpretable, threats culminating in his speech to the Reichstag on 30 January 1939 on the war to be fought against the Jews. Reinhard Heydrich proved to be the string-puller behind the scenes; in his capacity as armaments dictator, Hermann Göring claimed only formal authority in Jewish matters.

The Persecution Apparatus in Germany: The System of Justice, the SS, and the Concentration Camps

The German system of justice and the police had first responsibility for the deprivation of rights and for terror, but that was not their only task. In many areas of daily life, from directing traffic to divorce cases and the punishment of thefts, both continued to function according to traditional principles. But, in addition to the police, large parts of the German system of justice became accomplices of the unjust state.[15] For one thing, they were subjected to a personnel *Gleichschaltung*; the independence of the judiciary was eliminated. Training as well as recruiting made clear that they were now expected to fulfil a political function in the construction of the National Socialist state. Thus new offences were created, especially in penal law. Groups of perpetrators such as 'dangerous habitual criminals', 'national parasites' (*Volksschädlinge*), or 'economic saboteurs' were introduced into substantive law. In many cases penalties were made more severe, including possible execution. Even under the threat of a reduction of their authority, some judges resorted to giving the most severe possible sentences, so that the accused would not subsequently be arrested by the Gestapo. It even happened that prison sentences were demanded (for example for theft) and imposed more or less according to standard judicial norms to keep the accused from being exposed to the arbitrariness of the police apparatus for political reasons. In the beginning, the efforts of parts of the system of justice to exercise a restraining influence even on the Gestapo were successful in some cases, but this did not last long. The Minister of Justice, Franz Gürtner, who died in 1941 and who was a conservative German National and advocate of a powerful state, occasionally made himself unpopular with National Socialists in this way. After a harsh attack on the system of justice as a whole in Hitler's last speech to the Reichstag, Gürtner's successor devoted himself to carrying out a complete *Gleichschaltung* of the administration of justice.

Special courts with especially reliable National Socialist judges were introduced as early as 1933, and in 1934 a People's Court (*Volksgerichtshof*) was created as the highest authority for political crimes, becoming notorious under its presiding judge, Roland Freisler, during the Second World War. Of approximately 16,000 death sentences in Germany between 1933 and 1945, the People's Court issued 5,000. An independent system of military justice had existed in Imperial Germany; it was reintroduced at the beginning of 1934 with usually Draconian punishments, and came to serve as an instrument of suppression against desertion, insubordination, and similar offences in an increasingly hopeless war. There were 30,000 death sentences issued by this part of the judicial system.[16] In addition, the number for death sentences by field court-martial is estimated at 20,000.

But all these trials, which were formally within the system of justice, were surpassed by far by the core of the terror apparatus, which can be described as the SS state. The concentration camps were its most typical symbol.[17] The possibility provided in the Reichstag Fire Decree for 'protective custody' formed the legal starting-point for the expansion of the system of arbitrary rule which permitted the use of any measure to achieve its self-defined aims. In the first months of the regime the SA, the SS, party functionaries, and state authorities placed many people in protective custody. Both because the prisons and jails were soon overcrowded, and on their own initiative, National Socialist paramilitary organizations established their own, unauthorized concentration camps, in which the persecutors could treat their victims as they pleased, even torturing them to death. Soon, people arrested under 'protective custody' were no longer treated as ordinary prisoners. And the arbitrariness of the terror became the norm: 'protective custody' was no longer considered to be a punishment that had to be reversed if the reasons for which it had been initiated no longer existed. For this reason, many prisoners escaped the horrors of the concentration camps only after weeks or months. Moreover, the concentration camps were merged and placed under a systematic administration. Most were outside cities, but the notorious Columbia-Haus camp was in the middle of Berlin. In the Emsland, camps were established with the aim of making the swamps arable; their best-known prisoner was Carl von Ossietzky. The SA and party agencies as such lost the power to impose protective custody in April 1934. At that time, after the Nazis had eliminated most political opposition to their rule, it would have been possible to eliminate the camps, in which 27,000 people at most could be imprisoned at one time; but they were taken over by the SS.

As early as 20 March 1933 Himmler, who was then only the acting chief constable of Munich, announced the imminent opening of the Concentration Camp of Dachau, and released an appropriate press statement throughout Germany. Capacity and accommodation for the prisoners were stated as openly as the camp's political purpose and the enemies who would be incarcerated there. After the summer of 1933 Theodor Eicke was the commandant of Dachau, and made it a model for the entire camp system by attempting to channel the previously largely unauthorized terror into a system of penalties and classifications extending from arrest to whippings, deprivation of food, and post-hanging, in which the victim's hands were tied behind his back and he was suspended a few feet above the ground by the wrists. Prisoners subjected to post-hanging often suffered permanent injuries or even death. Such a system made it difficult for state agencies to interfere on the basis of traditional legal norms. It represented a systematization of torture. Newspaper readers were often informed that prisoners had been 'shot while trying to escape'. This became a cliché by means of which the victims were made responsible for the crime committed against them. The camp guards were indoctrinated with an image of the prisoner as the absolute enemy. They were trained to hate prisoners, but also, ideally, to practise only disciplined harshness towards them, so that totally arbitrary behaviour against prisoners declined between 1933 and 1939.

Eicke also organized the creation and training of the guard units in special troops of the SS. In 1934 he was named Inspector of the Concentration Camps and, beginning in the following year, supervised seven camps with 7,000 to 9,000 prisoners. While in 1933 most of the camp inmates were there for political reasons, new prisoner categories were added in the following years. Depending on their category, prisoners' clothing was marked with cloth triangles similar to insignia of military rank: political prisoners (red), Jehovah's Witnesses (lilac), asocials (black), criminals (green), homosexuals (pink), and emigrants (blue). Jewish prisoners had to wear a yellow triangle over the triangle designating their respective category, thus forming a six-pointed star. During the war, letter markings were added to designate prisoners of other countries.

The criminal system combined arbitrariness with method. In addition to subjecting its victims to direct torture, it was also intended to intimidate the rest of the population. The names of Dachau and other camps came to be synonymous with danger to life and freedom. After 1937 the camps were occasionally described as 're-education institutes for asocials'. And as Hitler's and Speer's gigantic urban construction programme required large numbers of labourers to quarry the necessary stone, new camps were built near granite deposits (Flossenbürg in Bavaria and Mauthausen near Linz in 1938, and Natzweiler in Alsace in 1940), just as brickworks were an important factor in the establishment of the concentration camps of Sachsenhausen at Oranienburg near Berlin and Buchenwald near Weimar. The SS also began to develop its own economic enterprises, and founded the German Earth and Stone Works Ltd. (*Deutsche Erd- und Steinwerke GmbH*) in the spring of 1938. In 1942 its chief administrator, Oswald Pohl, became head of the SS Economic and Administrative Main Office, a potentially gigantic economic enterprise. But until the war this aspect of exploitation of concentration-camp labour remained secondary to the function of stabilizing the Nazi system by isolating its enemies. This was made especially clear by the vastly increased number of prisoners and the consequently catastrophic hygiene conditions in the camps after the pogrom of November 1938.

THE WAR AGAINST ENEMIES WITHIN THE NAZI IMPERIUM IN EUROPE

The Expansion of German Rule in Europe: Occupation and the Apparatus of Terror

In 1939 the area of German domination already extended beyond the frontiers of 1933. Its every expansion brought more people whom National Socialists considered to be enemies within their reach. Many people who had fled Germany or emigrated since 1933 had found refuge and, they believed, safety in neighbouring countries such as Austria, Czechoslovakia, Holland, or France. Now, in so far as they were able, they had to flee again. But many lacked the means, and finding countries that would accept refugees was becoming increasingly difficult. Thus many victims were caught up in persecution for a second time. In addition to German émigrés, native Communists and Socialists, in so far as they had been active in those areas prior to the German occupation, automatically became enemies and therefore victims. The occupying German authorities lost no time in giving their attention to domestic political conditions within the occupied state, carrying out changes that always led to persecution. In so far as this involved 'bringing Germans home to Germany' (*Heimholung von Deutschen ins Reich*), as in Austria, the Sudeten areas, or Germans in Poland, the prevalent public mood in Germany was one of enthusiasm and jubilation, amplified by propaganda. But there, too, the terror claimed its victims from the start.

Amid the enthusiasm for the annexation of Austria in March 1938, special detachments (*Sonderkommandos*) of the Security Service (SD) of the SS entered that country with special operations groups (*Einsatzgruppen*).[18] In accordance with the original secret mission of the SD under Heydrich, they had prepared lists long before in order to begin searching for and arresting enemies immediately. In a more or less undisciplined fashion, the formerly suppressed National Socialists in Austria began to settle personal scores. These actions extended from the leaders of the previous Austro-fascist regime (in particular Federal Chancellor Kurt von Schuschnigg, who was arrested and, in 1941, sent to a concentration camp) to all categories of persons already subject to persecution within Germany itself. Between 20,000 and 70,000 people were affected. Beginning in April 1938, these Austrians were transported to Dachau and then to other concentration camps. In mid-1938, Austria received its own concentration camp, at Mauthausen, and the number of prisoners there grew rapidly. On the whole, the *Gleichschaltung*, which, as was now claimed, had taken 5 years in Germany before March 1938, was completed in Austria within a year. Its basis was created by an enabling law and the approval of the annexation in a plebiscite. The Austrian police, army, and administration were taken over, with the exception of a few top officials, and quickly integrated into their German counterparts. Though there were many administrative and reorganization problems, essentially the NSDAP set the pattern; its Gau organization provided the model for most state sectors. The name 'Austria' was struck from the maps in the new Greater Germany and replaced by the term 'Ostmark' ('Eastern Borderland'). Beginning in April 1940, the area of the former Austria was referred to as the Reich Gaus of the Ostmark, and 2 years later, when a very different borderland policy was being practised in the Soviet Union, there remained of Austria only the Alp and Danube Gaus. As in the German frontiers before 1938, plans for a fundamental reorganization of these areas were postponed until after the war and thus remained without significance.

The decision to annex Austria had been decisively influenced by that country's resources. The foreign-currency reserves of the Austrian State Bank helped the Reich Bank over a crisis by adding 1,368 million Reichsmarks to its reserves of barely 76 million Reichsmarks. As regards to raw materials, especially iron ore, the annexation provided welcome relief for bottlenecks in arms production. The comparatively smooth integration of Austria into the Third Reich, which was concluded at the outbreak of war in 1939, was not based on a uniform plan. On the contrary, it was marked more than in later cases by competition among private firms and state and party agencies for sinecures and privileges. Banks, private firms, Göring's Four Year Plan, every Ministry, old and new plenipotentiaries, the party, and the SS sought to expand and strengthen their often long-held positions, and to gain a decisive share of power there. This in turn, created a number of precedents for other parts of the Third Reich. Bitter conflicts developed between party functionaries which had to be decided by Hitler himself. The Jews in Austria were also quickly terrorized and deprived of their rights and, after brief hesitation, decided in many cases to emigrate. In this regard Himmler and Heydrich created an office that was to acquire enormous significance in future: in August 1938, Adolf Eichmann, the head of a sub-department, established the Central Office for Jewish Emigration (*Zentralstelle für jüdische Auswanderung*) in Vienna, where most of the 200,000 Jews in Austria lived. With money extorted from wealthy Jews (the 'emigration tax'), it financed the emigration of those less well-off. By the start of the war, 60 per cent of the Jews in Austria had emigrated. A branch office was established in Prague in March 1939. On 24 January 1939, Göring entrusted Heydrich with the organization of Jewish emigration, another consequence of the pogrom of November 1938. This was a development typical of many others, in which new forms and methods were tested at first outside the German frontiers as they had existed before March 1938, and then were later applied throughout Germany itself. Moreover, the tendency to force Jews to emigrate, with the knowledge or even assistance of the Gestapo and often to countries reluctant to accept them, became more pronounced.

The annexation of Austria was only a first step, from which lessons were learned for future territorial expansion, although not in the sense of co-ordinated total planning. Although the aim of 'bringing home' supposedly oppressed groups of ethnic Germans played a large role in German foreign policy and propaganda, there could be no second annexation like that of Austria. Of course the 'homecoming' of the 3 million Sudeten Germans was an occasion for much jubilation, but only for those who did not belong to one of the ostracized groups. But this was not true everywhere. Many people considered to be of German origin, like those in Alsace-Lorraine, did not identify with the Greater Germany ambitions of the Third Reich. In any case, such areas were usually incorporated directly into the Reich. The designations and exact territorial boundaries were determined later.[19] In April 1939, the northern Sudetenland became a Gau and kept its previous name. The southern areas became parts of already existing Gaus in Bavaria and what had been Austria. In the same way, the Memelland came under the authority of the Gau leader of East Prussia, Erich Koch, who also annexed previously Polish areas in the south and east to the area under his control in 1939 and the district of Białystok in August 1941. The formation of two other Gaus after Poland had been crushed was of great significance: Danzig-West Prussia under Albert Forster, and Wartheland under Arthur Greiser. Earlier both men had fought each other as Gau leader and Senate President respectively in Danzig; now they received separate 'playgrounds', in a very macabre sense of the term, as Reich governors. Other Polish areas were allocated to administrative districts in Upper Silesia. This was the pattern: leading party functionaries attempted to expand their territory beyond the frontiers of the

Reich to include areas which were then added, either formally or *de facto*, to Greater Germany. Eupen, Malmedy and Moresnet – parts of Belgium with a German population – were given to the Gau leader of Cologne-Aachen, Josef Grohé; in 1941 the Gau leader of Koblenz-Trier, Gustav Simon, united Luxembourg with the area already under his control to form the new Gau of Moselland. And Joseph Bürckel of the Saar-Palatinate, who had played a decisive role in the *Gleichschaltung* of Austria in 1938–9, extended his control over Lorraine (the Gau Westmark). From Baden, Robert Wagner incorporated Alsace into his sphere of influence. A similar development took place in April 1941, when the Gau leaders of Carinthia and Styria annexed parts of Slovenia. In September 1943, after Italy had changed sides in the war, two operations zones were formed: the Adriatic Coastal Area (including Istria) and the Foothills of the Alps (including Trent and Belluno). The Gau leaders Friedrich Rainer and Franz Hofer respectively considered them preliminary stages for their own territorial expansion. But these plans were never realized.

In so far as areas were not formally annexed as parts of the Reich, party functionaries there as heads of the civilian administration were directly subordinate to Hitler. As he explained in 1940:

> Creating a functioning administration such as is present in areas that were parts of Germany before March 1938 is not important. Rather our aim is the most rapid Germanization possible of the new areas . . . Any means serving to achieve this aim is acceptable . . . The party men will do the job right. They'll have to learn the hard way; mistakes are inevitable. But what difference will that make if ten years from now they can report that Danzig and Alsace-Lorraine are German although in Colmar three or four, elsewhere five and somewhere else ten mistakes were made?

This constituted an authorization for radicalization. The Gau leaders concerned were able to ignore existing administrative practices. Generally they were able to carry out their policy of Germanization as they saw fit, although they often found themselves in conflict with other National Socialist authorities.

It was the usual practice for a soldier to assume the highest executive authority in occupied areas and retain it until peace had been concluded. In Poland, as in the areas mentioned in the west of the Reich, as well as in The Netherlands and Norway, military leaders assumed executive power only for a short time, but the heads of the civilian administration, especially if they were high party functionaries, were often beyond military supervision, although they were formally subordinate to the military. Notably in Poland, killing operations took place in rear areas for which the military still had formal responsibility. When protests proved futile, the military tended to turn responsibility over to other agencies as soon as possible, a concession to the specifically National Socialist thirst for action. This development marked the beginning of the tendency of the Wehrmacht, which had been a self-confident partner of the regime until 1938, to look away, concentrating on military matters alone and so becoming active accomplices in the emerging total war. Military administrations remained in France, Belgium, the Channel Islands, south-east Europe, Serbia, and the part of Greece occupied by the Germans. In the Soviet Union, in accordance with a prior agreement with the SS, the military Commanders-in-Chief limited themselves to the (changing) army-rear and army-group-rear areas, and there, as the authority with executive power, they became *de facto* agents of the murder machinery.

Nevertheless, under military administration efforts to maintain at least a semblance of the rule of law were more likely to succeed, at least to a small degree, than under civilian administration, which was usually dominated by party functionaries and party aims. In the west, civilian administration consisted of the Reich commissariats for Norway under the Essen Gau leader Josef Terboven, while The Netherlands were under the last Minister of the Interior of Austria, the National Socialist Arthur Seyss-Inquart. The Protectorate of Bohemia and Moravia and the Government General, which included the remnant of Poland under Hans Frank, had the status of civilian areas, as did the Reich Commissariat Ostland in the Baltic States and part of Belorussia under Hinrich Lohse, previously the Gau leader of Schleswig–Holstein, and the Reich Commissariat Ukraine, to which Erich Koch extended his control from his territory of East Prussia. For the Reich Commissariats Moscow and Caucasus covering the Soviet Union to the Urals the core civilian administrations had been prepared; but they were never able to proceed to their designated areas.

More important than the difference between civilian and military administrations was the difference between German occupation in eastern and in western Europe. In the east, German authorities began a radical racial and colonial transformation during the war. There the far-reaching Nazi plans for the territory of the Soviet Union were stopped by the war itself. In the west, on the other hand, where, to use National Socialist terminology, not 'inferior' Slavic, but Germanic or neo-Latin peoples lived, the transformation remained a question of political expediency and necessity, which depended on the loyalty of the civilian population or their attitude towards Germany's enemies, Britain and America. The conclusion of an early peace was expected after June 1940 and then again in July 1941, which, it was hoped, would permit the German occupying authorities to proceed with the necessary severity against enemies in occupied areas in the west. These expectations continued until 1943, and hope for a final victory remained the official German propaganda line until the end of the war. Especially in the west, military administration seemed to be a provisional measure that would change or disappear after the victorious end of the war. Thus, German authorities believed, it had a calming effect on the civilian population of the occupied countries there, and at the same time it kept open the option of a radical transformation. This is the only possible explanation for the fact that, while Hitler considered establishing a civilian administration in Belgium after 1941, he actually took that step only in the last phase of the war, in July 1944, when Albert Speer urged the appointment of the Gau leader of Cologne and Aachen, Josef Grohé, as Reich Commissar there for reasons of the war economy.

The final category of German influence was that of German rule based on formally independent governments. In Denmark, whose protection Germany assumed, the government was dependent on the German plenipotentiary. After March 1939, Slovakia was a satellite state, as was Croatia after 1941. But especially in the Balkans and the pieces of the former multi-ethnic state of Yugoslavia, tensions developed because of German competition with Italian imperial and annexationist policies. In 1943, the Germans also took over Italian positions there, and occupied key positions even in Italy itself. Hungary, Romania, Bulgaria, and Finland, like Vichy France, only gradually became satellites. As a rule, the longer the war lasted, the more active became the requested and unrequested German advisers in these states, whether the Wehrmacht, the SS and intelligence services, or economic experts from the government bureaucracy. Under the protection of German hegemony, individual firms attained a disproportionate influence in some areas. Göring's Four Year Plan was involved almost everywhere. Construction gangs of the Todt Organization worked from the North Cape to North Africa and even in Turkey, which remained a neutral power until February 1945. In Spain, Portugal, Morocco, and Algeria, too, Germans were active at least as entrepreneurs. On the other hand, on the European continent only Switzerland, Sweden, and Portugal remained neutral until the end of the war, and at the high tide of German power and expansion in 1941–2, respecting their neutrality was only a question of political and economic expediency until 'final victory' had been achieved. The length and harshness of German rule over the greater part of the European continent thus varied, developing different forms of penetration and influence over public life which extended from transformations based on population policy and race ideology, to economic exploitation, forced labour, and genocide.

The Gau leaders (usually at first in their capacity as heads of the civil administration), Reich Commissars, and others were appointed by Hitler and were directly subordinate to him. But the SS became the most important force, usually in competition with others, but also exercising a considerable ability to overcome and eliminate any opposition. It distinguished itself by its aggressive attitude towards Germany's supposed enemies and its pronounced élitist consciousness. Here we shall mention only the Waffen SS, whose development from the SS Special Service Troops and the Death's Head formations to a military force has already been described.[21] By 1939, the Waffen SS accounted for 10 per cent of the entire SS. After the outbreak of war, the volunteer formations were expanded energetically but without advance planning. The voluntary character of this élite military group, which considered itself a rapid-reaction force to be used on various fronts, and which was recruited according to certain physical characteristics, could not be maintained. Increasingly, conscripts were taken into the SS and not only the Wehrmacht. At the beginning of 1945 it was planned to put 17 per cent of the next age group of men to be called up for service into SS uniforms. On 30 June 1944, the Waffen SS had almost 600,000 members, of whom almost 370,000 belonged to combat units (the total strength of the German armed forces was approximately 9,000,000). One army was commanded by a full SS general; seven commanding generals belonged to it, and nineteen SS generals were division commanders. But the concentration camps, too, operated with Waffen SS personnel. When Heinrich Himmler became Commander-in-Chief of the Replacement Army in 1944, and thus responsible for replacements in the Wehrmacht as a whole, the distinctions between the top echelons of the Wehrmacht, which were increasingly pushed aside, and those of the Waffen SS began to fuse into a National Socialist people's army.

Ethnic Germans from outside Germany, especially from south-eastern Europe and Denmark, were also pressured into joining the Waffen SS, which sought to develop the image of a pan-European volunteer organization. At the beginning of 1944, the SS volunteers numbered 300,000 men. First of all, they were soldiers with a 'Germanic' background and/or a German ideological orientation. Some were also mercenaries. On the whole, this appeal did not meet with any great success from Norwegians, Flemings, or Swiss, although, among others, approximately 55,000 Dutch were among the volunteers. In addition, there were Walloons and French, together with Estonians, Latvians, Ukrainians, Cossacks, and Islamic Turkic peoples. In the course of the proclaimed struggle against Bolshevism the Waffen SS lost not only its volunteer character but also its original character as an Aryan élite troop. But in view of the lack of equal treatment of foreign volunteers as well as ethnic Germans, the claim to represent a pan-Germanic army for all of Europe remained an unkept promise for the future. During the war Himmler and the SS continued, in a polyp-like fashion, to establish their own offices and activities in many areas, from race and genealogical research to medicine and economics, in a system of justice that extended beyond the SS itself, and in their own intelligence service (SD-International). In Europe two institutions became most important, to judge by their names and not their functions. On the one hand there was the Reich Security Main Office (*Reichssicherheitshauptamt* or RSHA), which was created on 27 September 1939 and which combined state and party police functions (the Order, Criminal, and Secret State Police as well as the Security Service). This was part of the tendency, never completely realized, to fuse the state parts of the police completely with the SS, which until then had been attempted only on an individual basis, using integration and the appropriate uniform. On the other hand there was Himmler's newly acquired title of Reich Commissar for the Strengthening of Germandom (*Reichskommissar für die Festigung des deutschen Volkstums* or RKF), acquired on 7 October 1939, which codified in the typically veiled granting of broad powers the authority to Germanize all persons who might be considered proper members of the Reich as well as to 'eliminate the harmful influence of such alien parts of the population that constitute a danger for Germany and the German national community'. While the RSHA was a thoroughly radical executive institution down to the lowest level, the RKF was at first only a central office that worked through other agencies in view of its manifold local activities, formally up to and including the appropriate Gau leaders. This was especially true as regards major aspects of Nazi rule in Europe; and it opened up possibilities for terror and persecution in the occupied areas and beyond.

Everywhere the SS became a synonym for the German reign of terror. To prevent its threatening disintegration into partial organizations, Higher SS and Police Leaders (*Höhere SS- und Polizeiführer* or HSSPF) were appointed. Originally created to ensure uniform representation of the interests of the SS during mobilization in Germany itself, they never acquired great significance there. But HSSPFs were gradually installed in most parts of occupied Europe. Each of them, Himmler wrote in 1943, 'is for me a representative of the Reich Leader SS in his area. Woe betide us if the SS and the police are separated.' The SS, he added, must remain besides its different branches and aims 'a [single] block, a [single] body, an order'. And for the HSSPFs this meant that, as representatives of the SS in their relations with other German authorities abroad, and even in the organization of sites and transport for the annihilation of human beings, they should act as decisive links to Himmler himself. In this capacity they were permitted to circumvent even the main offices (*Hauptämter*) of the SS Central Operations Office (*Führungshauptamt*) itself. The fact that this situation produced not only co-operation but also confrontation among the German occupying authorities, impaired only slightly the functioning of the terror machinery.

Kinds of Movement: Destination Death

In developed industrial societies, movement, mobility through space, is considered a positive criterion; under the conditions of German rule in Europe people began to move in previously inconceivable numbers. Migrations took place that often led to death. People left their places of residence for a limited time or permanently, some alone, some with their families, or in large social groups. This forced mobility often necessarily involved death – indeed, that was its goal – as the intention was that at their destination the human beings involved should die sooner or later. In many cases this can accurately be described as murder. Most of these migrations were known; they were mentioned in newspapers (even censored ones), and people not affected were aware of them. The Continent in motion meant the destruction of social relations on an enormous scale. Families were torn apart, local communities were destroyed; in certain regions cultural and ethnic identities disintegrated temporarily or permanently. The destruction extended to the extinction of entire peoples, to genocide. Here, too, the murder of the Jews stands out. Human beings disappeared from their familiar surroundings in broad daylight, the transports took place in public, and the foot marches were even more visible. The departures and occasional return of individuals subjected to these forced migrations were known; much more was suspected. But the decisive feature of this process, the genocide carried out with considerable technical efficiency, was so monstrous that even the National Socialist leaders attempted to limit the knowledge of it to as small a circle of initiated persons as possible, although the total number of such persons was probably at least a six-digit figure. This secrecy does not, of course, exonerate anyone, but it does make clear the extent to which what was done went beyond anything in the previous history of Western Europe.

The movements of large masses of people affected very different groups: soldiers, prisoners of war, refugees and resettlers, expellees, deportees, forced labourers, and people who were transported across Europe solely for the purpose of being killed in an extermination camp. The first large groups to be set in motion were growing numbers of soldiers, in Germany and, on an even greater scale, in the territories of all Germany's enemies together. Altogether the figure was about 40 million men. In so far as they were not defeated in short campaigns and then in many cases suffered death as prisoners of war, they experienced not only the change from the front to rear areas and between the fronts in west and east, but also home leave, and being assigned to help gather in the harvest, to work in the armaments industry, and even to study at universities. But during the war this became less and less frequent in the area under German control. As in most wars, being a soldier in the Second World War cost many people their lives. Their number far exceeded 10 million; many returned from the war mutilated for life. All were marked by their experience. Many suffered permanent psychological trauma through their fear of death or their participation in and experience of killing. The weapons used and their destructive power had been considerably improved since the First World War, but basically there was no difference. Indeed, because of fear of retaliation by the other side, Europe was spared chemical warfare and the use of poison gas, which had been used frequently in the First World War, just as it was spared the atomic bomb, which was used by the Americans at the end of the war in the Pacific. But losses resulting from phenomena quite normal in themselves attendant on the armed conflict, such as hunger, illness, and exhaustion, cost many more lives than the fighting itself.

The war resulted in the movements of large numbers of civilians or caused them to abandon their native countries. In 1938, Czechs living in the Sudetenland were the first. Areas in which fighting was expected were emptied, or 'evacuated', as it was called in official bureaucratic terminology. Millions of people fled at the approach of the fronts: approximately 8 million did so in France, for example, in 1940. After some time they were able to return when the fighting had ended. But that was definitely not the case in Eastern Europe. Where there was armed resistance – guerilla war in the Soviet Union or Yugoslavia, or the beginning of the *résistance* in 1943 in France – the distinction between civilians and military was lost in the face of the common threat of war and occupation. And people who were not involved were affected. The fronts were everywhere, and it was hardly possible to escape them.

The bombing war also led to movements of large groups of people. It threatened primarily urban populations, whose houses were destroyed. People lost their homes in the cities and fled to the apparent safety of the country. In the course of the war and the continued expectation of air attacks, however, they were increasingly taken to areas surrounding cities for longer periods of time, or were transported to less densely settled regions, from which the war still seemed distant at the time. These measures, in particular, affected millions of children. What the Germans had begun in Warsaw, Rotterdam, and Coventry in 1939–40 with the bombing of cities, including residential areas of the civilian population, was increasingly used in turn against them, affecting all the large German cities and many smaller ones as well. In parts of western and northern Germany in particular, the bombing attacks remained for many people the strongest and most lasting memory of the war.

Movement also meant rearranging the map of Europe according to the ideas of the German 'master race'. Other peoples were assigned subordinate positions ranging from economic and social dependence to enslavement. What the 'master race' was, or could be, or who could become members of it, was open to interpretation. In 1938 Hitler claimed that the world would one day belong to this great racial core of 110 million people.[22] In 1943 Himmler hoped to be able to recruit an additional 30 million people of Germanic stock; but that figure was only an empty calculation. In any case it was certain, and was proclaimed by Hitler as early as 6 October 1939, that after the war 'a new ordering of the ethnographic situation in Europe' would be carried out.

During the war this was both planned and begun. It was clear to Hitler that Scandinavians and many West Europeans were to belong to that Germanic racial core. Even in July 1944, Himmler still described the final aim as:

the winning and integration of the Germanic peoples, the Norwegians, the Danes, the Dutch, and the Flemings into this Germanic empire. If we can bring 25 or 30 million persons of this best blood into the body of our nation . . . who are brothers and sisters of our race, that will expand the [ethnic] basis of our people from 90 to about 120 million.

Using historical and ethnographic arguments, Himmler occasionally considered including not only the Flemings but also the Walloons, and even discreetly promoted efforts of the Bretons towards independence. But political considerations affecting the conduct of the war, as well as the usually negative response of most of the intended beneficiaries, precluded significant successes of the Germanization policy in Western Europe.

In 1940–1 only a few Alsatians and Lorrainers were forcibly resettled to Germany. Eastern Europe, however, became the main, lethal laboratory for National Socialist resettlement policy. Even some intended members of the 'master race' did not agree with the role assigned to them, that they should be expelled from their native regions against their will. In October 1939, in the process of delimiting definitively the German and Italian spheres of influence, the inhabitants of South Tirol were given until the end of that year to decide where they wanted to live. The 200,000 who voted for Germany were scheduled for resettlement, and approximately 80,000 did actually settle in Austria by the end of the war. Their final destination was intended to be the Crimea (*Gotenland* in Nazi parlance). But then the Germanization of the two new Gaus in the east, the Warthe Gau and Danzig-West Prussia, was given priority. As if the pact between Germany and the Soviet Union was actually a permanent arrangement, the resettlement of ethnic Germans from areas recognized as belonging to the Soviet interest sphere was initiated by the RKF: from eastern Poland (Volhynia and Galicia), from the still-independent Baltic States, then in 1940 from Bessarabia and Bukovina, but not, for the time being, from the Soviet Union itself. Beginning at the end of 1941 and then in the following year, after the delimitation of German and Italian spheres of interest, ethnic Germans from Yugoslavia and Bulgaria came 'home into the Reich'. And most of them were sent to the new eastern Gaus. At the end of 1940, agencies of the RKF were taking care of 500,000 ethnic Germans and, by the end of 1942, the figure was 800,000.[23]

In the new eastern Gaus, the official registration of the population was begun; and in 1940 a German 'national list' was created in which people were divided into four categories, from actual ethnic Germans to persons of German origin, who were either to be educated as Germans in the course of time, or given few or no rights as 'renegades', mere 'protected dependents' who had 'deserted' to the Poles. Many people living in these areas sought to prove their acceptability as Germans for economic reasons – indeed, simply to survive – but it was not planned to accept more than a million of them from the area of the former Polish state in any case. In the annexed areas of Yugoslavia and in Slovenia the development was similar. The negative aspects of this development were clear: the non-German population was expelled and deported, often to already densely settled areas. From the beginning the process was marked by great brutality. Poles were forced out of the annexed areas into the Government General, but they were also sent to concentration camps in Germany, and guidelines required that the number of Polish expellees be two to five times that of the new German settlers. By the end of 1941, 800,000 Poles had been expelled. As will be shown later, these operations were accompanied by the murders of Poles and Jews, and many of those expelled never reached their destinations. In Alsace, Lorraine, Luxembourg, and Slovenia, deportations were carried out in a similar fashion, but often less brutally.

The General Plan East

Population policy became a policy of murder. But this establishment of a new demographic order was given a distinctive quality when the settling of new 'territory for expansion' (*Lebensraum*) was planned at the same time as the attack on the Soviet Union. Most of the General Plan East, which was produced primarily by the RKF and the RSHA, but also by the Race and Settlement Main Office of the SS (*Rasse- und Siedlungshauptamt* or RuSHA), the race policy office of the NSDAP under Darré's, Ley's, or Speer's organizations, and many others, was never realized. What had been tested in Poland was put into practice in the Soviet Union. The mass killings there fitted in well with and prepared the way for the anticipated realization of final German plans for the newly conquered territories in the east. Moreover, Hitler felt that it was 'essential' not to 'announce our aims to the entire world', as Bormann noted on 16 July 1941, when expectations of early victory in the east reached their height:[24]

> Basically the main thing is to slice up the gigantic cake so skilfully that we first gain control of it, then administer it, and finally are able to exploit it. The rise of a [new] military power west of the Urals must never be possible again, even if we have to fight for a hundred years. We have to make a new Garden of Eden in the newly conquered eastern areas.

Millions of people lived in this area and, in Hitler's view, they were not needed there. Contrary to German expectations, however, it quickly became evident that prospective inhabitants for a Garden of Eden were very hard to find. The nation that was supposedly a 'people without space' was conquering a space for which it did not have the people. The prospective settlement area in the east could not be filled, even though in German officers' clubs the new knight's estates were already being distributed, soldiers were promised farms when they became veterans, and these acquisitions were already being registered. The RKF estimated that 3.8 million settlers would come from Germany, 100,000 from ethnic Germans in resettlement camps, 500,000 people from the 'scattered Germandom' in south-east and eastern Europe, and 150,000 'Germanic settlers' from northern and western Europe. They also included an 'undetermined number of Germans from Russia' in their calculations and hoped, moreover, for 750,000 Estonians, Latvians, Lithuanians, and Goralians who could be Germanized. Finally, they assumed that 150,000 'ethnic Germans from overseas' would return. Other expectations of 10 million Germans for the eastern *Lebensraum* could not even be realized on paper. It was intended to carry out the General Plan East over a period of 25 to 30 years; later this was reduced to 20 years. In September 1942, Himmler developed the plan to Germanize the area all the way to the Urals in 400 or 500 years; it would then be populated by 500 to 600 million people.

In so far as the General Plan East was carried out at all, it was done in a negative sense, through death, resettlement, and 'ethnic cleansing'. This began with taking children away from their parents to Germanize them. It was hoped to Germanize 50 per cent of the Czechs, 80 to 85 per cent of the Poles, up to 65 per cent of the West Ukrainians, and 75 per cent of the White Ruthenians (inhabitants of the eastern Poland and western Belorussia). Depending on the number considered necessary to support centres of German settlement and for the exploitation of raw materials, and the number of survivors of extermination measures, it was assumed that 40 to 45 million people would be expelled. 'Tens of millions of people will become superfluous in this area and will die or have to emigrate to Siberia,' State Secretary Backe declared on 23 May 1941 while preparing the attack on the Soviet Union. In August 1944, when National Socialist rule in the east was already in its death throes, Himmler presented his reduced but otherwise unchanged programme to a meeting of Reich and Gau leaders:

> It is our unchanging goal to expand the settlement frontier of our people by 500 kilometres, to establish a Germanic empire . . . It is our unchanging goal to settle this area, to plant centres of Germanic blood in the east, to push our defensive frontier far to the east . . . [In the next war, the Luftwaffe would have to be based in the Urals]: Anyone who does not have an air security zone of 2,000 or 3,000 kilometres for the next war has already lost it.

This was a monstrous programme of enslavement, which in its extent was unique in modern European history and which was begun with deadly seriousness. Mobility here meant transports to death and slavery, and was carried to its logical extreme. Agrarian strong points, exploitation of raw materials and, with the growing realization that the war might be lost, strategic security determined German planning from Hitler to Himmler, and even involved the new science of area planning.

As Himmler was making his speech, Soviet troops had already reached the earlier German frontier in East Prussia. The Germans, who had been declared to be a 'master race', had fled or were expelled. This sudden change, in which the eastern population of the nation of the perpetrators became victims, was only indirectly a result of this long-term planning, being much more nearly a consequence of real German rule in the occupied areas, in which flight, spontaneous expulsion, and deliberate expulsion overlapped. The widespread anti-Bolshevik image of the enemy gave reason to fear the worst from the Red Army. And indeed, many Soviet soldiers behaved as expected. Orgies of revenge were permitted, and the murders, rape, and plundering were used publicly by Goebbels's propaganda in a vain effort for a last mobilization. Later, after the experience of German occupation policies in their countries, not only the Russians but also Poles and Czechs took revenge after they were liberated. Moreover, among other reasons, because of the desire of the Soviet Union to keep the territorial gains from Poland on its western frontier achieved under the pact with Germany in 1939, the Polish government in exile persuaded the great powers to accept a shift of Poland's western frontier at the expense of Germany. The Polish and Czech governments had also been promised the resettlement of Germans living in their countries. That Britain, the Soviet Union, and the United States had agreed this should take place in an 'orderly manner' only served as a veil for what actually happened later.

Ethnic Germans and those who had collaborated with the occupiers retreated voluntarily along with German forces in the direction of Germany, or were deported by them. When the war ended, the mass flight and expulsion of native Germans from areas that had been parts of Germany prior to 1938, which affected approximately 7 million people, was still in progress. In addition, from the states of East Central Europe in 1939, from the Baltic States to Yugoslavia, 5 million ethnic Germans were expelled or fled by 1950. The 3 million Sudeten Germans formed the largest single group.

Labourers, Prisoners of War, and the Camp System: Exploitation and Death

Quite in contrast to the racist ethnic policies of the National Socialists, which can be rightly called 'ethnic cleansing' and which led to the expulsion of people designated as foreign or inferior, was the forced, often brutal migration of labourers to the Third Reich. The primary reason for the introduction of this policy was the need for labourers in German war production. The bringing of foreign labourers to Germany and their exploitation there did not represent any basic conflict between race policy on one hand and economic needs on the other, for the conditions of 'service in the Reich' were largely dictated by the racist logic of National Socialist ideology.[25] Seasonal and migrant workers, notably from Poland, had long been a familiar sight in Germany, especially in the Prussian eastern provinces. This situation did not change after 1933. There were approximately 375,000 such foreign workers in Germany in 1939, primarily Poles, Italians, Yugoslavs, Hungarians, and Bulgarians. But in spite of the conscription of about 1 million Germans for what was considered essential work, the booming armaments industry was still suffering from a labour shortage at the beginning of the war. In February 1939 the shortage was estimated at 1 million workers. In March it was calculated, although on an unclear and exaggerated basis, that 17 million would be needed for the 'Production Programme Final Aim' of the army. The solution was obvious: only the war, already planned for other reasons, could provide the necessary labourers. Moreover, conscripted German workers were only slightly limited in their ability to change jobs. Nevertheless, acute social problems arose. Cuts in social programmes envisaged for wartime were therefore put into effect only in modified form, and were partly cancelled after the victory over Poland. This approach did not change during the entire war: the National Socialist leaders were extremely cautious about demanding sacrifices from the German population, with the result that the labour shortage became increasingly severe as the war became a total one. The growing number of dead and wounded soldiers, the expanding fronts, and the military occupation of large areas meant that more and more German workers were put into uniform and had to be replaced. A constant tension developed around the question of which persons with which jobs should be considered fit for active duty and which were indispensable for the war effort in their civilian positions. And in spite of numerous, repeated attempts to cull out and register workers centrally, the patronage practices of powerful individuals in the German polyocracy protected an astonishingly high number of people from being called up for military service. The party and state bureaucracies in particular proved to be relatively resistant to all efforts to achieve a total labour mobilization for Germans. The only remaining possibility was to employ more women but, as will be shown, Hitler resisted all plans in that direction.

The increased use of foreign labourers in Germany was thus an inevitable result of the war, and the recruiting of such persons soon became a real hunt. There were indeed motives for foreigners to seek employment in Germany (including the Warthe Gau and the former Austria). In many countries, particularly in East Central Europe, and especially in Poland, there had been much unemployment before the war. In view of the murderous conditions under occupation in their own countries, living conditions in Germany as well as wages and the availability of food there undoubtedly seemed attractive to some non-Germans. Work in Germany thus meant, for some, an escape from immediate oppression and mortal danger for themselves or their dependents or the ability to provide better for them. But as a rule, labourers were taken to Germany by force and at best changed from bad to worse conditions, from a hopeless and distressing situation created by the German occupation of their country into another, equally undesirable one in Germany itself. By September 1939, 100,000 workers, among whom, in addition to farm labourers, there was a large number of qualified skilled workers, had been recruited more or less voluntarily in the newly established Protectorate (formerly Moravia and Bohemia); but prisoners of war were by definition not volunteers, and were entitled to at least minimum protection under the Geneva Convention. In Germany 300,000 Polish soldiers were employed in agriculture soon after their capture. After the summer of 1940 their status was changed to that of civilian workers; but this was no more than a completely inadequate stopgap measure.

From the very beginning German policy in the east had as one of its main goals the plundering of the occupied areas. On 19 January 1940, Hans Frank, the governor general of occupied Poland, admitted this: 'Until now the main idea has been to regard this country as an area to be plundered.'[26] Now, however, it was decided to put it into production for the German war effort, so that, for example, the output of Polish munitions factories was to be increased fourfold compared with the previous year. On the other hand, Göring continued to insist that unrestrained deportations would create wage and working conditions that would 'make available efficient labour at the lowest possible price'. The question of whether and under what circumstances production in the occupied areas or in Germany itself should be increased led to as many conflicts as the treatment of the workers themselves. In the same month in which armaments production in the Government General was to be raised, Frank and Göring ordered the transport of 750,000 agricultural and industrial workers to Germany. This shows a typical feature of National Socialist planning, its failures as well as its limited successes. In May 1940, approximately 1 million Poles were working within the pre-1938 frontiers of Germany; in the course of the war the figure rose to 2,826,000. This also meant that over 10 per cent of the total population of the Warthe Gau and the Government General were affected, together with 3.5 per cent of the population of Danzig-West Prussia. The lower figure in the latter Gau (as in Upper Silesia) was due to the fact that many workers in the armaments industry there were not deported. Some also had their names entered in the German national list, a classification system for people of German descent in occupied areas stating their suitability for Germanization. As early as the spring of 1940, when the desired number of voluntary labourers could not be recruited, police raids, in which German police forcibly rounded up people in villages, in busy streets, in churches and other places where they congregated, and in trams, buses and other forms of transport, were begun in Poland. Those who were not performing what German authorities considered useful activity were transported to Germany.

These actions confronted German labour policy with an additional dilemma: for racial reasons all social contact between the 'master race' and Slavs was undesirable. The only solution was a rigorous policy of separation that forbade Poles in Germany the use of public facilities, from parks to churches and public transport. Outside working hours, contact with them was forbidden for Germans. Polish men who had sexual contacts with German women were to be punished by death (but not the reverse situation of sexual contacts between German men and Polish women). This was one reason why German planning required that the number of men and women among foreign workers, especially those from the east, should be equal. And in 1944, 34.5 per cent of all Polish workers in Germany were in fact women, although this was the highest figure reached. As a rule, foreign workers were young, between 20 and 30 years of age; but children, too, and occasionally older people were sent to forced labour in Germany. They came from all social classes and were generally compelled to perform physical labour beneath their professional qualifications. Poles were only the first group among the foreign workers, but they remained the most numerous until the end of 1941.

After the occupation of northern and western Europe, their populations became available after mid-1940. Due to the high degree of industrialization in that part of Europe, there was at first no shortage of labourers. Between 90 and 95 per cent of the approximately 1.6 million French prisoners of war were sent to work in Germany soon after being captured. As the Vichy government attached great importance to the welfare of these men, they were treated relatively well. In addition, they were soon joined by voluntary civilian workers recruited in France. During the war their total number was estimated at between 850,000 and 922,000.

In planning for the war against the Soviet Union, the use of Soviet prisoners of war was not envisaged, as a quick victory was expected which would permit an early return of the majority of German soldiers to civilian jobs. It was clear that a large number of prisoners would be taken in the coming war in the east, but they were intended to remain as labourers in the pacified areas occupied by reduced German forces. But in the Soviet Union in particular, the basic approach and foreseeable consequences of National Socialist racial ideology were immediately evident. As early as May 1941, an expert German group of state secretaries expected that 'millions of people' would starve in the east.[27] The preparations made by the Wehrmacht, which traditionally had initial responsibility for prisoners of war, were completely inadequate.

As expected, millions of prisoners were taken in the first months of the war against the Soviet Union. They were often sent on foot marches to planned camps in the hinterland, and many were sent to the Government General and the newly conquered areas; and the food stocks available for them were completely inadequate. Until 1942 there were hardly any camps for prisoners of war. Those that did exist consisted only of barbed wire fences. Shootings during the long marches to rear areas were a frequent occurrence. Exhaustion, hunger, and cold, coupled with the fact that the guards were often not equal to the psychological and physical demands of their duties, aggravated the effects of the barbaric treatment. By the spring of 1942 probably almost 2 million Soviet prisoners of war had died of various causes. This began with the selection and murder of certain categories, but it was also the result of the inadequate, poorly organized system to which the allegedly Bolshevik 'subhumans' were subjected from the start. Of approximately 5.7 million members of the Red Army who were captured by the Germans, probably 3.3 million, or 57 per cent, died while they were prisoners of war; and only a small portion died in Germany itself. It was this treatment of Soviet prisoners of war that proved such a decisive factor in the later treatment of German prisoners of war in the Soviet Union, of whom 1.1 million (approximately 35 per cent) died.

As early as October 1941, under the impression of the failed blitzkrieg, the treatment of Soviet prisoners of war changed. Soviet citizens could also be used as labourers in Germany itself. Initially this saved only a few. It was hoped to recruit civilian workers voluntarily, but where this was unsuccessful the Wehrmacht conducted roundups to meet the required quotas. The local civilian population, mainly in the Ukraine, often found itself in a hopeless situation. The people soon discovered that the Germans classified them, according to racial criteria, at the lower end of the scale. Many therefore escaped if they possibly could and became partisans. If they did volunteer or were forced to report for work, they were often attacked by the growing partisan groups. In 1943 approximately 224,000 persons were registered for compulsory labour service in Kiev. Of these, 50,000 were sent to Germany, 80,000 fled, and the others were exempted or deferred for economic, social, or medical reasons.

As even existing German production facilities were still often unable to operate at capacity because of a worsening labour shortage, German skilled labourers were conscripted in growing numbers, although they had initially been exempted or released. Albert Speer, king of armaments since the beginning of 1942, urged the creation of a central office to direct the distribution and assignment of labourers. Hitler appointed the earlier Gau leader of Thuringia, Fritz Sauckel, as General Plenipotentiary for Labour (*Generalbevollmächtigter für den Arbeitseinsatz* or GBA). With energy, brutality, and a complete disregard for international law, Sauckel attempted to obtain the necessary labourers. Efforts to recruit volunteers were never very successful. Sauckel claimed to have brought 2.7 million foreign labourers to Germany in 1942 and over 5 million by the end of the war, of whom, as he himself admitted, only 200,000 were volunteers. Labour conscription was also extended to Western Europe; while in the Soviet Union, especially in the Ukraine, actual hunts were organized to round up potential labourers. No other factor made German occupation more hated than forced labour transports, which particularly affected the younger population groups of all countries. In the autumn of 1944, 7,906,760 people from twenty-six countries, civilian workers and prisoners of war, were working within the frontiers of Greater Germany.[28] Foreigners made up 20 per cent of the working population in Germany. The figure probably reached at least 10 million by the end of the war, although it has been variously estimated at 12 or even 14 million. In the autumn of 1944, the largest group of labourers, numbering 2.8 million, was from the Soviet Union. The number of women civilian workers, often young women from the Ukraine, many of whom were employed as housemaids, exceeded the number of men. The Poles were the second largest group (1.7 million), followed by the French (almost 1.25 million) and the Italians (715,000). In September 1943, after Italy changed sides, many Italian soldiers were seized as 'traitors' and taken to Germany or held there as forced labourers.

For the treatment of the various nationalities a mass of rules was developed based on the racist principles of National Socialist ideology, extending from wages and food rations to lodging and type of employment. Basically, German workers were to be treated as superior to all workers from the east. Foreign labourers were employed in agriculture (they accounted for almost half the employees in that sector in Germany) and industry. State enterprises, large concerns, small companies, and private households all sought to obtain foreign workers. This demand led to some loosening of the strict guidelines for their treatment. Workers from the east suffered especially under the concentration-camp system and its deprivations, and an unknown number of them died as a result of the living conditions to which they were subjected in Germany. Foreign workers became a common sight there for all Germans, many of whom were their direct employers or supervisors. This army of labourers were sometimes objects of sympathy, but they were also objects of scorn, as even many non-Nazi Germans considered them to be inferior. In Berlin alone there were 400 camps for foreign labourers, and Germany as a whole contained approximately 30,000 camps and details. Usually they were established by the Reich Labour Service, but they were also created by individual firms. Employers had considerable influence on the lives and living conditions of the forced labourers, as they decided how strictly or loosely guidelines and regulations were to be enforced. Eastern workers in small enterprises or agriculture were often able to live better than elsewhere. Food rations for labourers from Western Europe reached the approximate level of those for Germans (which, however, continuously declined until 1945). Beginning in 1943, in bitter conflicts with Sauckel, Speer attempted to transfer a large portion of armaments production to other countries, especially France, where he hoped to achieve good co-operation with ministries of the Vichy government. But he did not achieve any lasting success. In this way, however, beginnings were made for European co-operation which were resumed under completely different circumstances after 1945.

After Stalingrad, as the labour shortage became even more critical, ideological considerations assumed a less important role in the treatment of Slavic 'subhumans', especially as the use of Russian labourers had been uneconomical. Many of them soon became physically unable to work and even died. Food rations and training were improved so that, on the whole, the productivity of foreign workers rose in spite of constant bombing and the shrinking area under German domination. The highest production rates in the armaments industries were achieved in 1944. Draconian punishments were inflicted on foreign workers for resistance and attempts to escape. Hundreds of forced labourers were shot, often under pretexts, only a few weeks before they would have been liberated. Survivors became 'displaced persons'.[29] In part on their own, and in a chaotic fashion, and later in regular transports organized by the Allies, they sought to return to their homes. In Western Europe this presented no serious problems, but in the area under Soviet control returnees as a group were suspected of collaboration. Understandably, they therefore sought to remain in camps established by the Western Allies as long as possible; but many were nonetheless returned to their homelands under Soviet rule, often with fatal consequences.

The labour shortage continued in spite of the use of prisoners of war and forced civilian labourers. The economic exploitation of concentration-camp prisoners presented itself, therefore, as another source of workers. In terms of living conditions, prisoner-of-war camps or labour camps in many cases were not basically different from concentration camps, although Himmler attached great importance to proper official use of the latter term, and in that sense concentration camps existed only in Germany until 1940. In official German terminology there were approximately twenty different kinds of camps. But for those affected, the victims, such distinctions were a matter of indifference. On 3 September 1939 the following order was sent to the HSSPFs: 'Any attempt to undermine the unity and the will to fight of the German people is to be ruthlessly suppressed.' 'Brutal liquidation' was suggested as a final means to deal with such attempts.[30] This meant the introduction of execution by shooting as official policy in the concentration camps. Arrests within the framework of what National Socialists considered necessary for internal security were carried out both within and, more especially, outside Germany. The number of concentration camps grew rapidly, from Natzweiler in Alsace to the first camp in Auschwitz, begun in February 1940. By March 1942 their capacity had reached 100,000, a fourfold increase since the start of the war. Socialists and Communists were often arrested a second time. New camps were built but, partly because of overcrowding, the number of deaths increased rapidly. In the winter of 1939–40, in Buchenwald near Weimar, 20 per cent of the prisoners died within 5 months.

Moreover, the concentration camps underwent a change of their basic function in two respects: they became economic enterprises, and they became installations for the immediate mass killing of human beings. The occasional use by the SS of prisoners as slaves in the construction industry became an established entrepreneurial activity during the war. It was no accident that in March 1942 all concentration camps were placed under the newly established SS Economic and Administrative Main Office (*Wirtschafts- und Verwaltungshauptamt* or WVHA), headed by SS General Oswald Pohl. It was a time of serious reverses in the east, and Speer and Sauckel now began total mobilization. From this point on, the SS began specifically to expand its capacity for forced labour in the hope of raising the productivity of prisoners. No more prisoners were to be released during the war.

But, because of the conditions in the concentration camps, the SS economic enterprises achieved only 17 per cent of the normal per capita productivity elsewhere. Their contribution to the armaments industry as a whole is estimated to have been no more than 1 per cent. In the autumn of 1941 the SS planned an investment and construction programme for after final victory of 13 thousand million Reichsmarks for all of Europe, and included a plan for the expansion of the camp system throughout the entire area under German rule. In 1981 Albert Speer rightly described the system thus envisaged as a 'slave state', but this had already become a reality during the war.[31] The SS, for its part, began to take advantage of the conditions under which concentration-camp prisoners were forced to labour in Germany and to make them available to the relevant sectors of private industry. The SS became a rental agency for slaves, by charging set rates based on the qualifications of the slaves they provided. In this respect I. G. Farben played a pioneering role; since 1940–1 it had been considering erecting a branch factory near Auschwitz. The town had good railway connections, and the SS promised an adequate number of workers from their prisoner reserves. In the spring of 1942 prisoners began the construction of the Monowitz camp at Auschwitz for the production of synthetic rubber (Buna), but because of Allied air attacks the plant there never produced any rubber, in spite of large sums invested in it. Exhausted prisoners faced almost certain death in the main camp at Auschwitz. This remained the biggest attempt to shift private industry to the occupied areas, with other firms, such as Krupp and Siemens, also erecting facilities at Auschwitz.

In Germany itself, beginning in 1943, Speer supported the increased use of concentration-camp prisoners in numerous large enterprises. Large concentration camps extended their nets of subcamps like spider webs all over Germany, in accordance with the wishes of industrial enterprises and in their service. Increasingly the aim was to send as many foreign workers as possible, as well as Germans, to labour education camps (*Arbeitserziehungslager*) or concentration camps under the pretence of punishing a violation of some law or regulation. In addition to the generous use of force, even in the camps a graduated system of rewards was introduced to raise productivity. It extended from special privileges for prisoners, to money payments, and even to permission to visit a brothel. Concentration-camp prisoners were used especially for construction projects under the Todt Organization. Moreover, as Allied air attacks became increasingly severe, the transfer was begun of production of especially important armaments, such as fighter aircraft and rockets, to underground factories. This was done primarily in the foothills of the Harz Mountains, in the concentration camp of Dora Mittelbau, which had an extensive system of branch enterprises. A maximum of approximately 140,000 prisoners eventually worked on such projects. Approximately 500,000 prisoners, 90 per cent of them foreigners, were being employed in this way, as a special category of labour slaves in Germany, by 1945. But they also worked in other parts of the concentration-camp system within the shrinking area under German control.

But there was still one more level of brutality beyond the mere concentration camps. The final form of forced migration under National Socialism led to only one remaining destination: death in an extermination camp, where systematic mass murder was added to the functions of the concentration camps previously described. This primarily affected Jews and formed the central (though not the sole) aim of the Final Solution. In relation to this forced migration's destination – that of the extermination camps – the movement itself, the uprooting and the transport of all the Jews of Europe, was unimportant. This was the most frightening extreme of National Socialist rule: for one group the population movements caused by the war led only to the places where their lives were to be terminated, to gas chambers, to the crematoria, where murder was carried out on a mass industrial scale, almost as a form of assembly-line technology.

This development, in a direct sense, had nothing to do with the other functions of the concentration camps; nor could it be justified by any action taken by members of the ostracized group; nor, in spite of *Kristallnacht*, was it solely the result of a dynamic process set in motion by previous persecution of the Jews. The murder of the European Jews was rather a principal, fundamental goal of National Socialism. More precisely, it was one of Adolf Hitler's first and most important aims. As late as mid-1940, in a long memorandum about 'Foreigners in the East', Heinrich Himmler still rejected the 'Bolshevik method of the physical extermination of a people' as 'un-Germanic and impossible'.[32] A year before the systematic effort to exterminate the Jews was actually begun, and in which he was to play a decisive role, he clearly had no idea what was going to happen to them. In the view of the leaders of National Socialist Germany the Final Solution was a self-imposed historic mission dictated by race ideology, objective circumstances, and the short-term emergency situations of war. In addition, a number of favourable temporary factors came together which, most importantly, gave the murder apparatus freedom of action and guaranteed the greatest possible secrecy. This particular and essential dimension of National Socialist policy could not serve any socially cohesive purpose, and even National Socialist functionaries recognized this. Shortly after the occupation one official reported the massacres with the observation: 'It will only still be possible to carry out the liquidation for a short time. Then the German administration as well as other factors outside the NSDAP will make direct operations impossible.' While the wish of Hitler and his followers to annihilate the Jews developed from intention to actual execution, the failure to achieve a final victory in the war in the east excluded the possibility of further deportations in that direction, and this 'crisis' was overcome with deadly radicalism. The method of killing had only recently been tested in its final form of poison gas in the murder of mentally ill people and of other forms of human life considered to be 'unworthy'. This was also true of the Special Operations Groups (*Einsatzgruppen*), which only slowly developed into new kinds of killing detachments. And, finally, it was also true of the way to genocide, although the fact that it was a recent and slow development does not explain its origins.

The Way to Genocide: Jews, Poles, Russians, and Others

The murder of the Jews was prepared, planned, and finally carried out largely outside Germany; its repercussions, however, affected both Germany and the rest of Europe.[33] More precisely, it was connected with the murderous treatment of important parts of the populations of countries east of Germany, especially of Poland and the Soviet Union, and it can only be presented within that framework. In *Mein Kampf*, Hitler wrote regarding the First World War:

> Had one at the beginning and during the war exposed twelve or fifteen thousand of these Hebraic corrupters of nations to poison gas, as hundreds of thousands of our best German workers from all classes and professions had to endure it in the field, then the sacrifices of millions at the front would not have been in vain.

Behind this view was the idea that Jews were basically to be suspected of revolutionary and subversive ambitions, and that killing them during the war was therefore a kind of social prophylaxis. But in spite of all tendencies to make the German people into an army of auxiliary police to keep the Jews among them under surveillance, the murder machinery was not set in motion immediately upon the outbreak of war in 1939. In fact, expulsion continued to be the dominant aim of German policy towards the Jews; only in October 1941 was it officially stopped. The outbreak of war presented enormous practical difficulties for the continued pursuit of such a policy. While it had been difficult earlier to find states that were prepared to accept large numbers of German emigrants, and especially Jews, the war closed the seas and increasingly also land frontiers. Approximately 10,000 German Jews whose departure for Palestine had already been ordered were no longer able to leave Emden and Hamburg.

There remained, therefore, the method of expulsion to newly conquered areas. In addition to the east, in 1940, France was considered as a possible destination and, from July 1940, 20,000 Jews were expelled from Lorraine and Alsace to the unoccupied part of France. In October of that year they were followed by 6,000 Jews from Baden, the Palatinate, and the Saar, expelled on the initiative of the Gau leaders of those areas. These Jews suffered in camps under the anti-Semitic Vichy regime, but nevertheless found limited possibilities there to flee. A quite different possibility resulted from the German victory over France and the hope for an early peace. Even before the end of hostilities, Heydrich and Himmler turned their attention to a 'territorial final solution', the deportation of all Jews in the German sphere of influence to an African colony, namely Madagascar.[34] Similar plans with various destinations had been considered even before the war. Madagascar had been mentioned as a possibility by Polish officials, in France, and even by

German geopoliticians. Now the German Foreign Ministry began to promote the project, and even Hitler gave his consent for a time. The National Socialists did not, however, envisage such a mass deportation – in December 1940 one 'final solution' plan calculated the figure at 5.8 million European Jews – as an autonomous settlement colony. Rather, it was clear that a large number of these Jews 'with much hand luggage' (as the plan of the Foreign Ministry put it), under Gestapo guard, would inevitably die on board ship on the way to Madagascar or in a large ghetto in the inhospitable climate because of inadequate nutrition. Thus the Madagascar Project, as it was called, was also intended to exterminate Jews. The failure to conclude peace with France, which would have made it possible to demand the cession of the island, and the continuation of the war with the dominant sea powers, led to this plan being forgotten and replaced by an even more far-reaching 'solution'.

In Germany the legal and bureaucratic curtailment of the most elementary rights of Jews continued after the start of the war. Such curtailment included the restrictions placed on their use of public transport, the loss of driving licences, the confiscation of radios and private telephones, limitations on the use of public telephones, and the prohibition for Aryans to provide services (such as haircuts) for Jews. After their passports, the food ration cards of Jews also had to be stamped with a large 'J'; and finally, beginning on 1 September 1941, all Jews over 6 years of age were required to wear a six-pointed yellow star with the label 'Jew', which they were not permitted to cover in public. Jewish tenants could be given notice to leave, with the result that they came to be concentrated more and more in 'Jewish houses'. Social contact between Jews and non-Jews was increasingly restricted on a formal and informal level and surrounded with arbitrary sanctions including, in some cases, the death penalty. The rights of people in mixed marriages of Jews with non-Jews were codified in extreme detail, which did give the Jewish partner some protection, just as 'half' or 'one-quarter' Jews were subjected only to graduated forms of discrimination. All alleged or actual violations by Jews of discriminatory regulations and laws were subject to Draconian penalties. Death sentences were often given for the most trivial offences. Only with the help of Jewish organizations were Jews in Germany able to preserve any personal or property rights at all; and most eventually lost their lives.[35] The Reich Union of German Jews still had 164,000 members on 1 October 1941; on 1 January 1943 the figure was 51,257, and on 1 September 1944 it was 14,574. Most German Jews had been sent east after October 1941, to ghettos in Poland, and were then killed in various murder operations. It has been estimated that approximately 15,000 Jews survived in Germany, either openly or in hiding; and 13,677 German Jews were eventually liberated from camps in Germany and other countries.

Murder operations directed against parts of the Polish civilian population began with the German attack on Poland. They were initially carried out primarily by several special operations groups (*Einsatzgruppen*) of the

Security Police, formed *ad hoc* from members of various police and SS units. They consisted of a total of approximately 2,700 men and entered Poland, so to speak, as a second wave directly behind and in close co-operation with the Wehrmacht. As with other operations involving the direct killing of civilians, because of the strict secrecy and the fact that orders were often issued only orally, we do not know their precise instructions. We have contemporary or later testimony by the persecutors, but most of it does not deal with the actual events. It is therefore necessary, more so than is usually the case in studying history, to reconstruct probable and possible sequences of events and connections. The results of such an interpretation are presented here; there is, however, no doubt that the murders themselves did take place.

The 'combating of all elements hostile to the Reich and Germans in enemy territory behind the fighting troops', in the words of the guidelines agreed upon by Heydrich and the Army High Command (*Oberkommando des Heeres* or OKH), seemed to be a normal and relatively harmless phrase.[36] But, as Hitler remarked a year later (2 October 1940): 'For Poles there must be only *one* master, the German. For this reason, all members of the Polish intelligentsia are to be killed. That sounds brutal, but it is simply the law of life.' The same policies had been pursued earlier, but German operations had been presented as reactions, as defence against dangers. No other incident had played a greater role for German bystanders as well as for German propaganda as a whole, than the 'Bloody Sunday' in Bromberg, a town in the Polish corridor. On 3 September 1939 approximately 700 ethnic Germans were killed there by Poles in a pogrom-like fashion. It is highly probable that this massacre was preceded by deliberate German provocation. Goebbels' propaganda soon spoke of a total of 5,800 ethnic Germans killed during the campaign, and somewhat later of 58,000, although even this was no justification for the 'retaliation'. In fact, the special operations groups had entered Poland with prepared proscription lists containing at least 8,700 names, such as those of members of nationalistic Polish organizations, such as the West March Union. But soon doctors were being killed, together with teachers, lawyers, salesmen, artists, scientists, landowners, and finally everyone with a leading position in Polish public life, including master artisans and chairmen of organizations. This was done in part on the spot and in part in improvised concentration camps, from which, however, many prisoners were released after the end of military operations in Poland. Killing operations began during the hostilities, but were continued with the same intensity in the following months. On 2 July 1940, Heydrich himself mentioned that the 'police operations . . . were unusually radical' (e.g. liquidation orders for numerous Polish leadership groups which claimed thousands of victims).[37] In September 1939 alone 16,000 Polish civilians were shot. The later total figure was undoubtedly many times higher than that. Moreover, it was not only the special operations groups which carried out the killings; paramilitary groups such as ethnic German self-defence units also participated during the war, in an atmosphere that had been emotionally heated for months.

Finally, field courts martial, special courts, and soon the German administration, in the new Gaus as in the Government General, and especially the Higher SS and Police Leaders to whom the police troops were subordinate, participated in the killings. When the war in the west began and worldwide interest in events in Poland declined, a new 'extraordinary pacification operation' against Polish enemies of Germany was begun – against the early manifestations of a resistance movement as well as against 'professional criminals'. And euthanasia, too, was first pushed forward at a rapid pace in Poland.

Jews were persecuted from the very beginning of the Poland campaign. Synagogues were burned as early as mid-September 1939. Many orders for killings referred specifically to Poles and Jews. The Germans were, after all, in the process of conquering a country with approximately 3.2 million Jews, who often possessed a strong religious or ethnic consciousness clearly different from that of most Poles. Some 2 million additional Jews came under German rule. Whereas, at first, killing operations were directed primarily against Polish intellectuals, the 'elimination' of the Jews was never forgotten. Beginning with the six-pointed star, legalized discrimination against them was introduced faster in the Gaus established in the annexed areas than it had been within the frontiers of Germany before the war. 'The Jews must be annihilated,' Goebbels noted in his diary on 17 October 1939. After visiting the Łódź ghetto on 2 November, he wrote: 'They're not human beings; they are animals. That's why [killing them] is not a humanitarian [question] but a surgical task. We have to perform radical surgery here. Otherwise Europe will one day be destroyed by this Jewish disease.' While being driven through the Łódź ghetto, he observed: 'That's already Asia . . . Radical [measures] against the Poles and the strongest protection for the Germans.' Goebbels and other leading National Socialists held equally hostile images of other 'sub-humans', but those peoples were to be treated differently; Poles, deprived of their leadership groups, were intended to serve as slave labour, but Jews (and Gypsies) were considered to be an even greater, because racial, threat to Germans. In the Government General, established on 26 October 1939, forced labour for Poles was administered by ordinary labour offices; but the Jews were administered by the SS and the police.[38] While the killing continued, especially in the areas nearby, uncoordinated deportations began to the area of the soon-to-be-established Government General, which affected some 40,000 people. And from the beginning of December 1939 these operations were systematized. The aim was largely to 'cleanse' the new areas of Poles and Jews to make room for German settlers. By the spring of 1941 at least 365,000 Poles and Jews had been deported to the Government General, some in an orderly fashion, by train, but most without any overall plan. No provision had been made for accommodating the new arrivals in the often overcrowded cities of the Government General, which inevitably led to chaotic conditions in this 'reservation' as a 'homeland for Poles' (as Hans Frank described it on 2 March 1942).

While these actions affected both Poles and Jews, another major project to transport large numbers of people affected only Jews. Even before the German occupation some 200,000 of them had fled over the River San to territory occupied by Soviet forces. In the 21 months during which its forces occupied the formerly eastern parts of Poland, the Soviet Union carried out a similar policy of deportation and murder, directed primarily against Poles but which also affected many Polish Jews. The murder of some 11,000 captured Polish officers was only the best-known such operation. On 21 September 1939, Heydrich informed the special operations groups: 'As a first advance measure the first precondition for the final aim is the concentration of the Jews from the country in the cities.' The annexed areas were then to be 'made free of Jews'. In the remaining areas and the later Government General 'as few concentration points as possible are to be established to facilitate later measures'.

The exact nature of the final aim was to be keep strictly secret and was not explained for the time being, at least not in writing. It was to be organized by newly established councils of Jewish elders. And that is what happened. Jews were moved from small towns, the surrounding countryside, and the new Gaus in territory annexed by Germany, to major Polish cities, many of which already had large Jewish populations (29 per cent of Warsaw's population was Jewish, and 45 per cent of that of Białystok). In many such cities there had been no separate residential areas or even closed ghettos for Jews for decades. Now they were re-established, under catastrophic conditions for those affected; and some time passed before the Jewish population, many of whom belonged to the lower or middle classes, realized that the measures taken by the Germans were aimed not only at a small upper class.

It was clear to the Germans from the very beginning that the concentration of Jews in urban areas could not be a permanent solution, nor was it intended to be. In Warsaw alone, where the largest ghetto in Poland was surrounded by a wall, the number of Jewish residents rose from 100,000 to 425,000, people crowded together in an extremely small area. Fifty per cent of the Jews and 10 per cent of the Poles from the new Gaus were deported. Under these circumstances, living conditions in the ghettos deteriorated rapidly. In the first 2 years, 100,000 Jews died in Warsaw as a result of terror, epidemics, and malnutrition. Even Hans Frank protested to the SS against the pace and extent of the transport of Jews to his territory. Although he approved of the aim, after January 1940, in the interest of an orderly administration and later of economic efficiency, he sought to moderate the rigorous methods of his rivals, including Greiser and Forster, and was actually able to persuade Göring to issue an order temporarily stopping all deportations. Shortly thereafter they were resumed in a form acceptable to Frank, but for a year, until March 1941, the pace was slowed considerably. Hans Frank's influence slowly declined, although he was able to continue his brutal regime from his office in the castle in Kraków, the earlier residence of the Polish kings.

But it was not only Jews from Poland who were affected. On 21 September 1939 Heydrich reported that Hitler had also approved the deportation to what remained of Poland of all Jews within the German frontiers of 1938 as well as the annexed areas of Poland. On Eichmann's initiative the first transport carrying Jews from Vienna arrived by train at Niško on the San in October 1939. Their task was to erect buildings for themselves and for the settlement of later Jews there. This attempt was not successful, however, and was quickly stopped. Because of the overcrowding in the established ghettos, social problems developed that were made worse by the arrival of over 1,000 Jews from Stettin, who were deported without any prior notice to three villages near Lublin in February 1940. Many soon died. Thereupon plans were developed to build a large ghetto near Lublin, to which all Jews and Gypsies from the Greater German Reich, including the Protectorate, were to be sent. In the summer of 1940, the Madagascar Plan received more attention. Only in the spring of 1941 was the establishment of a ghetto zone in Lublin begun. But this, too, proved to be only a temporary solution.

In the meantime, plans for an attack on the Soviet Union had assumed concrete form. Since the beginning of 1941 millions of German soldiers had been waiting in assembly areas in the Government General, and their presence placed enormous strains on the transport system there. The forced expulsion of Jews and Gypsies to the Government General was temporarily disrupted. On 25 March 1941, Frank mentioned a new stop to the transportation of Jews ordered by Göring because of the priority of military preparations.[39] Frank had also spoken with Hitler, who told him: 'With the Jews, the Poles will also leave this area.' The intention was to make the area completely German within 15 or 20 years. In future there would be no question of a 'homeland for the Polish people' there. This reflected some features of the General Plan East already mentioned, as did the hunger strategy approved by the state secretaries, which was intended to leave for the Soviet population only what the Wehrmacht in the east and the German population did not want, and which was based on the assumed death of millions of people. Behind all these plans was the old, but now revived and active image of the main enemy, 'Jewish Bolshevism'.

At present, our knowledge of the criminal plans is based primarily on Wehrmacht records, as is our knowledge of the Wehrmacht's veiled agreements with the SS. On 30 March 1941 Hitler made a speech to between 200 and 250 senior Wehrmacht commanders, in which he equated Bolshevism with 'asocial criminality' and spoke of a 'battle of annihilation', in which 'commissars and GPU people' would have to be treated as 'criminals'. In several orders that violated international law, the Wehrmacht put these views into practice. Among them was the order that political commissars of the Red Army, 'if captured in battle or while offering resistance', were 'as a rule to be killed immediately', together with the decree concerning the administration of justice during Operation Barbarossa, the attack on the Soviet Union, which stated that crimes committed by Germans against Soviet civilians could not be prosecuted. Similar crimes had still been occasionally investigated and prosecuted during the Poland campaign.

Little is known about the missions of the newly reorganized special operations groups [*Einsatzgruppen*] of the Security Police and the Security Service, each of which was divided into special operations detachments.[40] Their activities were more clearly separated from those of the Wehrmacht than had been the case in Poland, but they remained subordinated to the Army for marching orders and rations, and in practice often co-operated closely with it. This time Special Operations Groups A to D were used. They were fully motorized, and had a total strength of 3,000 men. As in Poland, they consisted of personnel from various police and Security Service units, and were to operate in the rear areas behind the advancing front. There are several indications that when they were formed in May–June 1941, they received a general authorization, originating from Hitler, to kill the arch-enemies of the National Socialist ideology. Its wording was probably similar to what Heydrich told the Higher SS and Police Leaders (who were not identical with the commanders of the special operations groups) on 2 July 1941:

> All functionaries of the Comintern (and professional Communist polit-
> ical figures), the senior, mid-level and radical functionaries of the
> Communist Party of the Soviet Union, of the district and regional
> committees, people's commissars, Jews in party and state positions,
> and other radical elements (such as saboteurs, propagandists, snipers,
> assassins, agitators etc.) are to be killed.

But this was probably the usual veiled language. From the very beginning not only 'Jews in party and state positions', but also women and children were killed. Moreover, there may have been a general order framed in the usual terminology – such as 'elimination', 'radical solution', 'combating anti-German tendencies', 'immediately render harmless' – that need not necessarily be understood as a direct order to kill. Similar statements even before the German attack on the Soviet Union, such as Heydrich's remarks about the 'annihilation of the eastern Jews', were in any case at first interpreted by the special operations detachments (*Einsatzkommandos*) more as direct orders. But with the start of the war in the east, these detachments advanced immediately behind the fighting troops and began systematically to kill civilians. In these operations, and especially in the Baltic States, they often used local 'self-defence forces' (*Selbstschutzeinheiten*), which were incited to carry out pogroms. After a year under Soviet rule, such groups often had their own scores to settle; they were also often motivated by a deep-rooted anti-Semitism. The special operations detachments herded people together, shot them indiscriminately, and then levelled entire villages. They killed everyone considered to be an enemy, but especially Jews, who were numerous in the newly conquered territories, particularly in the cities. Bolshevik activity was all too easily assumed in the case of any subjective suspicion towards the population. And Jews were considered politically dangerous simply because they were Jews. One special operations detachment reported with astonishment: 'The Bolshevik apparatus is by no means identical with the Jewish population.' The Germans themselves decided who represented a threat to them. Individual special operations detachments, on their own initiative, concentrated on different categories of victims. Special operations groups also murdered prisoners of war, whom Wehrmacht commanders, often voluntarily, turned over to them.

After the first weeks of the attack on the Soviet Union the special operations groups quite possibly received clearer orders to kill all Jews. At any rate their actions marked the beginning of a part of the genocidal Final Solution, although it became clear to the National Socialist leaders and the participating units only in the autumn that they would not be able to kill all the Jews for a long time. One reason for this was that, as far as they were able, Jews fled from the invaders. The killing units reported their successes in great detail. A total of approximately 220,000 Jews were killed in the Baltic States by mobile special operations detachments; the estimated figure for the total area of the Soviet Union in the frontiers before the German attack is more than a million. But it was not only the special operations groups which were involved in killing. After the largest individual operation of this kind, Special Operations Group C reported: 'On 29 and 30 September 1941 Special Operations Detachment 4, in co-operation with the Group Staff and two details of the Police Regiment South, executed 33,771 Jews in Kiev'.[41] That happened in the ravine of Babi Yar, where the victims had been compelled to go to be 'resettled' and where they were shot in front of open graves. The executions were carried out by police troops of the Higher SS and Police Leaders, but units of the Wehrmacht actively assisted them, and other Wehrmacht units willingly escorted the Jews to their executioners. In the autumn of 1941, the special operations groups were assigned permanent duty stations, where they remained until the German retreat. It has been estimated that 90 per cent of the victims of the killings they carried out were Jews. But Gypsies, Communists, partisans, the mentally ill, Poles, prisoners of war, Armenians, and others are mentioned separately in the reports the groups sent in and in which the victims were transformed into at least potential perpetrators of acts directed against the occupying forces.

Carrying Out the Final Solution

It was reported that participating in the shootings resulted in a great psychological strain for the perpetrators, whose superiors placed maximum value on maintaining discipline within their units. Himmler once praised some of his SS lieutenant generals (*Gruppenführer*) specifically for having remained 'decent' and done their duty, 'apart from a few exceptions of human weakness', and there were indeed enough of those.[42] Very probably for this reason other methods of mass killing had to be found, and these were taken from the killing operations of the euthanasia programme, in which gas chambers with carbon monoxide had been used. The chambers were moved by lorries, whose exhaust fumes were eventually diverted directly into the load space. These lorries were intended to serve the special operations groups and were used by them, but they were also used in completely new kinds of camps. The decisions concerning these, taken in the later summer and autumn of 1941, and the reasons involved, still have not been completely explained. At that time Hitler was still initially opposed to the deportation of Jews from Germany to the east, although this may have been due only to problems with transport capacity; but after that he gave his consent. It was repeatedly rumoured in National Socialist circles that the Jews were to be sent even farther to the east after the war. It is not clear whether the authors of such rumours really meant to do this, or whether it was a deliberate deception. In any case the deportation of more Jews from Germany began in October 1941 (from Berlin, Munich, Prague, Vienna, and Hanover) to Minsk (Belorussia), Łódź (Litzmannstadt), Kovno, and Riga. When they arrived in the latter two cities they were murdered immediately, together with the residents of the ghettos there, by special operations detachments. In Łódź, on the other hand, conditions became intolerable after the arrival of the transport into the massively overcrowded ghetto for the very reason that its inhabitants were not murdered immediately.

But it was not primarily the chaotic conditions during the deportations caused by the failure to achieve a lightning victory in the east, nor Hitler's disappointment at that failure, that led to the construction of the extermination factories. In reality they were not camps at all.[43] They were built as a part of Hitler's specific plan to make Europe free of Jews, which began now to be realized on a grand scale. In the area of Lublin, in the administrative district of the especially brutal SSPF Odilo Globocnik, new camps were constructed, occasionally disguised as prisoner-of-war-camps (which some of them had in fact been earlier) in Belzec in October 1941 and in Sobibór; and also, probably because total killing capacity was still inadequate, in Treblinka near Warsaw from March to July 1942 and in Chelmno (the German Kulmhof) in the Warthe Gau, which was put into operation on 8 December 1941. In addition there were Majdanek, near Lublin, and Birkenau (Auschwitz II), both planned after September 1941, with room for over 100,000 prisoners each. People were brought to the first four camps solely for the purpose of being killed and to the last two for 'extermination through labour'. The locations were probably chosen for transportation connections: railway sidings could be easily constructed; and the chosen sites were largely protected from outside observation. The arriving prisoners were only unloaded to be killed as quickly as possible. Gas lorries (mobile gas chambers) as described above were used in Chelmno, but otherwise mostly stationary gas chambers were used. After September 1941 people were mostly killed in these camps with Zyklon B, a commercial pesticide, although shooting, injections, and other means were also used. Killing capacities, and the problem of disposing of the bodies, proved to be more important limiting factors than the resulting reduction in the transport capacity of the railways available for the war effort. Between 2,500 and 10,000 people were killed every day.

The victims of the death camps were primarily the Jews of Europe who could be caught. From Western Europe they were brought in passenger trains, or otherwise they travelled in wagons of trains, often in transports lasting several days, without food or sanitation facilities. The transport guards were often forcibly recruited ethnic Germans; the killers in the camps themselves were euthanasia specialists from Germany. Most of the construction gangs that built the extermination facilities and the prisoners who worked there were killed in the end. The facilities themselves were not merely closed, but levelled after their task was accomplished, before the approach of the Red Army or earlier. Where the victims had only been buried their bodies were exhumed and burned whenever possible to destroy the evidence. Very few inmates survived the extermination camps.

After the Soviet prisoners of war, Jewish and non-Jewish Poles were sent to Majdanek, and it remained a camp with two functions. This was also especially true of Auschwitz-Birkenau, which combined the functions of a forced labour camp and a murder camp. Its slogan was 'extermination through labour'. At the arrival ramp in Birkenau, SS doctors decided, on the basis of a cursory look at the physical condition of the totally exhausted prisoners, which ones were to work for a time until they were ready to be murdered, and which were to be sent directly to the gas chambers. The average life expectancy in Birkenau for newly arrived inmates who were put to work was 1 to 3 months. Beginning on 3 September 1941, Soviet prisoners of war were gassed in Birkenau. In January 1942 the first Jews, from the surrounding area in Upper Silesia, were gassed there. The number of victims killed at these extermination camps cannot be determined precisely: in Chelmno it was approximately 152,000; in Belzec 600,000; in Sobibór 250,000; in Treblinka 900,000, and in Majdanek 200,000 (of whom 50,000 to 60,000 were Jews). In Auschwitz the estimated figure is 1,000,000 to 1,500,000. These figures give one an idea of the extent of the killing in the camps, and offer a rough idea of what is usually referred to as the 'Final Solution of the Jewish Question'. But 'extermination through labour' was also practised in the expanding camp system in the rest of Europe. Many people died in the transports to Poland, and the killing done by the special operations groups has been described above. Only the inclusion of these factors provides a complete picture of the true dimension of the Final Solution.

But how did the systematic murder primarily of Jews in Poland and the Soviet Union develop into a plan to kill all European Jews? There are many indications that Hitler originally intended this last stage of his self-imposed historic mission for the time immediately after the lightning German victory over the Soviet Union and had already given the necessary orders earlier; and when the victory was not achieved in the autumn of 1941, the extermination machinery was nevertheless set in motion throughout Europe. Earlier, on 31 July 1941, Heydrich had obtained from Göring, his nominal subordinate as head of the Gestapo in Prussia, an order to 'submit a comprehensive draft concerning organizational, technical, and material preparations for carrying out the desired final solution of the Jewish question'.[44] But this was hardly more than organizational cover in connection with the task which Heydrich had been given, on 24 January 1939, of organizing the emigration of the Jews, and it was certainly in accord with Hitler's known aims. At this time and afterwards Hitler repeatedly stated, publicly and privately, his intention to annihilate the Jews, and he later also described it as completed.

The 'Wannsee Conference' in Berlin on 20 January 1942 had originally been planned for December 1941. It was called to co-ordinate with other Reich authorities the bureaucratic measures involved in the 'Final Solution', which was already being carried out. The conference was attended primarily by representatives of the ministries that co-operated in carrying out the deportations all over Europe. In 1961, Adolf Eichmann, who kept the minutes of the conference, claimed that he had moderated the open language of the discussion in his written record. In his minutes it appeared that a 'further solution', in addition to emigration, namely that of concentrating the Jews 'in so-called ghettos in order to transport them farther to the east', was to be initiated only after Hitler had given his approval. Heydrich mentioned the annihilation of the Jews through forced labour, 'in which undoubtedly a large number will cease to be available because of natural decrease'. The most robust 'last remnant' would 'have to be subjected to appropriate treatment', as the murder was obliquely termed. The number of European Jews to be included in this gigantic plan of transports to the east was revealing. Heydrich expected a total, probably exaggerated, of more than 11 million Jews. Under Point A, he enumerated the Jews already in the area under German domination: from within the pre-March 1938 frontiers of Germany to Estonia ('free of Jews') and from Norway to occupied France. But under Point B, he included the Jews of the rest of Europe, from Britain and Ireland to Portugal, from Sweden to European Turkey – a 'solution' that clearly showed the continental dimensions of his bureaucratic planning.

In the end these plans were never realized. The high point of the Final Solution was reached in 1942–3, when the National Socialists' last hopes for victory disappeared. After Heydrich's death, Himmler and Ernst Kaltenbrunner continued to pursue the same aim with single-minded determination. On 2 November 1944, Himmler ordered the end of operations connected with the Final Solution. Only a few prisoners survived the concentration camps, and most of those who did survive were in slave labour camps, where it was intended to work them to death and where conditions contributed to the deaths of many even after liberation. The number of Jews who were actually murdered is estimated at between 5,290,000 and slightly over 6 million, although it may have been higher.[45]

How this was possible is difficult to explain. It was inconceivable without Hitler's firm will and dictatorial authority. But to recognize this is not to exculpate the hundreds of thousands of others who were involved in carrying out the Final Solution. Beyond isolated cases of protest and attempts to avoid participation, there were no clear acts of opposition among the perpetrators. They included not only members of the SS, but also members of the Wehrmacht, the state bureaucracy, and the party; they were to be found in the upper classes as well as among the lowest-ranking functionaries. Even violent criminals were used. Certainly some were sadistic perverts intent on enriching themselves. But those functionaries who confined themselves to the narrow field of their assigned tasks and took advantage of their possibilities without any moral restraint or scruple were just as important. Moreover, those people also played an essential role who overcame initial moral reservations because of their bureaucratic mentality or ideological convictions, who committed or assisted in crimes in the service of the 'cause', who carried out their small part of the larger murder operation, and in that sense did their 'duty'. 'Work Will Make You Free' were the words that greeted prisoners at the gate to Auschwitz, and indeed, many Jews went to Auschwitz with the hope of 'only' having to perform forced labour. Many were only too eager to hold on to that illusion until immediately before their deaths. Revolts and resistance did occur, but rarely, and in view of the vastly superior forces available to the persecutors, they were doomed to failure from the very beginning. Only the approaching liberation by the Allies increased the chances of successful revolts in 1944–5, such as that organized by prisoners in Buchenwald.

The dimensions of the mass murder in the specially constructed extermination camps in Poland – Belzec, Sobibor, Treblinka and Chelmno – comprised the most frightening form of persecution, as it involved killing people solely on the basis of certain 'racial characteristics', regardless of any other physical factors, political opinions, or the activities of the victims. These murders were even incompatible with the forced labour system, the 'extermination through labour', for which Majdanek and Auschwitz were the most important locations. Even the most fanatical National Socialists did not think they could expect the public to accept passively an open acknowledgment of the existence of extermination camps.

OCCUPATION POLICY AND POWER STRUCTURES IN GERMAN-DOMINATED EUROPE

Genocide was an essential component of German rule in Europe, but because of the different social and political structures of the occupied countries it was often not the aspect that attracted the most attention. Many non-Jews in the occupied countries were so concerned with their own suffering that they were simply not interested in the fate of the Jews. When applied to Jews, the Christian commandment to love one's enemies still implied that they were enemies. In many places in Europe Christians even staged their own pogroms. Elsewhere, however, the 'final solution of the Jewish question' and the form in which it was carried out in particular united society against the occupiers as effectively as did forced labour.

The Soviet Union

Those parts of the Soviet Union occupied by the Germans after June 1941 had seen the most intense anti-Semitism and persecution of Jews since Tsarist times.[46] Approximately 5.1 million Jews, defined according to nationality by the census, lived in that area at the time of the German attack on the Soviet Union; of these, more than 3 million came under German occupation; and of those, 2 million lost their lives, many in what had been eastern Poland, the Baltic States, and areas bordering on Romania. Using all the means at their disposal, including genocide, the Romanian authorities conducted an especially intensive persecution of Jews. The massacre of 50,000 Jews in Odessa, which was occupied by Romanian forces, as retribution for alleged resistance in October 1943, is a particularly striking example. But in other cases, the Romanian occupiers were quite prepared to leave the killing to the Germans. The special operations groups and stationary police units with additional troops under the HSSPFs took the leading role, and made use of local and national 'self-defence' units. Wehrmacht units also participated spontaneously in some pogroms and killings. After the initial impulse had been provided by the German authorities, loose supervision of killings carried out by the non-Jewish population was often sufficient. By mid-1942, most of the Jews in Poland and the western parts of the Soviet Union were already dead. The (open) ghettos in medium-sized and small towns had been 'combed out' repeatedly. Jews were able to survive only if they worked in firms fulfilling priority orders for the Wehrmacht. On Himmler's orders, the remaining ghettos were converted into concentration camps and placed under the SS Economic and Administrative Main Office on 21 June 1943. A small number of Jews were sent to concentration camps farther west, from Dachau to Auschwitz, and murdered there.

The total losses of human life in the Soviet Union caused by the war are still undetermined even today. Until the end of the 1980s, the figure was usually given as 20 million. At the present time it is given as between 27.5 and 40 million, among them 7.8 million soldiers and 20 to 25 million civilians. How many of these civilians died as a consequence of military operations or as a direct result of German occupation and deportation policies is not known.[47] Likewise, the number of victims of Stalin's internal policies during the war has not been determined. At any rate the Soviet government treated all cases of suspected collaboration, even if they were only a pretence, with Draconian harshness. And most of the approximately 3 million German soldiers killed in the war fell on the eastern front. The war against the Soviet Union lasted from 1941 until 1945, and indeed the Second World War in Europe was decided there with the German advance and retreat. From that point of view, but also because of its racially ideological nature, the war in the east differed in character from the war in the rest of occupied Europe. The army rear areas and army-group rear areas extending approximately 500 kilometres behind the front were under the authority of the responsible Wehrmacht offices, which organized security divisions. Although these territories changed with the course of the front, the close co-operation agreed upon earlier with various SS and police commanders continued.

The remaining area in the east was nominally under Alfred Rosenberg and his Reich Ministry for the Occupied Eastern Areas (*Reichsministerium für die besetzten Ostgebiete* or RMO), but Rosenberg never had a decisive influence in the areas for which he was responsible on paper. Before the attack on the Soviet Union he planned a gigantic bureaucracy organized in departments, and during the war he occupied himself with writing drafts for ambitious projects which, however, remained mere pieces of paper. Rosenberg was a Baltic German, and his views were marked by a strong anti-Semitism and an anti-Russian attitude; he wanted to smash the Soviet state and then grant the other peoples within its former frontiers a limited independence under German hegemony. In Lithuania, Latvia, and Estonia, and above all in the Ukraine, and to a limited extent even in the Crimea, there were hopes that the arrival of German forces would lead to a promotion of national independence. But such hopes were usually dashed within a few weeks, as most offers of collaboration were disregarded or even answered with indiscriminate persecution. In addition to Rosenberg's Ministry, the Reich commissars, the SS and police, and the Wehrmacht, the Economic Staff East under Göring was of central importance, as it was in charge of organizing the exploitation of the occupied areas. This was done under the Central Trade Association East (*Zentrale Handelsgesellschaft Ost*), which consisted of approximately 250 individual 'Eastern Companies' (*Ostgesellschaften*). In addition to trade, these companies were involved in the operation of firms and were organized according to sectors. They employed both persons from the state economic bureaucracy and private industry, who were in charge of individual branch firms and, moreover, acquired property themselves. In the interest of greater production, large Soviet industrial and agricultural enterprises were not broken up for the time being; only socialist structures were eliminated. The naïvely optimistic expectation that Soviet peacetime production could be used to support the German economy was quickly shattered. This was due to the failure to achieve a lightning victory, the destruction caused by the war, and the growing strength of partisans, who controlled an estimated 20 per cent of the occupied area in the summer of 1943. It was possible, however, to supply the food requirements of the Wehrmacht by brutally enforcing delivery quotas, and industrial concerns in the Baltic States were put back into operation. But the monthly production of coal from the Donetz Basin was only 4 per cent of the pre-war figure; the figure for iron ore (Krivoi Rog) was 12 per cent. Production of small quantities of steel ingots was begun there only in May 1943; the production of crude oil (Maikop) was also small. But, on the whole, production was increased considerably, or at least begun, in the first months of 1943. Sauckel's deportations of labourers from these areas had to be stopped for a time. Generally speaking, Germany received considerably more during the period of economic co-operation with the Soviet Union (1939–41) than during the occupation. The main cause of this was the contradiction between the policies of annihilation and exploitation. In the words of one German economics official, on 2 December 1941:

> If we shoot the Jews, let the prisoners of war die and a considerable part of the urban population starve, and also lose part of the rural population to hunger in the coming years, the question remains as to who here is supposed to produce anything of economic value.

The General Commissar for Belorussia, the earlier Gau leader Wilhelm Kube, came to a similar conclusion but, in spite of his protests, could not stop the shooting of Jews and the murder of the non-Jewish population in his area. In addition to racist considerations, feudal expectations of future booty also played a role.

Only after mid-1942, as a result of German policies of deportation and mass murder, did the number of partisans increase significantly, influenced also by Stalin's appeals to the nation for a 'Great Fatherland War' instead of Bolshevik internationalism. The German policy of annihilation, officially described as a war against 'bandits', continued and was carried out by all armed German forces in the occupied areas, including the Wehrmacht. Leading generals issued murderous anti-Jewish and anti-Bolshevik orders, although the Commissar Order itself, which many German commanders had obeyed, was withdrawn. Most front-line Wehrmacht units were not involved in the murder operations, but many behind the lines were. At present, the debate continues as to whether this was due primarily to acceptance by the Wehrmacht of the radical, racist image of the enemy or to the subjective belief by staffs short of personnel, and by incompetent, anxious individuals, that such behaviour was required by what they considered to be an emergency situation in enemy territory. It is likely that both factors were often involved. Nevertheless, and in spite of all the differences among themselves, the occupiers can be considered as a single group who erected prisons, ghettos, concentration camps, and forced labour camps in hundreds of locations where prisoners were executed, especially during the German retreat. Statements about the brutality of both sides are certainly accurate, but they often fail or refuse to recognize that the Germans and their allies attacked a country that then defended itself with all means at its disposal. Moreover, such statements usually neglect or deny the planned, premeditated nature of the racist ideology behind the policy of annihilation, as well as the fact that this policy itself did not develop as a mere reaction to Stalin's practices of annihilation and oppression of the population of his own country as well as of the invaders.

Poland

At the beginning of 1942, over 2.3 million Jews were living in the Government General and the Polish areas that had been annexed to Germany. They were brought from the ghettos, where most had been performing forced labour, to nearby concentration and extermination camps. In this desperate situation, the Jewish elders and councils were assigned the responsibility of guaranteeing the required number of persons for the transports. The murder operations reached their high point in the second half of 1942. Then, for a time, armaments production was again given priority in the remaining ghettos, which gave many Jews new hope. But in February 1943 the annihilation process was accelerated again. In several places there were revolts. On 19 May 1943, the Jews still in the Warsaw ghetto began a hopeless battle. The Polish underground remained largely inactive. Within a month SS forces, supported by all types of other available armed units, including those of the Wehrmacht, had liquidated the ghetto. More than 60,000 people perished during this liquidation or as a direct consequence of it. By mid-1944 the only ghetto still in existence was in Lódź; and most of the 68,000 Jews there were gassed in Chelmno. In absolute figures as well as in terms of percentage of the population, the largest number of Jews died in Poland. About 80 per cent of the Jews there, some 2.7 million people, were killed, 2 million in concentration and extermination camps.

Based on 1939 figures, Poland lost the largest proportion of its population of any participating country during the war. From the very beginning, German occupation policy (and, between 1939 and 1941, Soviet occupation policy) in Poland consisted only of oppression. This led to the development in the Government General of an independent Polish administration, an underground state which finally became an alternative government and whose co-operation with the exiled government in London was not without friction. This development was rooted in Polish traditions since the nineteenth century, and it extended from the social services to the police, schools, and universities. Members of the underground often performed their functions in addition to their official co-operation with the occupiers. It was even possible to equip a Home Army that in the end reached a strength of 350,000 men. Moreover, political groups that had often been enemies before the war (the Communists played a small role only after 1941) co-operated in the organization of a Polish society to resist the occupiers.

Under these conditions, created by the occupation, the German policy of harsh reprisals for sabotage, but also for major acts of resistance, was continued and finally co-ordinated through special 'anti-bandit' units. Moreover, the Germans attempted (with limited success) to carry out a policy of graduated discrimination towards a population one-third of whose members had not been Poles in 1939. The Poles were treated somewhat better than the Jews, the Ukrainians, and the White Ruthenians (the inhabitants of eastern Poland and western Belorussia), most of whom, however, lived in the Reich Commissariat Ukraine. The policy of rigorous Germanisation was continued in the annexed areas, where German was made the only official language. But even there the number of Polish 'protected dependents' (6,454,000) still exceeded that of the Germans (3,102,000) in 1944.

The Government General was an assembly and support area for the Wehrmacht in the east, and approximately 500,000 soldiers were normally stationed there. The first resettlement operations in the Government General were begun in 1940, when the Wehrmacht took over large areas for training facilities. The surrounding areas were to be secured by German settlers, including future military veterans. This was the core of the General Plan East, which, after the spring of 1941, concentrated increasingly on a resettlement of most Poles to the vast conquered spaces of Russia, with devastating consequences. It was obviously also intended to make the Government General German, and to settle it with Germans and Germanized Poles. In 1942–3 a beginning was made on this in Globocnik's district of Lublin, which was already largely 'free of Jews'. Beginning in November 1942, the population in the area around Zamość were driven from their homes, with often fatal consequences. The more than 100,000 expelled and deported Poles were replaced by 9,000 German settlers brought from Bessarabia. It was planned to settle more Germans in the area, but the operation was stopped in mid-1943 because of the military situation. Plans were also made to convert Warsaw and Kraków into German cities; the former was already used as a support area and furlough city for the war in the east.

German policy in the annexed Polish areas was primarily one of forced emigration, and this was also true in the sense of economic exploitation. A Central Trustee Office East (*Haupttreuhandstelle Ost*), in which the Four Year Plan and co-operative combines of German firms in individual industrial sectors participated, prepared for re-privatization for German companies in the annexed areas. Göring's Economic Staff East (*Wirtschafts-stab Ost*) was also responsible for the Government General. In the first 6 months of the German occupation, the spontaneous, unauthorized removal of economically important goods was carried out to the largest extent possible, after which a system of organized deliveries was introduced which placed especially valuable foodstuffs at the disposal of German authorities, including, for example, 60 per cent of meat production. Consequently the misery of the Polish population increased and their living standards declined. Beginning in 1943, among other reasons because of the relative safety there from Allied bombing attacks, large sectors of the armaments production industry were transferred to the Government General, and this resulted in the highest level of production being reached there in May 1944. General Governor Hans Frank, who basically advocated a relatively moderate policy for security and economic reasons, was deprived of much of his real power in the confusion and authority conflicts of the various German agencies in the Government General. But Hitler would not accept Frank's resignation. When the mass graves of Polish officers who had been shot by the Soviets were found in the Katyn Forest in April 1943, Goebbels attempted, without significant success, to exploit this for propaganda purposes to mobilize support in Poland and worldwide against the Soviet Union and to divert attention from German atrocities.

With the approach of the Red Army, the Polish Home Army attempted, with an initial force of 25,000, to liberate Warsaw itself in a large-scale revolt. But, as the Red Army stopped on the east bank of the Vistula, the initially outnumbered German forces, using all the means at their disposal, were able to put down the revolt in bitter house-to-house fighting by 2 October 1944. In Warsaw a total of 170,000 people died. Shortly after the start of the uprising, Hitler ordered the city to be levelled. And unlike Moscow and Leningrad, which the Germans never conquered, or Paris and Bucharest, this was actually done in Warsaw. It was an act of revenge unique in the Second World War.

South-East Europe

Yugoslavia had been completely crushed and divided among its neighbours. In addition to Germany and Italy, Hungary and Bulgaria seized parts of the country. The especially bitter partisan war was typical of conditions in Yugoslavia; it was fought not only against the German and Italian occupiers, but also, at the same time, as a civil war. Hitler, who was not especially interested in German rule in south-east Europe in the long term beyond the annexed areas of Slovenia, left Yugoslavia and Greece to a military Commander-in-Chief South-East, under or in addition to whom the SS and various representatives of German industry, the Foreign Ministry, and other agencies were able to assert their claims. In this entire area of influence, which it was planned in the long term to leave to Italy, Germany occupied the territory of Serbia for the duration of the war, and proceeded, with limited success, to make use of a puppet government there. The independent state of Croatia became a protectorate under its 'poglavnik' (leader) Ante Pavelić, but German and Italian troops were stationed on its territory. Its Ustascha Movement erected concentration camps, including extermination camps, carried out mass murders, forced Serbs to convert to Catholicism with the support of the Catholic Church, or simply expelled them in large numbers. The national Serbian monarchist resistance movement, the Četnici, and Colonel Drazha Mihailovič, co-operated only occasionally with each other, but fought more and more together against the Communist partisans under the Croat Josip Broz Tito, who was able to expand his activities from Serbia over the entire country and attract support for his idea of a single Yugoslavia. Although the Četnici occasionally co-operated with the Axis powers, especially with Italy, they basically placed their faith in the Allies. Mihailovič, who became Minister of War in the government in exile in London in 1942, was not, however, able to maintain his position in the long term. His followers lost their positions of power to Tito's partisans in 1943, and in the end Tito's followers were the only group to enjoy Allied support. They opposed the Croat Ustascha of Pavelič, the Germans, and the Italians, against whom they were able to fight pitched battles as of 1943.

A total of 1.7 million people died in Yugoslavia during the war; two-thirds were civilians. This figure includes 65,000 of the approximately 85,000 Jews living in the country. Like the Gypsies and the Communists, in Serbia they were segregated and placed in ghettos and then in concentration camps at an early stage, shot at a ratio of 100:1 as reprisals for partisan activities, and, beginning in late 1941, gassed in the camp of Zemun (in German, Semlin) at the same time as the first Jews were gassed in Chelmno. Here, as in Croatia, the Wehrmacht not only supported but carried out murder operations itself. In Croatia the German police attaché requested the approval of the government there for the 'resettlement' of the Jews to the newly conquered areas in the east, which led to their being murdered primarily in Auschwitz by 1944. In the parts of Yugoslavia occupied by Italy, the Jews were drawn into the Final Solution after Mussolini was overthrown in 1943. The Jews from parts of Macedonia and Greece were killed in Poland. In Yugoslavia, and especially Croatia, secure deliveries of raw materials (lead, bauxite, chromium, and nickel) were important for the German war effort. Ethnic Germans and the Reich Interior Ministry attempted without success to promote plans for the creation of a new Reich Gau in Yugoslavia, with Belgrade as a 'Reich fortress'. In November 1943, Tito was able to form a government in exile in London, and his partisans liberated Yugoslavia from German occupation themselves, an achievement unique among partisan movements in the Second World War.

In Greece, on the other hand, where strong rival Communist and non-Communist partisan groups became active after 1941, British support played an important role. After the collapse of the Italian occupation in 1943, the partisan groups were successful in preventing an expansion of German-controlled areas, but they became involved in conflicts with each other which expanded into a full-scale civil war after the German withdrawal in 1944. Of the 180,000 Greeks who died during the occupation, 94 per cent were killed in German anti-partisan operations. The shooting of hostages and mass executions of entire villages were a common occurrence. Of the approximately 70,000 Greek Jews, 80 to 90 per cent died. The 45,000 Jews in Thessalonica formed the largest group in Greece. After forced labour and life in a ghetto, they were deported to Treblinka or Auschwitz in March 1943, where their extermination required the full capacity of both camps for a time. In 1944 they were followed by a large number of Jews from Rhodes and Kos, which had been under Italian occupation until then. There, too, the Wehrmacht supervised the deportation.

With the exception of chrome ore, the Greek economy was of little interest to the Germans. Their main concern in the region was the strategic importance of the south-east flank and thus the position of Allied and neutral states. A German diplomatic representative remained accredited to the puppet government installed in Greece by Germany and Italy. But there was little co-ordination between him and the Wehrmacht, the real occupation authority in the country. As in Yugoslavia, the German occupying authorities in Greece attempted by increased brutality and shootings to pacify the areas formerly controlled by Italy; but this only strengthened the partisans.

Germany's allies in south-east Europe had already had authoritarian governments. Fascist movements, as in Hungary and Romania, received only limited support from Berlin, and that support came more from the SS than from Hitler, who rightly feared that such movements would only destabilize their countries. They were too weak to exercise power alone. The authoritarian-clerical regime of Monsignore Tiso in Slovakia was able to preserve limited internal independence at home by turning over its foreign policy to Germany. But there was no fascist international movement, either in Slovakia or elsewhere in Europe, especially as national expansion was an important principle of many fascist movements, and the danger of conflicts with similar movements in neighbouring states was always present. Germany was primarily interested in maintaining the role of the countries of south-eastern Europe as suppliers for the German economy. This orientation had already been strong before the war, and it was based above all on Germany's need for agricultural products and raw materials, especially oil from Romania and Hungary. Increasing German military difficulties, however, led to increased economic demands on Germany's Balkan allies; and after 1941 in Hungary, for example, it led also to a decline in their standard of living which greatly reduced the popularity of what had begun as alliances of expediency with Germany. These alliances had been attractive primarily because of the territorial expansion they made possible at the expense of neighbouring states: Romania had received formerly Soviet, Yugoslav, and Greek territory, but had to cede parts of the Siebenbürgen area to Hungary. Increasing economic exploitation, and growing German demands for military involvement on the eastern front, together with the declining prospects of a German victory, however, eroded the bases of the Balkan alliances. The varied forms of German domination in economic, military, and security matters, as well as German 'advisory activities' in the Balkans, also played an important role in this development.

In spite of its membership in the Anti-Comintern Pact, Bulgaria did not declare war on the Soviet Union (although it did issue a largely symbolic declaration of war on the United States and Great Britain at the end of 1941). It was thus later able to change fronts more easily than Germany's other Balkan allies. But in September 1944 it became involved for one day in hostilities with all the main warring states in Europe. German influence in Bulgaria had been strong in many areas; but the strong pressure applied by Germany over the Jewish question had led to nothing more than anti-Semitic legislation. The Jews within the frontiers of Bulgaria before the war were saved by the skilful maneouvring of King Boris III, and were the only group of European Jews to escape the Holocaust completely. Those Jews in the parts of Bulgaria that had formerly belonged to Yugoslavia and Greece, on the other hand, died in the gas chambers.

In Romania probably over 200,000 of the 750,000 Jews living within the pre-war frontiers died. Anti-Semitic laws were enacted without German pressure, and major pogroms organized by the Iron Guard were tolerated by the government. Beginning in 1941, after the government had suppressed the Guard, the regime pursued a relatively moderate anti-Semitic policy. Many Jews were able to emigrate half-legally. In the frontier areas, however, they were often placed in ghettos and subjected to expulsion and deportation, especially to the north-east. From there, areas of the Soviet Union occupied by Romanian forces, Jews from Romania were also sent to the German death factories.

Central Europe

In Hungary the Regent and acting head of state, Admiral Miklós Horthy, gradually accepted governments with increasingly friendly policies towards Germany; and he also yielded to German pressure to enact anti-Semitic laws, although Hungary initially resisted German pressure to deport Hungarian Jews. The number of religious Jews in Hungary was increased from 400,000 to 725,000 by annexations. Of these Jews from the Carpatho-Ukraine area, 12,000 were deported to the Government General in 1941, with fatal consequences. On 19 March 1944, German forces occupied Hungary because of the general war situation and began, with the help of members of the fascist Arrow Cross movement, whom they placed in key positions, to persecute energetically all presumed enemies of National Socialism. In the course of this development some 450,000 people from rural areas, including almost all Hungarian Jews as well as many Gypsies, were transported to the extermination camps. For the time being there remained a ghetto containing 200,000 Jews in Budapest. In spite of Horthy's dilatory maneouvring, some of these Jews were deported after mid-1944. When Horthy attempted to change sides and reach an armistice with the Soviet Union – the Red Army having already entered Hungarian territory – he was overthrown on 15 October 1944 in a *putsch* staged by the Arrow Cross leader Szálasi and supported by Germany. Szálasi's regime was prepared to 'lend' the remaining Hungarian Jews to Germany as labourers. Most of them died, however, in pogroms in Hungary, on foot marches to the frontier or during railway transports, and in German camps. Approximately 120,000 of the Jews in Budapest survived.

As in Hungary, forced-labour service with military discipline in camps was introduced for Jews in Slovakia in the autumn of 1941. In spite of a certain resistance by the Slovak government, half of the 137,000 Slovak Jews (defined according to their religion) died in the Final Solution. In 1942 they were deported to Auschwitz and Lublin. When a Slovak uprising was bloodily put down by the Germans between August and October 1944, and German forces then took complete control of the country, the Jews who until then had been protected from persecution by letters issued by the Slovak government, or at least by nominal conversion to Catholicism, were also deported. In addition to Wehrmacht units, a special operations detachment was used to suppress the uprising, which also led to the destruction of villages, mass murders, and deportations of the non-Jewish population.

Occupation policy always meant the use of force combined with terror, persecution, and exploitation. Having said that, we should note that German occupation policy in central Europe differed significantly in many respects from occupation policy in eastern Europe, especially in Poland and the Soviet Union. An example of this was the Protectorate of Bohemia and Moravia.[48] Formally, the Czech president, Hácha, was subordinate to the German Reich Protector. Nevertheless, notwithstanding all professions of loyalty and congratulations for German victories, he and his government initially retained some independence, and were able to defend Czech interests and maintain contact with the exile government under Eduard Beneš in London. But this freedom of action was lost at the latest by 1941–2. Hácha's co-operation was based not on any affinity for Germans or National Socialists, but was the result of considerations of expediency, although he and his government thus compromised themselves in the eyes of most of the Czech population. Both the conservative Reich Protector von Neurath and his radical deputy, the Sudeten German Karl Hermann Frank, who was also HSSPF in the Protectorate, advocated a policy of assimilation of the Czechs and settlement of Germans in the Protectorate. And the number of Germans living there did rise, from 189,000 in 1940 (compared with 7.25 million Czechs) to 242,000. But the number of Germans from other countries, often settled in evacuated military training areas, remained small: 8,824 by the end of 1944. National resistance manifested itself in the Protectorate for the first time in student demonstrations in the autumn of 1939 and led, through Frank's efforts, to the closing of all universities there, and to 1,200 Czech students being sent to concentration camps. The main aim of German policy was to depoliticize the Czechs, which, in spite of all efforts to promote the German language and German culture, meant permitting a limited Czech cultural development, social measures for workers, and a food rationing policy that maintained the nutritional level for Czechs at almost that for Germans in Germany, even in the last 3 years of the war.

Reinhard Heydrich, in addition to his other offices, became the *de facto* Protector in Prague in September 1941 and continued this policy. He declared a state of emergency, and had more than 400 people tried by court martial and shot within a short time, among them the head of the Czech government, Eliaš. Between 4,000 and 5,000 other people were arrested. Thereafter, however, Heydrich introduced positive social measures. He was seriously injured in an assassination attempt ordered by the Czech government in exile, and died on 4 June 1942.

His death led to a new wave of terror. Although between 10,000 and as many as 30,000 people were not shot, as Hitler ordered, all 199 men of the village of Lidice and all residents of Lezaky were shot. Courts-martial sentenced 1,357 people to death for reasons such as 'approving of the assassination'. Organized Czech resistance was largely broken; it carried out several acts of sabotage, but concentrated primarily on providing intelligence for the Czech government in exile and the Allies. In the end Karl Hermann Frank, after the usual in-fighting with rivals, was able to consolidate his position in the Protectorate. He gave top priority to armaments production, and steered a relatively mild course in other areas, for the Protectorate remained largely safe from Allied bombing attacks until July 1944. As it was also a highly industrialized area, it became increasingly important for the German war effort. The liberation of the country in the Prague uprising of May 1945 coincided with the end of the war.

Many German opponents of Nazism had first emigrated to Bohemia and Moravia, and people whom the National Socialists considered to be political and racial enemies there were persecuted after March 1939. Approximately 40,000 Jews in that area were able to emigrate; 14,000 who remained survived. But 77,000 Czech Jews lost their lives. As in Germany itself, the first Jews from the Protectorate were sent to their deaths at the end of 1941. In the little town of Theresienstadt a ghetto was established at that time which, despite what the Jewish religious congregation there expected, did not serve to provide labourers for the German war economy. At first it was a temporary ghetto, overcrowded and with intolerable hygiene conditions. A total of 141,000 people were sent to Theresienstadt, the highest number at any given time being 50,000. Although Jews were not systematically murdered in Theresienstadt, 35,000 people died there. Most of the camp's occupants were, however, deported to extermination camps. In addition to Jews from Prague and Brno, Jews from Germany and Western Europe were sent to Theresienstadt. After the end of 1942, it was presented as a model camp, a pleasant ghetto for elderly Jews. As part of this deception, a film was produced entitled *The Führer Gives the Jews a Town.*

Northern Europe

Finland participated in the war against the Soviet Union with its own, limited political aims, but it also served as a staging area for German troops. Nevertheless, it remained relatively independent until the conclusion of an armistice with the Soviet Union on 19 August 1944. As was the case with Finnish deliveries of raw materials, Swedish shipments of iron ore also had a decisive influence on the German conduct of the war. Sweden managed to preserve its neutrality in spite of its strong economic orientation towards Germany, while its neighbour, Norway, was forcibly incorporated into the area under German domination. German planning for the occupation of Denmark and Norway in April 1940 was based on the assumption that the monarchs and governments of those countries would remain in office under German protection, and that they would become parts, as it were, of a 'community of Germanic blood', as the Nordic Society in Germany had already believed they were before the war. In fact, however, the Norwegian monarch and his government remained important politically in their London exile, where they had fled after the German invasion of their country. Reich Commissar Terboven (who was involved in conflicts with the Wehrmacht commander in Norway, von Falkenhorst, as well as with the navy) was never able to base his authority on any significant political group in the country. The various bodies he created to help him govern Norway never had any influence. Vidkum Quisling's policy of ethnocentric ideas and co-operation with the Germans was unsuccessful. Even with German support, his Nasjonal Samling was able to attract only opportunists. Quisling's installation as Minister President on 1 February 1942 did not strengthen his position, although he sought to preserve remnants of Norwegian independence as he understood it. Plans for the future, such as the project to convert Trondheim into a gigantic 'Reich' port connected by motorway with Germany, were never realized; but the fact that the occupation consumed three-quarters of Norway's national income made Norwegians painfully aware of the cost of German rule. In addition to deliveries of agricultural products, aluminium production based on Norway's hydro-electric resources played an important role in the German war economy, but it remained far below expectations, and capacity was not expanded after the end of 1942. Widespread resistance and sabotage caused Terboven, in agreement with the HSSPF responsible, to establish a regime in which 366 Norwegians were executed. A total of probably more than 2,000 resistance fighters were killed. Almost half the 1,800 Jews in Norway and those who had emigrated there were able to save themselves by fleeing to Sweden.

It is remarkable not only that most of the 6,000 or 7,000 Jews in Denmark were able to reach safety, but also that German authorities, including the Reich plenipotentiary, the high SS functionary Werner Best, actively or passively assisted them in August and September 1943. Of the almost 500 Danish Jews deported to Theresienstadt, 116 died. Denmark submitted to German occupation, and the Germans promised to maintain Danish sovereignty. Denmark long remained the only country in the entire area under German domination with a democratic regime – king, government, and parliament – that had its own police and armed forces. The previous German minister in Copenhagen, Cecil von Renthe-Fink, served as the first German plenipotentiary in occupied Denmark (after October 1942 he was succeeded by Werner Best), and this secured the dominant position of the Foreign Ministry in that country. As Denmark's agricultural production was important for the German war economy, co-operation with Germany was relatively good. When the situation in the country became increasingly tense as a result of the harsh policies pursued by the Wehrmacht commander there, the government in Copenhagen was removed on 29 August 1943. The Danish armed forces were disarmed, and finally, in mid-1944, over 2,000 Danish policemen were sent to the concentration camp at Buchenwald. In the end, a policy of open repression also had to be practised in Denmark, but it was considerably less thorough than the scorched-earth policy pursued by the Wehrmacht during its withdrawal from northern Norway.

Western Europe

The German victory in western Europe in May and June 1940 provided the chance to create a 'new order' which was primarily economic but also political, after the early conclusion of peace. In a conversation with Marshal Pétain in December 1941, Göring emphasized that political good behaviour towards Germany would be a central factor in determining the position of states in Europe after the war. But although most of the French population, in the expectation of a lasting German domination of Europe, were prepared to accept this condition, their attitude changed to one of more or less determined opposition after a few years as a result of German actions. France, Belgium, and The Netherlands all had fascist or National Socialist movements which, however, did not come to power under German domination. The National Socialist movement in The Netherlands, led by Anton Mussert (in competition with other people and groups), the Vlaamse Nationaal Verbond of Staf de Clerq, the Walloon Rexists under Léon Degrelle, and various French groups (especially those of Marcel Déat or Jacques Doriot), were supported more or less discreetly by the Germans; but, like Quisling in Norway, they never developed beyond opportunism into a really strong mass movement able to secure even minimum loyalty towards the Germans among their countrymen. Moreover, exile governments or organizations for all three countries, whose influence on their homelands differed greatly, were soon formed in London. Free France under General Charles de Gaulle in London was hardly able to exert any influence until the end of 1942. The Belgian government in exile there was also in a difficult situation, as King Leopold had chosen to remain in his country, although he regarded himself as a prisoner of war and co-operated only to a very limited extent with the German occupiers. Queen Wilhelmina of The Netherlands and her government in London were able to exert a unifying influence on their country comparable to that achieved by the King Haakon VII and the Norwegian government in exile.

Drawing its conclusions from the murderous operations behind the front in Poland, the Wehrmacht prepared 'purely' military administrations for the countries occupied in 1940; however, these were circumvented or replaced with varying degrees of rapidity by party offices and other competitors. In The Netherlands, Seyss-Inquart took office as Reich Commissar at the end of May 1940, but could not push his views through against his fellow Austrian general commissars in the co-ordination of German occupation policy. Especially in matters relating to the use of the police and terror, as well as in economic questions, the latter were directly responsible to Himmler or Göring. The Dutch bureaucracy continued to function under general secretaries, who made compromises with the occupiers to maintain peace and order. And the police were largely converted into an instrument of the occupation. The German police apparatus itself grew to approximately 5,000 men, which was not quite double the strength of German police units in France (3,000). The strong anti-parliamentary political currents in the country quickly led to an all-party union whose aim was to establish a corporative organization of the state. But this union was dissolved by the German authorities at the end of 1941. As in Norway, the hope that the Dutch would slowly become National Socialists themselves was quickly dashed. In spite of superficial acceptance of the occupation, symbolic expressions of loyalty to the royal family, hidden gestures of political nonconformity, and minor acts of sabotage were frequent. But the German police reacted with extreme brutality to a mass strike in protest against the first deportations of Dutch Jews to Mauthausen on 22 and 23 January 1941.

The fact that the government had not been able to overcome mass unemployment prior to 1940, and that the occupation cut off The Netherlands from its traditional markets, was also important. For these reasons the Dutch economy, including the trade unions, developed a relatively strong orientation towards Germany. German authorities established agencies for controlling armaments contracts and labour similar to those introduced in France and Belgium. As elsewhere in Western Europe, reserves of foreign currency and raw materials in The Netherlands were plundered to support the German war effort. Approximately one-third of the goods produced in The Netherlands in 1943 and almost half in 1944 went to Germany. Secure jobs and, until 1942, voluntary employment in Germany were part of this situation. Sauckel introduced forced deportations, against which a proper job in The Netherlands provided protection. But beginning in 1943, resistance increased. When it became known that all Dutch soldiers held as prisoners of war were to be sent to work in Germany, a general strike was called at the end of April, to which the German authorities responded with new mass arrests and shootings. In the expectation of an early liberation, the Dutch staged an effective railway strike in September 1944. As a result, 50,000 people were sent to concentration camps, many resistance fighters were shot on the spot, and the Germans imposed a food embargo that resulted in the deaths of some 10,000 people by the time The Netherlands was liberated.

Depriving Jews in The Netherlands of their rights (in 1941, 140,000 Jews were living there, 112,000 of them Dutch citizens) and placing them under the responsibility of a Jewish council (*Joodenrat*) together with the establishment of a Central Office for Jewish Emigration did not, with the one exception mentioned of the 1941 mass strike, result in any general protest. In July 1942 the expropriation of Jews and their confinement in ghettos were superseded by the measures of the Final Solution. Some time passed before the Jewish Council, which was responsible for providing contingents of Jews for transports, realized that 'work in Germany' meant the early death of those sent, rather than being, as had been thought, the lesser evil compared with confinement in concentration camps. Most Dutch Jews went to Auschwitz and Sobibór via the transit camp of Westerbork; others went into hiding. Of the 107,000 Jews deported from The Netherlands, 105,000, or nearly 70 per cent of all Jews in the country, died. Of the 3,751 deported to Bergen-Belsen, a 'holding camp' built on the edge of a military training area in 1943, over 2,000 survived. Originally, 'privileged' Jews had been held there to be exchanged for Nazis and other internees in other countries (which was actually done); but in 1944 it became a typical concentration camp, with extreme overcrowding and a corresponding death rate, and it remained in existence until it was liberated on 15 March 1945.

Until mid-1944, General Alexander von Falkenhausen remained the German military commander in Belgium and northern France. Two French departments were added to the area under his administration, probably because of their high degree of industrialization, as bargaining chips in negotiations for a permanent peace treaty with France, and because of hopes that they could be Germanized in the long term. But the policy for German occupation in this area did not have a clear and consistent aim. While Falkenhausen gave priority to the immediate needs of the military administration, security, and the armaments industry, Eggert Reeder, his chief of administration and previously District President in Cologne, was more interested in promoting ethnic and cultural ties to bind Flanders more closely to Germany. The continuing presence of the monarch in the country stabilized the German occupation, but many Belgians still remembered the brutal

German occupation in the First World War. On the whole, political and economic co-operation with the occupiers in Belgium was similar to that in The Netherlands. But providing food for the population in Belgium was less well organized than in the rest of Western Europe, although the country had been largely, if reluctantly, incorporated into the German war economy.

Falkenhausen succeeded in preventing the appointment of an HSSPF for Belgium, although there was a security police and SD office subordinate to him. He carried out the *Gleichschaltung* of the police and the race policy measures himself. In November 1942 the Germans began a policy of deportations and shooting of hostages to combat resistance and sabotage. The resistance movements responded with counter-terror and the murder of Rexists, among others, and accelerated the escalation. When the Final Solution in Belgium began with deportation quotas in August 1942, Jews were often deported to the camp at Mecheln by the security police and the SD. The first victims were numerous foreign Jews who had fled to Belgium, but from mid-1943 onwards mostly Belgian Jews, who had already been confined to ghettos in four cities, were also deported. Falkenhausen and Reeder and, independently, the Belgian authorities attempted with some (although ultimately limited) success to delay meeting the prescribed quotas. Approximately 25,000 Jews from Belgium died in the extermination camps or in transports to them, but almost as many were able to hide or otherwise escape deportation.

The fact that, in France, a military commander remained the highest German authority at first moderated the direct persecution of the Jews there. On the whole, the development of German rule in France was more complicated than in other areas, both legally and in other respects. The military commanders (three generals succeeded one another) were only responsible for the occupied part of France. The German ambassador in Paris was Otto Abetz, a National Socialist from Ribbentrop's office, who sought to develop a close alliance with right-wing French groups and who also propagated and practised a policy of co-operation with France in cultural matters. He was not officially accredited in Vichy as, technically, a state of war still existed between Germany and France. Concrete decisions regarding occupation policy were taken by the armistice commission in Wiesbaden, where in economic questions the sub-commission under Minister Hemmen came to play a central role. France was the only great power in the area under German domination and, in spite of Hitler's intransigence, this fact had to be taken into consideration. Because Vichy still had instruments of independent power at its disposal, such as colonies with their own troops and naval forces, several alternatives presented themselves to various influential groups in France and Germany: a complete alliance (advocated by the second most influential men in Vichy, Pierre Laval and Admiral Darlan), or subjugation to Germany; resumption of hostilities against the Germans, or the occupation of all of France; or flexibility and waiting. Pétain chose the last policy. The Vichy government's choice among the possibilities available to it depended on the expected result of the war and thus France's future role in a German-dominated or free Europe.

With Pétain as president, an authoritarian regime was established in France which reflected widespread anti-democratic tendencies in the French population. It was not, however, a complete dictatorship, and it attempted, under the slogan 'Fatherland, Labour, Family' together with absolutist touches, to present itself as the government of all the French people. In all of German-occupied Europe, no other government made a greater effort to co-operate with the occupiers on the basis of its own values. Although opportunism was certainly a factor, the Vichy French began to enact anti-Semitic legislation on their own as early as July 1940, and in July 1941 they created, without German prompting, a not very well-received volunteer legion for the war in the east. Only after the German attack on the Soviet Union, when the Communists (as in other Western European countries) abandoned the waiting policy they had adopted after the signing of the German-Soviet non-aggression pact of 1939, did significant resistance develop in France itself. Hostage-taking and shootings by occupation authorities, as well as court-ordered executions, increased after October 1941. At the beginning of December the German military commander in France, Otto von Stülpnagel, ordered a hundred French hostages to be shot at one time, but such measures made him quite uncomfortable and he soon obtained a transfer.

After 1 June 1942 an HSSPF, Carl Oberg, also resided in Paris; his arrival marked the beginning of a policy of increased terror. The Wehrmacht reinforced its units in France, as it wanted to be able to occupy all of France in the event of an Allied landing in North Africa. The landing took place on 11 November 1942, the anniversary of the Armistice of 1918, and the HSSPF in France expanded the area under his authority to include the rest of that country. The German military established a separate Command-in-Chief for the West. Many who had previously found refuge in the unoccupied part of France now fell victim to the policy of persecution. Although co-operation with the French police was practised whenever possible, German terror was now open and unrestrained. After a bomb attack on Germans in Marseilles at the beginning of 1943, Himmler considered deporting 100,000 people from the 'large mass of criminals' in the city. In May 1943 the various resistance groups (including the Communists) overcame their political differences to form the National Resistance Council under de Gaulle's plenipotentiary, Jean Moulin, who, however, was then betrayed to the Gestapo. In the underground (the Maquis), partisan troops were formed from the networks previously used to exchange information and occasionally carry out acts of sabotage. They were able to liberate Paris in 1944, but compared with the regular troops of the Allies they were not, on the whole, of major importance. Not only were the German military leaders increasingly pushed aside, but Pétain and his government had already lost most of their influence.

Beginning in June 1940, Dannecker, the RSHA representative in Paris responsible for Jewish matters, worked closely with the French General Commissariat for Jewish Affairs (as it was called after February 1941) in carrying out the Final Solution. At first the Vichy government sought to protect native-born, assimilated French Jews, but it also created the conditions for carrying out the Final Solution in France, from the registration of Jews, to police raids and deportations, to assembly camps. It refused only to introduce the 'Jewish star'. On 27 March 1942 the first transport, carrying over 1,000 Jews in passenger trains from the camps at Drancy and Compiègne, left France for Auschwitz. The passengers had been interned earlier in normal hostage-taking operations. Beginning in June 1942, goods trains containing Jews left Drancy regularly, most of them headed for Auschwitz, but several also for Sobibór, Majdanek, or elsewhere to 'annihilation through work'. Vichy had also already agreed to transports from the still-unoccupied part of France. The German quota system affected not only Jews of approximately sixty different foreign nationalities in France – most were Poles, Germans, Austrians, or Romanians – but also Jews with French citizenship, which had traditionally been granted to only a very limited number. Of the approximately 300,000 Jews in France in 1940, almost 76,000 were murdered; fewer than half of the victims had French citizenship. In Morocco, Algeria, and Tunisia the French enacted discriminatory legislation against Jews living there which was similar to the laws in force in France itself. But in spite of the temporary German occupation of Tunisia, Jews there were able to survive.

After occupying France and other Western European countries, the Germans plundered their raw-materials reserves to support German armaments programmes. These reserves brought in two–six times the German stocks at that time. Moreover, from the very beginning France had to pay a financial tribute in the form of occupation costs amounting to 20 million German Reichsmarks a day, 20 per cent of the total German war costs at the time. This sum was reduced for a time, but was later raised to 25 million marks, at a fictitious exchange rate. Part of the hard currency thus obtained was used for purchases on the French black market. The French were thus forced to finance to a great extent their own exploitation. The value of German imports from France was twice that of German exports there in 1941, and five times as high in 1944. In 1944, 87 per cent of exports from France and its colonies went to Germany, whereas before the war the figure had only been 3.2 per cent.

Until the second half of 1942, this bilateral economic co-operation developed satisfactorily. German firms took advantage of the opportunity to secure extensive holdings, and in some cases majorities, in French companies. And beginnings were made for the future investment of French capital in the east. On the whole, in large industrial firms and small banks in Western Europe the development of a 'New Order' under German leadership made good progress. In 1942 the entire French locomotive industry, together with 95 per cent of the machine tool industry, was working to fill German orders. The decisive factor was the economic rationale for participation in what was assumed would be a single, German-dominated large economy, and the disappearance of traditional markets in future. Beginning in the spring of 1942, the growing number of French people sent to forced labour in Germany placed a heavy burden on economic relations between France and Germany, as did agricultural deliveries to Germany, and declining productivity, Vichy's agrarian ideology notwithstanding. The French sent 15 to 20 per cent of their food production to Germany, and that meant, for their country as a whole, a level of nutrition below the generally accepted minimum. Because of Hitler's view of France as Germany's traditional enemy, from the very beginning that country, potentially the most important partner of a German-dominated Europe, was never really able to be more than a satellite. In the end, as a result of Allied military successes, more intensive German economic exploitation, and the policy of annihilation and deportations to forced labour, France was reduced to the level of a plundered state attempting to free itself from foreign oppression and its own collaboration with the enemy.

Italy

The parts of areas under Italian control which remained unaffected by the change of regime and the armistice of July to September 1943 came under German occupation.[49] The difference between the two related political systems of National Socialism and Italian fascism was evident not only in the German and Italian dictatorships (in spite of Mussolini's puppet regime in Salo), but also in the much more thorough, and thus more brutal, German rule. Italy had pursued racist policies, especially in Africa, and, beginning in 1938, had enacted anti-Jewish legislation that largely excluded Jews from public life. But, at first, Mussolini did not turn the more than 46,000 Jews in Italy over to the Germans, only having foreign Jews in Italy interned. After the Axis powers had occupied all of France, numerous Jews from its previously unoccupied parts fled to the Italian sector. In September 1943 the first large-scale raids to find Jews were carried out in northern Italy and then in Rome by the SD and the Security Police. The *Repubblica Sociale Italiana* (RSI), the puppet regime in northern Italy that Mussolini established after being freed by German paratroops in September 1943, also sent Italian Jews to concentration camps. The most important camp, Fossoli, was turned over to the Germans at the beginning of 1944 and for a time served as a transit camp primarily for transports to Auschwitz, until it was replaced by a new camp near Bolzano. The developments in Italy in 1943 placed some 33,000 Jews in areas under German domination, of whom, because of the solidarity of the Italian population, only 19 per cent could be deported. Jews deported earlier by the Italians from Libya, as well as those from areas in the Balkans formerly occupied by Italy, were also drawn into the Final Solution.

In the use of violence and the cynicism they demonstrated these actions were not significantly different from those used in the disarming of the Italian armed forces, whose members were also taken into the German forced-labour system. Compared with other countries, German occupation in Italy developed quickly. The Italians had concluded an armistice with the Allies because they feared a defeat; the Germans, however, still placed their hopes in holding out and final victory. The so-called Italian 'betrayal' caused German authorities, especially the Wehrmacht and the police and SS, to develop a brutal persecutor mentality towards their former ally. This was also true of the role assigned to Italy in the German war economy and its armaments production. In addition to deportations for forced labour in Germany and the aim of transferring production there, the German author-ities concerned themselves with reducing the Italians' standard of living in the interest of Germany. Attempts by the RSI to introduce social reforms received little more than polite consideration. Under these circumstances it is not surprising that a partisan movement soon developed in the parts of Italy occupied by German forces. The Wehrmacht and the SS adopted radical measures to 'combat the bandits', a group in which almost any Italian could be included. By the end of the war 44,720 'partisans' and 9,980 civilians had died as a result. As of mid-1944 the SS was able increasingly to strengthen its position in Italy, as became obvious when HSSPF Karl Wolf independently conducted surrender negotiations with the Americans in April 1945.

Change in the German System of Rule

During the Second World War Germany dominated large parts of Europe. Other nations and states could be Germany's allies only on paper, not in reality. In fact, for them there could be only submission and subordination in an order prepared during the war that was to be given a clear form only after final victory had been achieved. Economically this order was to be a new kind of single, large economy; politically it was to be the living space of the Germanic 'master race'. Within this framework, talk of European unity served only a tactical function, such as in the idea of a European crusade against Bolshevism when the war in the east did not develop as originally expected; or in its use by parts of the SS to promote a European-Germanic élite army; or again as a European economic union of states mobilized for total war, as advocated by Albert Speer. But economic questions in particular were dominated by the rule that a German must never be materially worse off than a foreigner. It is clear that under the conditions of massive bombing and (as of the autumn of 1944) increasing occupation, Germans received fewer foodstuffs and other material necessities from outside. But, in contrast with the First World War, people in Germany between 1939 and 1945 did not die of hunger, nor, as a rule, did they experience it. Everywhere in Europe, non-Germans were not only discriminated against or killed according to their racial classification, but, in addition to different degrees of terror depending on their nationality, other peoples or foreign inmates of camps in Germany were subjected to various degrees of material deprivation in favour of the 'master race'. Nevertheless, until the final phase of the war in each country, the living conditions of north and west Europeans were much closer to those of the Germans than was the case in the east, where extermination and annihilation through material scarcity had determined German policies in the occupied areas for years.

A high degree of efficiency in the conduct of the war, the exploitation of resources, and the murder of ostracized individuals and groups was maintained in areas under German rule to the end. This was the result, too, of Hitler's very real use of his dictatorial powers, although because of illness and the necessity of conducting the war he was increasingly unable to fulfil his function as a general co-ordinator of policy. This placed limitations on the efficiency of the mobilization for the total war; most sectors of the German war economy reached their highest level of production only in 1944.

The polyocracy in which everything depended on the favour of the Führer remained.[50] At the beginning of the war in 1939 Göring had been named chairman of the Council of Ministers for the Defence of the Reich (*Miniserrat für die Reichsverteidigung*), but the council never became a war cabinet, especially as it never met in formal session. In fact, in terms of political power, Göring's empire disintegrated into its constituent parts under the men he had appointed, although to all appearances he remained the second most powerful man in the Third Reich. Nevertheless, many people sought for purely tactical reasons to obtain a title from him and thus a secure position within the framework of the Four Year Plan. Much more important, on the other hand, was the tactic the SS used to protect its own interests. Since the 1930s Himmler had bestowed honorary SS ranks (with uniforms) upon other powerful individuals, seeking through these formal ties to create personal loyalty to the SS and its ideology, and to expand his own information network. High-ranking SS officers also moved into many other offices and bureaucracies. In general it is difficult to determine whether these men felt more loyalty to the SS or to their new offices. Above all, however, Himmler sought to create a formal and informal system beyond the SD apparatus for obtaining information on all developments within the state, as Göring, for his part, had already done by creating a 'Research Office' and a 'Central Surveillance Office' (*Abhörzentrale*) in 1933. The disintegration of Göring's empire into this and other information networks reflected the erosion of his power.

The diverse organizations of German rule in the occupied areas, from the annexed areas to military combat zones, were all in one way or another under the formal authority of Hitler, who was still able to exercise that

authority in matters he considered important. But increasingly, power centres became involved in direct competition with each other. The same was
true within the Reich, from the party to the state bureaucracy and the
Wehrmacht. In 1943 Interior Minister Frick, who had attempted repeatedly
to introduce long-term bureaucratic co-ordination into this chaos, requested
to be relieved of his position and, with considerable relief, became Reich
Protector of Bohemia and Moravia. Especially near the end of the war, the
number of special-tasks assignments (*Sonderaufträge*) with differing legal
bases for authorization increased again. During the battle of Stalingrad it
appeared that the three heads of offices with direct access to Hitler would
divide the organization of state and related business among themselves:
Keitel for the Wehrmacht, Hans Heinrich Lammers for other state affairs,
and Martin Bormann as head of the party chancellery (and Hitler's secretary). None of these three men was motivated by ambitions of personal
power, although Bormann seemed to many to be an *éminence grise* and an
ersatz Reich Chancellor. He did carry on feuds and alliances, such as his close
co-operation with Goebbels, who personally made great efforts to gather the
reins of domestic policy in his own hands. His activities as Reich Plenipotentiary for Total War Mobilization (*Reichsbevollmächtigter für den totalen
Kriegseinsatz*), a position to which he was appointed on 25 July 1944, were
largely limited to ineffective gestures, in spite of his co-operation with Speer
in this area. Because of his accumulation of offices and achievements in
organizing the war economy, Speer viewed himself as Hitler's crown prince
in 1942–3, but he then fell out of favour and thus lost much of his power.
Some of the more active young functionaries in Speer's ministry were so
dynamic that they made alliances with other clients (like the SS) and thus
abandoned their protector. And the Gau leaders, who were also Reich
defence commissars, did not want to support the mobilization of the entire
population for total war. Especially in the last phase of the war, as a result of
the destruction of housing space, transportation, and production facilities,
much authority again shifted to the local and regional levels, where party and
government bureaucracies down to the municipal level, as well as business
leaders who had been carrying out many state tasks in 'self-administration'
since 1941, co-operated to maintain public functions and essential services.
In spite of all the morale-boosting slogans, the realization was widespread
that Germans would have to prepare for life after losing the war. And in the
western parts of Germany the hope for an early occupation was widespread
after September 1944.

   In addition to Speer's rise and fall, the growth of the SS state was the most
striking development within Germany during the war. This was true not only
with regard to the organization of racist mass murder. Himmler expanded
his empire into almost all areas of society. There is no evidence that his close
subordinates went beyond the scope of the 'the order under the Death's
Head' or even endangered his position as Reich Leader of the SS by their
various activities. The SS was active as a fighting organization, although the

formations of the Waffen SS in general cannot be regarded as mere soldiers like any others. In July 1944 Himmler took over the organization of the replacement army, and thus was in a position to push forward his long-held aim, which he had been developing for some time, of creating a National Socialist mass army. In 1945 he commanded military formations on the Vistula and the upper Rhine. As Frick's successor, Himmler headed the Reich and Prussian Ministry of the Interior after 20 August 1943 and attempted, mostly through plenipotentiaries, to place the entire German population in the service of the war effort. But, as shown by many of his speeches to mayors or Reich governors, especially in Posen in 1944, his appeals were largely without effect; given the obstacles and the established chaos in the power centres, Himmler, too, reached his limits. And finally, the SS expanded its influence on the economy and made the empty shell of the Reich Economics Ministry into a new power centre by placing its own people in key positions there. Towards the end of the war the concept of a National Socialist economy advocated by party functionaries was increasingly aimed at Speer's efforts to achieve a total mobilization. And in the SS Economic and Administrative Main Office, Oswald Pohl encountered obstacles in his efforts to expand the SS concerns, German Economic Enterprises, some of which were of a legal nature but which were also due to Hitler himself. Hitler did occasionally say that he expected to see Himmler as the head of a great concentration-camp industry after the war, but that was no longer a serious statement of real intention. In the disintegrating Führer state, Himmler courted the Reich Organization of Industry (*Reichsgruppe Industrie*) in his speeches. It was as impossible to make prognoses about a future National Socialist regime without Hitler as it was to make predictions about its development after victory in the world war. Although Hitler had expressly forbidden it, the problems that Germany would face after the war were discussed in the highest circles, and especially among business leaders. That the country was facing a total defeat was clear to almost all Germans in the final months of the war.

A change of course could not be expected from the existing power apparatus in Germany. A few Germans had come to this conclusion even before the war, realizing that a change of course would require not only the arrest but also the killing of Hitler and his closest associates. This would require the use of organized force, which during the war only the Wehrmacht could provide on a large scale. The origins of resistance were varied, from the realization that the chaotic structures of the Third Reich were destroying the German state, to the insight that the war had been started irresponsibly and that the dictator was unable and unwilling to end it. A further motive for many people was the knowledge of the regime's policy of murder and terror in occupied countries, of persecution and oppression in Germany itself, or of acts of genocide. Such knowledge formed the basis for an ethical rejection of the regime, a return to humane principles that had to be re-established by any means necessary. Several of those who joined the resistance had earlier participated actively and openly in racist declarations and measures. Whether and how independent thinking led to opposition that in turn resulted in a readiness to participate actively in resistance depended on the political starting-point of the individuals involved, on their critical view of developments in certain areas of policy together with their agreement with the actions of the regime in other areas, and on changing political constellations. There was not a single, general resistance movement, but a diversity of relationships between people who, given the surveillance capabilities of the regime and its vast number of informers, could only work together clandestinely and who increasingly came to see the violent elimination of the dictator as their main aim.

In the early years of the Third Reich many opponents of the regime emigrated after they had not only been deprived of any possibilities for legal opposition but also, in many cases, had been threatened, arrested, or tortured. But one did not have to be against the regime to be ostracized and forced to emigrate, for racial reasons, for example. Between 1933 and 1945, as a result of the emigration of approximately 30,000 people persecuted for their political views (in addition to the persecuted Jews), German history took place to an unusual extent outside the area of German influence and beyond the reach of German authorities.

After the 1934–8 period, therefore, any prospect of successful resistance movements was dependent on their members occupying positions in state organizations with access to instruments of force; thus military opposition acquired a significant role. Such a group began to form around General Ludwig Beck because of the risk of war in 1938, and after his departure that same year it remained dependent on support in the active officer corps. Murder operations in Poland, fear that a campaign against France would not be successful, and later declining prospects of victory in the east became important motives for a German military resistance at the beginning of 1942. However, prior to July 1944 several attempts by people from that group to assassinate Hitler failed.

In addition to groups of active and former officers, several civilian resistance groups were formed, often among higher public officials or in the diplomatic service. Carl Goerdler, the former mayor of Leipzig who advocated national conservative views of the state and Germany's position as a great power, became their most prominent member. Younger members of this group, on the other hand, from both aristocratic and commoner families, both officers and civilians, were more interested in social and political reforms. Beginning in the autumn of 1942, the Kreisau Circle, to which Social Democrats, trade unionists, and representatives of the Protestant and Catholic churches belonged, met at the country estate of Count Helmuth James von Moltke. They sought to break with anti-democratic German traditions, while older national conservatives advocated a corporative and authoritarian socio-political order. Moreover, the circle established loose contacts with Communists, whose most important group, the Rote Kapelle, was smashed by the Gestapo at the end of 1942. Only in the final phase of the war did clandestine Communist or Social Democrat information networks again become significant.

Opposition among students to the regime reached its high point in the distribution of leaflets by members of the White Rose group around Hans and Sophie Scholl. In February 1943 this group was smashed after distributing leaflets in Munich; its leaders were executed. The longer the war lasted, the clearer it became that, quite apart from any prospects for an indulgent treatment of Germany, for which the Allies in any case had made no promises, and regardless of the feared refusal of the majority of the population to accept an assassination, Hitler had to be eliminated for moral reasons alone. 'It is no longer a question of practical considerations, but of showing the world and history that the German resistance movement has dared to take the decisive step', Henning von Tresckow wrote in June 1944.[51] On 20 July 1944 the assassination attempt by Colonel Claus von Stauffenberg in Hitler's headquarters in East Prussia failed. Hitler was injured, but not killed, by the bomb Stauffenberg had planted. The far-flung conspiracy was able to seize positions of power in certain places, such as Paris, albeit for a short time; but not in Berlin, where the SS, the Gestapo, and loyal Wehrmacht units arrested members of the resistance or forced them to commit suicide. The core of the resistance was uncovered in the following months, and members and those who had known of their plans were tried by the People's Court (*Volksgerichtshof*). Most of them were subsequently executed.

Because of the terror apparatus, the resistance acted without the support of the mass of the population; but unco-ordinated resistance was widespread in many social groups. By 1935 at the latest, efforts to achieve the removal of the regime by direct methods, in themselves the essence of resistance, had come to be rejected as being without any prospect of success. Beneath the level of active resistance, there was, however, a broad scale of non-conformist behaviour, including the preservation of a non-National-Socialist identity. Incidents of completely non-conformist behaviour and dangerous expressions of dissent occurred even among convinced National Socialists. Contacts among illegal socialist groups were maintained in large cities. It was often also possible to help victims of the terror. Protestant pastors and, above all, Catholic priests in isolated rural areas sought, together with their congregations, to maintain ethical norms contrary to those ordered and practised by the regime. Although the churches accepted the regime in many respects, the earliest organized alternative sources of power to confront it developed within their ranks. Whispered jokes about the regime, opposition among the young, from conscious political criticism to acts of sabotage, enthusiasm for jazz, and theft of coal were typical examples of non-National-Socialist behaviour that extended to active resistance with the risk of fatal persecution. Under the conditions of the war and terror, and also of continued loyalty to Hitler, no mass movement against the regime developed in Germany, as it did in large parts of German-dominated Europe. But a general turning-away from the regime did begin during the battle of Stalingrad (in January-and February 1943), and grew stronger after the Allied landing in France and the attempted assassination of Hitler (in June and July 1944), which, nevertheless, was itself rather unpopular with most ordinary Germans.[52] The Führer myth lost its power over most Germans because the Allied successes destroyed the credibility of the victory and morale-boosting slogans, but also because many Germans began to experience dire need and fear for the first time. Most who were not among the persecuted probably awaited the end of the war with apathy or caution, hoping for liberation but fearing defeat. In the spreading chaos of the fatal evacuation marches from the camps, fanatical National Socialists practised naked terror to prevent local surrender negotiations with the Allies. But even many National Socialists had by this time accepted the inevitability of defeat. An Alpine fortress to be defended to the end or German youth prepared to fight on as underground 'werewolves' existed only in the final propagada mobilization and, correspondingly, in the fears of the Allies. The National Socialist regime collapsed with its military defeat, and there was no successor. People attempted to adjust to the new situation and the rule of the victors, who themselves soon arrested a large number of leading representatives of the regime. On the whole most Germans were concerned with their own survival when the collapse finally came.

Germany, which had wanted to conquer the world and for a time had ruled and spread death over the greater part of Europe, was defeated by an alliance of European powers, and above all by the Soviet Union as well as North America. As early as 16 June 1941, Joseph Goebbels had confided to his diary: 'We already have so much to answer for anyway that we have to win. Otherwise, our whole people with everthing that is dear to us will be wiped out. Well, let's get to work.'[53] True to this conviction, he, as well as Hitler and several other leading National Socialists, resorted to suicide in the hour of defeat. Germans as a people, however, for whom the dictator in his defeat had prophesied a well-deserved destruction because of their alleged weakness, faced at first an uncertain new beginning in destitution and suffering under the governance of the victors.

|6|

Origins, Breaks, and After-effects: On the Social History and Politics of the 'National Community'

With increasing distance from any period of history, it becomes easier, in addition to the obvious breaks, to recognize continuities. This is especially true of the 12-year National Socialist rule in Germany and Europe, whose total destruction was accomplished half a century ago. At first, the end of the National Socialist policy of conquest in Europe led to an expansion of political power for the two world powers, the United States and the Soviet Union, whose basic ideological positions had been clear since the First World War. As it was necessary to completely eliminate the National Socialist regime, their common victory brought the power blocs centred around these two world powers into direct contact in a divided Germany in a way that probably contributed essentially to the Cold War.

But from the very beginning the positions of the super powers in this conflict were not equal. There were great differences in the amount of suffering and destruction which had been inflicted on them by German military action and rule; in the extent of their military participation in the victory; and finally in the socio-political systems under which the power blocs were organized.

To consolidate their victory they extended their respective systems over the former enemy states as well as over large parts of the rest of Europe. The German attempt to reduce much of Europe to the level of colonies, like the Japanese attempt in East Asia, contributed greatly to the acceleration of decolonization, which had been in progress since the First World War and which, for their different reasons, was also supported by the United States and the Soviet Union. But only the weakening of the positions of the traditional European colonial powers resulting from the Second World War made possible the rise of the 'Third World', after the Europeans had been able to re-establish their colonial rule for a short time after 1945.

It is still unclear to what extent the rise of the defeated powers in the Second World War to a position of leading industrial nations by the 1970s was due to their earlier expansionist policies. In the case of Germany under National Socialism, there was a technological and industrial impetus during the last years of the war which, in spite of the destruction and the dismantling programme thereafter, left many elements intact that contributed to later recovery. The post-war effects of this impulse were stronger in the western part of Germany, but were also noticeable, in weaker form, in the east, under the conditions of the new socio-political system. In addition, however, other factors, from the Cold War to economic aid, specific attitudes, and technical knowledge contributed to this development. All this was, however, only an indirect result of National Socialist rule.

Here we are dealing with the concept of modernization or progress that, like its contrary, atavism or regression, derives from a teleological view of history and thereby, in addition to its analytical use, also has positive connotations. This is especially true if modernity is viewed as an all-encompassing political state or as a goal of action, though less so if it refers to clearly defined aspects of modern developments. Democratic-participatory, technological-industrial, social-welfare, or artistic aspects of 'modernity' never coincide perfectly in historical reality; they are never accepted once and for all, but are always found in a changing, mixed relationship. Moreover, to define 'modernity' by the standards of subsequent conditions, or to give an automatically positive value to devopments which, whether as sources or simply precursors, have led to what is now considered 'modern', is to lay oneself open to criticism. Such an approach is taken in journalistic and scientific usage when referring to other epochs, but it is ambivalent and easily misunderstood when transferred to the National Socialist system. For heuristic purposes three questions must be answered separately:

- During the 12 years of their rule, what did the National Socialists initiate deliberately and purposefully?
- What was in fact promoted by propaganda or actually prepared, possibly against the intentions of National Socialists, for the time after the 'final victory' which never came?
- In the real course of events, what determined the development of German history beyond the National Socialist period, even if it was possibly contrary to the intentions of leading political figures?

For key aspects of the Führer state, Adolf Hitler's aims were decisive. In spite of the variety of other views and plans, no ideas that were basically incompatible with his main aims could be effectively articulated; 'polyocracy [was] an essential condition of monocracy'.[1] All things considered, the National Socialists, and above all their Führer, claimed that their aim was to ensure that the Germans would prosper and that they would have a good life in the future. Not only did this reflect Hitler's view of the world, being a central driving force behind his actions; but most Germans let themselves be convinced by it, and were only too ready to believe that 'the Führer wants the best for us'. And although this faith was severely tested and did occasionally weaken, many Germans – whether active National Socialists or unconnected with politics – believed it would be fulfilled, worked for the same or similar aims, or accepted professional responsibility for ensuring the fulfilment of parts of it. Even after the end of the regime it was possible, with or without mental or opportunistic adjustment to the new situation, still to advocate projects conceived as parts of that faith, although the original National Socialist framework had collapsed.

The 'national community of all Germans' formed a basic idea in two senses. Firstly, everything that allegedly threatened that community had to be radically isolated; race ideological war and genocide were the key elements of such a view, and the concept of such a community also formed the justification for the power of the Führer over life and death. It was often stressed that this way was 'harsh but necessary'. Secondly, in German society itself the community was intended to overcome traditional barriers of station and class. It would not only eliminate the remnants of the privileged position of the nobility, but also the social position of the often-ridiculed middle class. The slogan 'Make the Way Free for Ability' was intended to appeal to those who wanted to improve their socio-economic situation.[2] This was especially true of the lower classes, the 'little people'. But it did not refer basically to the total economy in liberal-capitalistic competition, or to state policy (which was supposed to direct the economy). Hitler believed that only he himself was able to achieve the desired elimination of socio-economic conflicts within German society, although he felt that illness and old age would overtake him before he could so so. For a time he considered creating a 'Führer council' to determine his successor, but he eventually rejected that idea. The question remained open as to how, immediately after victory in a war of annihilation, social mobility could be promoted in a 'national community' which was actually expected to develop in the course of several centuries. Even the visions of what the 'national community' should be like after all enemies of National Socialism had been annihilated remained unclear.

On the level of actual history, Hitler and his paladins could never accept a society with a competition of ideas in which individuals made their own political decisions and acted on their own responsibility. The National Socialists rejected on principle not only the contemptible (in their view) Weimar Republic, but also all forms of democracy and parliamentarianism. Authoritarian tendencies, which had traditionally formed a framework for competing policies in German history, were now carried to their logical extreme and for a long time attracted many followers. Tolerance, respect for differing opinions, and the resulting peaceful competition to achieve political goals were quite incompatible with National Socialist ideas of social Darwinist struggle, and also with the ruthless, chaotic careerism it fostered.

And this constituted a serious lack of what can be called modernity. Most of the developments discussed below reflected not only anti-democratic but also racist aims: aims which it would not be legitimate to separate in any discussion of the National Socialist period. None the less, although anti-democracy and racism were constitutive parts of National Socialism, deliberately forgetting them while at the same time continuing many National Socialist policies beyond 1945 was a fact of life for most of those Germans not accused of criminal deeds.

Often this could be put down to opportunism in the post-war period. In each case, however, it also showed the extent to which the policy of racist ostracization had been accepted by individuals only for reasons of expediency. In addition, the shock of finding out the details of many inhuman aspects of National Socialist policies initially caused many Germans to place their hopes for the future in traditional values, institutions, and standards. Some people, for example, confused National Socialist mass mobilization with democracy, and began to propagate other, supposedly safer values against a mobile mass society.

The National Socialist period also resulted in a decisive break with many modern artistic trends, in which conflict and feelings of danger for people as individuals or members of society were expressed. National Socialist ideas of art became official policy not only in the vision of a distant future, but also in reality. A very specific, usually kitschy and superficial aesthetic, which had existed earlier, was demanded by the state. Only what was officially considered beautiful was acceptable; anything, or anyone, officially regarded as ugly was not only decadent, but also pathological and therefore had to be eradicated. 'Degenerate art' was presented as a model of what to avoid, with comments about the subjects portrayed and their artists. A classical ideal of art was promoted as an antidote; it idealized and, at the same time, by treating them solely as examples of Germanic greatness, presented an extremely narrow, one-sided view of Rembrandt, Schiller, Dürer, Goethe, Beethoven, and Wagner. 'The SA is marching for Goethe, Schiller, Kant, Bach, for the Cologne Cathedral, for the Bamberg Reiter, for Novalis and Hans Thoma,' it was claimed in justifying the battle against political enemies in Germany itself in 1933.[3] When the commander of an SS special operations group or a concentration camp attended a concert or played the piano for pleasure while on holiday or in his leisure time, in addition to providing psychological relief such activities also had the function of giving meaning and justification to his own murderous actions. For he had been indoctrinated and preferred to believe that works of real culture were endangered by Jews and Communists, and that such persons had to be killed so that his own children would be able to enjoy classical violin concerts.

There were other aspects to the anti-modern National Socialist aesthetic. In the official aesthetic hierarchy, National Socialist imperial architecture was dominant. From the works of Richard Wagner to the sculptor Arno Breker and the 'poet' Hans Jost, the heroic element was emphasized. In addition there was the rustic idyll of human beings, animals, and the countryside existing in a harmonious or trite symbiosis, and this was partly connected with ideals of 'blood and the earth of their forefathers'. These attitudes, towards art as the kingdom of the 'beautiful' reflected a long tradition in Germany. Their underlying mentality survived the collapse of Hitler's Reich in 1945, although its specifically National Socialist forms disappeared along with the aesthetic of that period. We must also mention that another cultural trend, 'non-political' entertainment, such as that in films or novels, was not institutionalized by the Reich Chamber of Culture; but it was more or less tolerated, and even promoted, especially by Goebbels. Moreover, for a long time after 1933 it was possible to buy or borrow books by banned authors; and American dance music, including the officially condemned jazz, was often tolerated with only slight camouflage. Such continuity during and after the National Socialist period was possible not because it was officially sanctioned, but because the first priority of the regime, especially during the war, was to preserve the loyalty of the population. This produced often astonishing degrees of freedom side by side with the determined persecution of 'degenerate' artists.

The situation is different when we consider National Socialist economic and social policy, which had as its final aim the creation of a complete 'national community'. The political transformation that began in 1933, with its waves of arrests and expulsions, destroyed so many established political ties, interest networks, and social structures that the collapse of the regime offered a chance for a completely new beginning. The youth cult was pervasive. Not only the self-image of children and young people as heralds of a new age played a role; under the new conditions great numbers of relatively young people moved into leadership positions. Luftwaffe generals in their thirties were only one example. In their personnel policies, Goebbels and Speer deliberately promoted youthful dynamism. Compared to the opportunities such policies offered, the prospects for advancement during the Weimar period were poor. And many politicians involved in the reconstruction of Germany after 1945 had to work with the young technocrats of the National Socialist period, who were already in key positions.

National Socialist policies did create new possibilities for personal advancement. But in spite of all the dynamism of National Socialist society, experts and technocrats did not attain their new positions by being members of any pressure group. The established system, they believed, gave them the opportunity to participate in the 'great construction work' of the Führer, to create a new human being in a new society. Technicians received unprecedented chances for advancement within the established socio-political framework. On the other hand, basic research in areas like the natural sciences was often neglected. Many scientists, especially if they were Jews, did such research in exile. But in Germany itself, opportunities were primarily available to persons in fields of applied knowledge, such as engineers, doctors, jurists, urban planners, pedagogues, and geographers, whose task it was to build a new society for the happy and satisfied people of the future 'national community'. In some cases only as a tried means of promoting their own influence or advancement, such people often readily accepted and shared the enormous arrogance expressed in the intention to create such human beings. It must be emphasized that most of the developments to which these individuals contributed served to prepare for war. Although they did not provide its initial impulse, these new experts systematized the deadly 'ostracization'. Many of them believed they were performing great tasks for the future; but many also thought solely in terms of feasibility within the larger task of creating the 'national community', and ignored the question of the dignity of the individual. After 1945, they continued to practise their professions, but without National Socialist aims, swastikas, or the persecution of supposed political enemies.

Hitler admired technology. Assembly lines and the rationalization of production were, for him, obvious preconditions for further developments. For this reason, Fordism and Taylorism continued to replace traditional production technology in National Socialist Germany, at least in large firms. That Hitler did not oppose this development was due to his appreciation of the potential of the United States as the world's greatest industrial power, with which Germany would eventually have to compete for world domination. For this reason, too, it was planned to build a new area in the west of Hamburg, clearly on the model of such American cities as New York or San Francisco, with a skyscraper-like high-rise building and an enormous bridge across the Elbe. New technologies were often developed to prepare for or conduct war. As an autodidact, Hitler concerned himself with the calibre of battleships' guns and the thickness of their armour and, increasingly, with details of the large-scale technology of weapons and armaments production. The technicians and engineers had to talk him out of pursuing some ideas, but his interests usually gave them considerable freedom. The direction they chose is demonstrated by the so-called 'miracle weapons' (*Wunderwaffen*) and the myth that technology, whether in the form of rockets such as the V2, or of research to produce an atomic bomb, could save Germany from imminent defeat. Such efforts were certainly quite different from Himmler's suggestion of obtaining oil from herbs or fir-cones, although that, too, was intended to promote new technologies.

More important was the fact that its policy of autarchy and disengagement, from the world market created a need for the exploitation and development of raw materials within Germany itself. This gave rise to gasoline synthesis from brown coal, synthetic rubber (Buna), new methods for the smelting of low-grade iron ore near Salzgitter, and the production and processing of cellulose for the textile industry, for which decreasing quantities of cotton were available. Not only war-related technologies were involved. The idea of producing a 'people's car' (*Volkswagen*) for all members of the 'national community' was inspired by developments in the United States in the 1920s. The 'motorways of the Führer' (*Autobahnen*) in particular were intended to make efficient transportation possible for private individuals. The propaganda to promote saving for the 'Strength through Joy' car, later rechristened the *Volkswagen*, or 'VW', was launched at the same time as the car itself, which was designed by Ferdinand Porsche and opened, for hundreds of thousands of people, the hope of self-realization through increased individual mobility. Broad, straight streets in new German cities were intended to serve as monuments to the regime and at the same time to facilitate military deployments. But in 1938 Hitler already envisaged cities built for cars: 'The new streets [are] built less for 1938, 1939, or 1940, than to accommodate the certain, gigantic increase in traffic in the coming decades and centuries.'[4] The Reichsmarks which German savers put away towards the purchase of a VW disappeared in the moloch of the armaments budget, but this had not been deliberately planned as a fraud to obtain funds.

Technology and physical mobility were also intended to help the ordinary members of the 'national community' and give them an awareness of national greatness through the contemplation of the beauties of Germany. Workers in large firms were mostly alienated by their work environment, and Hitler could not imagine how, for example, a worker who laboured in a chemical factory, 'a stink-pot', in an 'incredible stench' for 9 hours every day year after year could develop any enthusiasm for his job.[5] He had to be offered possibilities in his free time that would give him true satisfaction and at the same time the chance to rise beyond the possibilities normally available to him, and all this could best be accomplished in party organizations. In spite of all the middle-class rhetoric and the special inclusion, from 1937–8 onwards of small firms in the armaments boom, when the major German enterprises were being used to full capacity, (a tendency strengthened by Allied bombing after 1942), the trend towards the creation of large firms continued throughout the National Socialist period. And this development meant new tasks and possibilities in the internal social policy of companies.[6] Discipline and order were certainly pervasive in German enterprises, as all trade-union activity had been suppressed. But the view that the head of a firm was the 'master in his own house' was, increasingly, indirectly undermined by the welfare policies of the German Labour Front. Existing social programmes within firms had now been given greater legal protection. The official general wage and price freeze led to an expansion of bonus systems, and social programmes within companies, even small- and medium-sized, ones, were improved, not least by an agency called 'Beautification of Work', which was part of the DAF. This demand, that aesthetic considerations be incorporated into policy, was to be found in works of art and even in the designing of motorways and roads to preserve the countryside. And it was part of an overall programme: beauty was intended to promote what was considered good; the preservation of beauty was a task of policy and thus acquired an ethical quality. This was one side of the totalitarian system: in a very specific sense the National Socialists set about restoring the classical unity of the beautiful and the good through their policies.

Of course, reasonably priced meals at the workplace and bright, cheerful canteens or wash-rooms could not replace the activities of trade unions or works councils; but beyond their aim of mobilizing labour for the purposes of the regime, they were typical National Socialist concerns. Another aspect of this policy was the elimination of distinctions, still emphasized as late as the 1920s, between workers and much better-paid, and socially more respected, salaried employees. The Ergonomics Institute (*Arbeitswissenschaftliches Institut*) of the German Labour Front became a social-policy think-tank in the pre-war period, and, at the high point of German expectations of final victory in 1940, with Hitler's approval, began to plan for the post-war period. Among other aims, full employment was to be guaranteed in the future through retraining and qualification programmes, which would also serve to control or at least influence the number of people entering various professions. Equal pay for equal work was to be realized; and for this purpose, a precise analysis and evaluation for each workplace was made. Beginning in 1940, DAF planners with Robert Ley as Reich Commissar for Publicly Financed Flats developed a strong interest in housing construction. Housing shortages and resulting attempts to steer housing construction had been widespread in the 1920s.[7] The necessary instruments, such as rent freezes and protection against unwarranted notice to quit, were usually strengthened in favour of tenants. In accordance with Gottfried Feder's ideas, it was initially planned to build many new small towns with a maximum of 20,000 residents each, and with names such as Hitlerburg, Göringen, Frickhausen, or Federfeld. But the new towns that were built, such as Wolfsburg (VW) and Salzgitter (for iron-ore production), were considerably larger. A home of one's own, in a style that conveyed a sense of strength and protection (*Heimatschutzstil*), surrounded by nature, emphasized the idyllic search for beauty and security; but this could not solve the growing housing problems. And so a tendency in the DAF gained acceptance which envisaged, in addition to large-scale construction of settlements in the east, mass housing construction in large cities, using assembly-line methods that would be standardized and cheap.[8] Rationalization was also dominant in this area, and even more in emergency and immediate-aid programmes begun during the war because of the destruction of housing in German cities. Financing agencies (such as the Neue Heimat, taken over from the trade unions) made possible state control in this area; and such methods were, continued after 1945.

The hostility towards large cities in parts of the National Socialist movement never became a dominant influence in government policy. The large cities of central Germany, although not those with a million or more inhabitants in 1933, grew significantly during the National Socialist period. The large numbers of architects and urban planners who had begun to level parts of German cities for the purpose of constructing major thoroughfares and squares for mass assemblies before the war continued their planning after 1939. Everything 'unhealthy', even in the area of housing, was to be eliminated. In this regard, Allied bombing later helped the planners by levelling many old parts of cities. Beginning in 1943, many of these planners began to prepare for the post-war period by designing street plans and high-rise buildings without National Socialist monumental ornamentation. And more plans were made for a National Socialist welfare state as a reward for the citizens' good behaviour towards the regime.[9] In other words, those who did not conform to the desired degree were ostracized, and for many even conformity was not sufficient to enable them to continue to live as members of the 'national community'.

As late as April 1944, while planning social programmes for the post-war period, Robert Ley had the idea of extending the principle of equal pay for equal work to women, which, however, Hitler categorically rejected. Nevertheless, in certain cases, this principle was accepted after 1939, indicating the Nazis ambivalence towards it. The regime held particularly firm ideological views on the female part of the population, and sought more or less consistently to put them into practice: women were to be removed as far as possible from the working world outside the home; they were to marry and bear as many children as possible, in order to continuously enlarge the Aryan racial core group.[10] Women were intended for activities in serving, charitable, and domestic areas. The happy mother was publicly promoted as the preferred role-model through the officially sanctioned Mothers' Day and the 'Cross of Honour of the German Mother' (for four or more children) introduced in 1939. To combat mass unemployment, the NSDAP and other bodies organized campaigns against dual-income families before 1933 which aimed at the laying-off of women, who allegedly deprived men of jobs. As late as 1935–6, SA groups attempted to make this quite clear to leading men in German industry. In the civil service, women were deliberately laid off to provide jobs for men, or were placed in jobs below their professional qualifications. Only 10 per cent of university students were to be women. Although this decree was revoked in 1935, the number of women students declined faster than that of their male counterparts until 1939. In the schools it became possible to obtain a diploma in home economics. Indeed, in the training of girls and the influencing of their career choices, emphasis was placed on specifically domestic, caring areas, such as cooking or nursing. In *Mein Kampf* Hitler wrote, 'The aim of education for women must always be future motherhood'; and he never changed his opinion. There were no, women in leading positions of the National Socialist hierarchy. The Reich Women's Leader, Gertrud Scholtz-Klink, had no power in the state as a whole. Numerous incentives were introduced to support the party's family-policy goals. Generous state loans to young married couples were introduced in 1933, and they were maintained even when full employment was reached. Various new family allowances and tax breaks were created. In addition, measures to assist mothers, including holidays and household assistants, show that the regime actually intended to professionalize their desired domestic role for women.

Although the aim of this policy towards women was clearly to maximize the number of children they bore – and this tendency was reinforced by a prohibition of abortion and restrictions on the availability of contraceptives – parts of it were later retained in the quite different framework of the welfare state. But in many respects the real development of women's roles in National Socialist Germany differed considerably from the official ideal, and the reasons for this were also to be found in part in constitutive elements of National Socialist policy. On the whole, the number of working women did not decline; it rose. In 1939 2 million more women were working than in 1933. This figure amounted to 36.7 per cent as opposed to 34.4 per cent of the women of working age respectively. The attempt to redirect employment for women to social services and similar areas was unsuccessful. Instead, many women found themselves bearing the double burden of running both a household and a job outside the home.

The primary cause of this situation was the armaments boom. But after the outbreak of the war, the situation changed temporarily. Because of state support for families, many married women whose breadwinners had been called to military service stopped working for the time being. Beginning in 1938, a year of service in housekeeping or agriculture was required of all Germans, even of single women, before they began to work for a living, but this requirement was not consistently enforced at first. Beginning in 1941, in addition to half a year of labour service, half a year of service to support the war effort was required for young unmarried women, which could be performed in a state agency. In 1944, this requirement was made permanent, and it affected the general labour market, where many of these young women were already employed. Although armaments technocrats from Göring to Speer urged the introduction of such a general service requirement for women, not only mothers but also many other women were exempt. This was one reason for the use of foreign labourers in Germany. Especially in the last phase of the war, an increasing number of women became semi-voluntary Luftwaffe helpers, or worked not only in production plants but also in the service sector, in clearing away rubble, as concentration-camp wardresses and so forth, in what were considered to be normally men's jobs.

And the typical National Socialist methods of preparing women for life in adult society, too, offered girls possibilities outside the traditional woman's, role in the family. They could participate in the Union of German Girls (*Bund Deutscher Mädel*), the Reich Labour Service, the Winter Relief Programme (*Winterhilfswerk*), the National Socialist Public Welfare (*NS-Volksfürsorge*), the National Socialist Women's Organization (*NS-Frauenschaft*), or various other organizations beyond the traditional role of mother in a family, even when such activities were meant to be preparing them for what was supposedly their true feminine calling. For example, the percentage of women among German doctors rose from 6.5 per cent in 1932 to approximately 12.4 per cent in 1942, and possibly to 17 per cent in 1944.[11] In sports, in the harvest, and in the camps of National Socialist organizations, new areas also opened up for women. In spite of ideological views about the social separation of the sexes and thus specific activities for each sex, co-education was reluctantly accepted. In 1939 there were approximately 12 million women in National Socialist organizations in Germany. This fact undoubtedly reflected, in many cases, a corresponding mentality and blind faith in the Führer; but within the social framework and freedoms these women were permitted, new types of organizations for women evolved. They were hierarchical, but gave women and girls new kinds of responsibility and took them away from hearth and home. Moreover, they levelled social distinctions and privileges to an extent previously unknown in Germany, although the better-off were often able to avoid the experiences of belonging to the 'national community' resulting from membership and participation in National Socialist organizations and activities.

The 12 years of National Socialist rule in Germany were too short to permit well-founded conclusions about population policy trends, in which the losses in the war constituted the most important hiatus.[12] But the trend towards small families continued. On the whole, the number of families with many children did not increase. People did marry more frequently and earlier; at least between 1936 and 1942 women bore their first child earlier (subsequently the trend was reversed, until 1947); but on average they did not give birth to more children than earlier. The idyll of a tightly knit agrarian family offering security was the model; but because of the war and the preparations for it, because of conflicting tendencies in National Socialist preparation of individuals for life in society, it often bore little resemblance to actual developments. In the final analysis, this was also true of the return to agriculture, in accordance with the ideology of 'blood and the earth of their forefathers', which was in many instances a forced one. The percentage of the German population employed in agriculture continued to sink at a quite constant rate, while the percentage employed in industry actually increased slightly. On the whole, the percentage employed in the service sector increased rapidly, a trend that was accelerated by the war. In all sectors the number of self-employed people declined, or of family members employed in assisting another member of their family, which was the role intended for many women. The number of blue-collar workers stagnated, whereas the increase in the number of white-collar employees and civil, servants continued.

As far as the development of ecological awareness goes, the National Socialist period was marked by conflicting trends. In the area of industrial and other kinds of production no thought was given to limiting pollutants. But the very ideology of 'blood and the earth of the forefathers' was based on the cyclical model of the seasons and the succession of generations, and these ideas formed the basis for the first policies to regulate cultivation, the use of organic fertilizers (although artificial fertilizer was not frowned upon), and other such matters. However, because of the war the shortage of such fertilizers led to a completely unecological exhaustion of the soil. But even before the war, bottlenecks in raw materials essential to war preparations had led to the first recycling programmes. The efforts to achieve an autarchic economy in particular, strongly supported as they were by official propaganda and effectively carried out through National Socialist organizations, reminded Germans of the limitations of their own resources and the necessity of recycling; and it was not until the 1950s, with the development of an affluent, throw-away society in Germany, that these supposed relics of National Socialism and times of dire need were put aside. Recycling in Germany was an obvious result of the National Socialist economy of scarcity; the fact that the mortal remains and the belongings of the victims of mass murder in the concentration camps, from gold teeth to hair and shoes, were also included in that effort shows the extremes to which recycling as well as the policy of annihilation was taken. All positive social measures regulated and militarized in many respects the desired 'national community' and discriminated against ostracized persons and groups, often with deadly consequences. And this was occasionally justified by the regime, which pointed out the contributions such discrimination could make to the war economy.

This was especially true of urban planning. Such planning on a small scale had been carried out since the turn of the century. But only in 1935 was a Reich agency created, against the opposition of other bureaucracies, that asked more basic questions beyond urban and settlement planning: 'How can the best possible distribution of population in a given space be achieved? What is the most suitable use possible of available space?'[13] Within the frontiers of Germany before 1938, because of the war, the development of answers to these questions never went beyond initial planning, but after the war 'impact analyses' of the previous decade were useful in formulating industrial zoning policies. This represented a new degree of planning professionalism, but, in co-operation with state authorities, the expectation and, to a small degree, realization of colonization plans in the east offered an opportunity for developing a 'population economy', which grew as a field of study at German universities during the war into an enormous area of activity. Formulas were devised to determine the optimum population and food-production potential for a given area, which had very real consequences in the conclusion that optimum population in relation to available, or potential food resources could be achieved only by reducing the number of people or their standard of living. It is now clear that such figures could not be calculated with any degree of precision and that such efforts were based on a racist policy of ostracization. Working with these principles, 'population economists' determined for Göring the optimum number of Jews to be expelled from a given area. With the occupation of Poland and then parts of the Soviet Union, these 'experts' were given a deadly opportunity to experiment with the future form of society as a whole. From their purely technocratic point of view, 'excess population' (such as that in the Soviet

Union) could either be expelled (beyond the Urals, for instance) or permitted to starve, or killed outright. This was the particular framework within which National Socialist policy was carried out. It was an unrestrained passion for organizing and planning rather than simple opportunism which motivated one of the rising planners of the early 1930s (and, later, of the 1950s), Professor Konrad Meyer (-Hetling), who, as Director of the Main Department of Planning and Land Use of the RKF, was in charge of drawing up, editing, and revising the General Plan East. His was not an isolated case, and is one example of the potentially murderous organization and planning involved in the policy of ostracization.

This was also true of domestic policy: as the National Socialists understood the term, creating a 'good' society with beautiful human beings also meant promoting health, healing illness wherever possible, and destroying what could not be corrected or healed. From this point of view hygiene and biology became areas requiring organization and planning. A 1938 German propaganda film showed how insects that had infested a grain silo could be exterminated effectively and with few or no negative consequences: the silo was made air-tight, Zyklon B, a pesticide produced by I. G. Farben, was introduced into it, and after a short time the pests were dead and, the silo could be put back into use. In the same way, it was possible to promote attractive, clean work-places. And when buses with drawn curtains drove from factory to factory, it was assumed at the time that their task was to carry out mass examinations for the early diagnosis of illnesses such as cancer. Somewhat later buses with a similar appearance were used to transport human beings to places where they were killed in keeping with the policy of euthanasia.

Preventive medicine was accelerated. In an exaggerated sense, such medicine became at the same time an important part of new social policy. But preventive medicine was also the main concern of a new science, that of 'race hygiene', which had been developing within and beyond Germany since the last decades of the nineteenth century.[14] This was an interdisciplinary science in which psychiatrists, biologists, geneticists, and medical specialists worked together. But in the National Socialist period the new kind of 'race hygiene' crossed the threshold of inhibitions against the killing of human beings, who became guinea-pigs for all kinds of experiments, from research on twins (in itself a respectable activity under normal circumstances) to vivisection. In some cases, experiments were carried out for the sake of research, and it is probable that in these special conditions they even produced some knowledge of lasting value. But the methods were often unethical and the premises or conclusions questionable.

One assumption was that, if hereditary diseases could be diagnosed more precisely, it would be possible to prevent them in the long term. This approach had long been advocated by many psychiatrists who emphasized the assumed hereditary nature of some mental disorders, and who were supported by a broad political consensus extending even as far as the political left. In 1932 in Prussia, which was governed by Social Democrats, this assumption led to the introduction of a bill that, with only a few changes, was promulgated throughout Germany on 14 July 1933 as a law to prevent offspring afflicted with hereditary diseases. It involved the use of sterilization to prevent an entire group of diseases, from schizophrenia to feeble-mindedness, hereditary blindness, and even chronic alcoholism. It was obvious that the last-mentioned disease was actually a social problem, and the hereditary nature of other diseases was never proved. This approach was already outside the framework of traditional science, but it permitted those who practised it to claim to be engaged in scientific pursuits, a claim which was believed by outsiders. Since the beginning of the world depression, considerations of the cost of psychiatric institutions had also become important. Racial ideas, too, were a continued legacy of the past. There was, for example, a broad consensus that the children of German mothers and Black French occupation soldiers in the 1920s, the so-called 'Rhineland bastards', should be the first candidates for sterilization.

The sterilization of those suffering from or carrying hereditary diseases began on a large scale with scientific expert opinions and the creation of 'genetic health courts' (*Erbgesundheitsgerichte*) in 1934. By 1945, this programme had led to the sterilization of some 360,000 people. What in 1932 in Prussia still required the consent of those affected was made a measure that could be carried out against their will in 1933, a fundamental difference for such a serious infringement of personal liberty. Not only psychiatric institutions but many hospitals too participated in the programme. In accordance with National Socialist principles, doctors were given a new agenda: medicine became an élite science with the public task of 'maintaining and correcting the genetic health of the German race'. Doctors were to become 'bio-political block wardens' in the service of public health.[15] Approximately 45 per cent of German doctors joined the NSDAP, a higher percentage than in most other professions, but not all of them had to accept being assigned such a role.

The dynamic competition of various agencies and authorities in the regime played an especially significant role in the expansion and radicalization of the legal requirements for proceeding with new sterilization and health policies. But the co-operation of the Reich Committee for Questions of Genetic Health (*Reichsausschuss für Erbgesundheitsfragen*), whose members were mostly doctors, with the Party Chancellery of the Führer led to Hitler's personal order concerning euthanasia in the National Socialist sense of the term: primarily that of the annihilation of 'forms of life not deserving to live' (*lebensunwertes Leben*), rather than the giving of active assistance to dying persons in terminating their own lives. Such measures had also long been discussed among the general public and among experts, but for the first time it now led to the killing of human beings, 60,000 to 70,000 of them by 1941. The killing of handicapped or deformed children had begun earlier, resulting in approximately 5,000 deaths. The killing of adults, most of them patients in mental institutions from Munich-Haar to Hadamar, and from Brandenburg to Hartheim near Linz, was carried out within the framework of 'Action T4' (named after the seat of the office responsible at Tiergarten Street 4 in Berlin) until 1941. But this 'social measure' did not take place in public and was largely kept secret. The relatives of the victims subsequently received uniform letters; although many were horrified, several of them expressly supported the killing of their seriously handicapped relatives.

In August 1941, after protests from Catholics and Protestants, the action was officially stopped, but it continued to be carried out in certain areas, although not on a large scale. The murder of 'useless beings' (*Ballastexistenzen*) employed a large circle of recognized psychiatric experts, who in some cases thoughtlessly pronounced death verdicts that went far beyond the restraints set by earlier criteria. One reason for taking this course was in order to increase the capacity of crowded institutions for psychiatric cases considered to be curable. This was the starting-point for the new psychiatry.

Not the least reason for killing those considered to be incurable was their potential use for the purposes of medical research. Mass experiments which were intended to kill, or which accepted the deaths of subjects as part of the cost of scientific research, promised to increase the chances of curing or preventing mental illness in the population as a whole. Doctors wished to arrive at accurate medical diagnoses of hereditary diseases; but as well as this, there was a tendency to experiment to the point of death simply because it was permitted, whether on socially ostracized people, confined to psychiatric institutions, or simply on certain prisoners of war. Finally, during the war the greater number of beds needed for those who could be healed, such as wounded soldiers, was occasionally used as a justification for 'euthanasia'. Under these conditions a policy of ostracization developed which declared all 'foreign' people, or those not considered sufficiently fit, to be racially undesirable. The next step, killing such people, was easily taken.

More specifically, the increasingly perfected mechanics of killing, from injections to the use of stationary or mobile gas chambers, were developed in the euthanasia programme. The personnel of the Final Solution – of mass murder as a highly organized process – were largely recruited from the T4 operation. In occupied Poland, the special operations groups conducted a radical form of euthanasia in 1939–40 by shooting all the patients of psychiatric institutions. Not the least common characteristic connecting the euthanasia programme and the Final Solution was the fact that doctors in the concentration camps practised an inhumane medicine on inmates by using them as guinea-pigs for race hygiene experiments, experiments with pathogenic agents, or experiments in which the victims were subjected to extreme physiological or psychological stress. Some of these experiments did yield knowledge otherwise unobtainable at the time; but the majority involved absurd hypotheses, and a criminal delight in experimentation as an end in itself which had only a superficial connection with scientific criteria. However, as far as the victims were concerned, those people who had been ostracized for various reasons from the 'national community', the new aspect of these experiments was that inhibitions against killing were discarded without any scruples in the name of what claimed to be science, and in many respects the results were considered to be contributions to the future health and healing possibilities within the 'national community'. Mass murder became possible for quite different reasons, but it was also carried out in the spirit of modern scientific motivation, knowledge, and planning for the presumed needs of the 'national community'. The basic premise was that it was permissible to sacrifice the life – or, at the very least, the dignity – of the individual in the service of the nation as a whole.

During the National Socialist period such approaches in one form or another (such as a penal law commission in 1933) affected most sciences which set themselves the goal of 'eliminating the incorrigible enemies of the nation'. These tendencies were not, of course, part of science in themselves; rather, they were certain exaggerated ideas about the importance of knowledge to be gained through scientific research. Such ideas dominated the thinking of certain scientists. They allegedly served to increase human knowledge, and they exercised an effective, formative influence within the framework of National Socialist policies. They had existed earlier; but, in view of the total deprivation of rights of the individual under National Socialism, and its rejection of any legal restraints, they became a predominant influence in the years after 1933. This development depended not only on the career opportunism of young, successful people or established functionaries; even more important was the conviction of the participants that they were collaborating under ideal conditions in pioneering projects based on radical ideas.

Technicians and engineers were given undreamt-of chances during the National Socialist period, and this was all the more true of technicians and engineers in social fields, whose task it was to produce long-term plans for the development of society, and who wanted and were permitted to produce such plans. The 'national community', providing optimal care for its members, was an elastic and variously interpretable concept. In the process of ostracizing and exterminating its enemies, superficial arguments of scientific causality were transferred to social relationships and applied in practice, although the main aims of such actions were often political.

German society in the National Socialist period developed in a continuity of trends and mentalities, some of which had existed for generations and which were developed under National Socialist rule with deadly consistency to undreamt-of effectiveness. This was true of the murder operations actually carried out by 1945, including genocide; but it was also true of the many plans for the time after final victory had been achieved. The circle closes: the Führer state, centred around and essentially directed by Adolf Hitler, not only released enormous dynamism; within it, the readiness to sacrifice one's own life was accepted, to die in war for what was considered the 'good cause' in order to help achieve the victory of the 'beautiful' and the 'good', as National Socialists understood those terms. Not only did Hitler bring destruction and death to most of Europe; beyond the military events themselves he also initiated a planned and annihilating political and ethnic reshaping of Europe, of which the murder of a large part of European Jewry was the most conspicuous but by no means the only aspect. It was a return to behaviour previously considered barbaric, but it made use of the instruments of an industrial mass society which until then had been considered progressive and modern. From Hitler's political leadership to broad areas of German society, it was also an extreme development of the cult of the feasible itself, of the uncritical admiration of technical and organizational achievement and the belief, especially with regard to technology, that because something can be done, it should be done. The readiness to kill and to die was an important internal component of the developing 'national community'. War and mass murder were its central external aspects. Here traditional ethics and morality were turned inside out; National Socialist ideology had its own ethical claims. National Socialist aesthetics, too, which often elevated kitsch to a public standard, nevertheless enjoyed broad acceptance. The subjecting of ethics and aesthetics to a racially ideological transformation, and their appearance as political goals of National Socialism intended to eliminate previous social conflicts in the new 'national community', was new. Life in Germany was to be made more beautiful, even if the world were reduced to rubble in the process.

The way to this situation was a product of German history, but it led to qualitatively new crimes which cannot be explained solely in terms of that history. It was a break with what Western civilization had represented until that time. But it was only possible because ideas and instruments developed within that civilization were brought together in a new destructive quality and then unleashed. Although the basic conditions in which the National Socialist dictatorship developed were unique, the problems of the possibilities and dangers of technocratic development as an end in itself, and the reduction of human beings to its mere objects, were not limited to National Socialist Germany.

Notes

Chapter 1

1. Election results according to Eberhard Kolb, *The Weimar Republic* (London, 1988), 16-17.
2. On the foll. see in addition to Jürgen Falter, *Hitlers Wähler* (Munich, 1991); Michael H. Kater, *The Nazi Party: A Social Profile of Members and Leaders, 1919–1945* (Cambridge, Mass., 1983) and esp. Thomas Childers, *The Nazi Voter* (Chapel Hill, 1983).
3. Ibid., 264.
4. Quoted in Martin Broszat, *Die Machtergreifung: Der Aufstieg der NSDAP und die Zerstörung der Weimarer Republik* (Munich, 1984) 107.
5. Max Domarus (ed.), *Hitler: Reden und Proklamationen 1932–1945* (2 vols., Munich, 1965), 101.
6. Ibid., 88, foll. quote, 89.
7. Joseph Goebbels, *Die Tagebücher von Joseph Goebbels*, I: *Aufzeichnungen 1924–1941*, ed. Elke Fröhlich (4 vols., Munich, 1987), I, vol. 2, 9 (18 Jan. 1931).
8. Albrecht Tyrell (ed.), *Führer befiehl! Selbstzeugnisse aus der Kampfzeit der NSDAP: Dokumentation und Analyse* (Düsseldorf, 1969), 163, (foll. quote, 173).
9. Most recently, Martin Broszat and Klaus Schwabe (eds), *Die deutschen Eliten und der Weg in den Zweiten Weltkrieg* (Munich, 1989), 66.
10. Ian Kershaw, *The 'Hitler Myth': Image and Reality in the Third Reich* (Oxford, 1989), 13–47, foll. quotes; Goebbels, *Tagebücher*, I. i. (14 Oct. 1925 and 19 Apr. 1926).
11. Jochen Thies, *Architekt der Weltherrschaft: Die 'Endziele' Hitlers* (3rd edn., Düsseldorf, 1980), 56.
12. Domarus, *Hitler*, 62, foll. quote from Goebbels, *Tagebücher*, I. ii. 211.
13. Kolb, *Weimar Republic*, 120.
14. Heinrich August Winkler, *Der Weg in die Katastrophe* (Berlin and Bonn, 1987), 681.
15. Karl-Dietrich Erdmann *et al* (eds), *Akten der Reichskanzlei: Weimarer Republik (1918–1933)* (20 vols., Boppard, 1968–89), see Das Kabinett von Papen, docs. 132, 135, quote 173.
16. Erdmann *et al.*, see Das Kabinett von Schleicher, 101–17.

17. Hagen Schulze, *Weimar. Deutschland 1917–1933* (Berlin, 1982), 392.
18. Goebbels, *Tagebücher*, I. ii. 332 (10 Jan. 1933).
19. Wolfgang Michalka (ed.), *Das Dritte Reich* (2 vols., Munich, 1985), i. 15.

Chapter 2

1. Michalka, *Das Dritte Reich,* i. 27 (Liebmann notes); Konrad Repgen and Hans Booms (eds), *Akten der Reichskanzlei: Regierung Hitler 1933–1938* (2 vols., Boppard, 1983), i. doc. 180, 680 (6 July 1933); doc. 1, 2.
2. Josef Becker and Ruth Becker (eds), *Hitlers Machtergreifung* (Munich, 1983), doc. 19, 52.
3. Ibid., docs. 24, 25, 57–61
4. Domarus, *Hitler,* 264.
5. Becker, *Hitlers Machtergreifung,* docs. 4, 7. See also docs. 5, 32–34, and 17, 45.
6. Hans-Ulrich Thamer, *Verführung und Gewalt: Deutschland 1933–1945* (Berlin, 1986), 243; Becker *Hitlers Machtergreifung,* docs. 42, 74, 75 (17 Feb.) and 78 (3 Mar.)
7. Repgen and Booms, *Akten der Reichskanzlei,* i. docs. 34, 35, A7; *Reichsgesetzblatt* (Berlin, 1933), i. 35.
8. Goebbels, *Tagebücher*, I. ii. 383; foll. quote, *Reichsgesetzblatt*, 83.
9. Herbert Michaelis and Ernst Schraepler (eds), *Ursachen und Folgen: Vom deutschen Zusammenbruch 1918 und 1945 bis zur staatlichen Neuordnung Deutschlands in der Gegenwart. Eine Urkunden- und Dokumentensammlung zur Zeitgeschichte* (vols. ix–xxiii, Berlin, 1964–75), ix. 145–7.
10. Becker, *Hitlers Machtergreifung,* doc. 260, 309.
11. Becker, *Hitlers Machtergreifung,* doc. 337, 378; foll. quote, Repgen and Booms, *Akten der Reichskanzlei,* i. docs. 180, 629–36 (629, 631); Goebbels, *Tagebücher*, I. ii. 426 (4 June 1933).
12. Winkler, *Der Weg,* (chapter 1, n.14) 895.
13. Goebbels, *Tagebücher*, I. ii. 403.
14. Repgen and Booms, *Akten der Reichskanzlei,* i. doc. 93, 321, n. 33; Thamer, *Verführung,* 294.
15. Goebbels, *Tagebücher,* I. ii. 403.
16. The 'Gau' was the highest National Socialist party organization unit below the national level after the Nazis took power in 1933, and unofficially even earlier. In Nov. 1941 there were some 43 Gau, plus an organization for party members abroad.
17. Repgen and Booms, *Akten der Reichskanzlei,,* i. doc. 320, 1199 (22 Mar. 1934).
18. Ibid., doc. 372, 1347; cf. Dieter Rebentisch, *Führerstaat und Verwaltung im Zweiten Weltkrieg: Verfassungsentwicklung und Verwaltungspolitik im sogenannten Altreich 1939–1943* (Munich, 1989), 233.
19. Gottfried Feder, *Das Programm der NSDAP und seine weltanschaulichen Grundlagen* (1927), 81st–90th repr. (Munich, 1932), 31, 46, 48.
20. David Schoenbaum, *Hitler's Social Revolution: Class and Status in Nazi Germany 1933–1945* (London, 1967), 143.
21. According to Gunther Mai, 'Die nationalsozialistische Betriebszellenorganisation', *Vierteljahrshefte für Zeitgeschichte,* 31 (1983), 594; foll. quote, Martin Broszat, *Hitler's State: The Foundation and Development of the Internal Structure of the Third Reich* (London, 1981), 2; Karl Dietrich Bracher, Wolfgang Sauer, and Günther Schulz, *Die nationalsozialistische Machtergreifung: Studien zur Errichtung des totalitären Herrschaftssystems in Deutschland 1933/34* (2nd

edn. Cologne, 1962), 321 and 333; Hans Mommsen and Susanne Willems (eds), *Herrschaftsalltag im Dritten Reich: Studien und Texte* (Düsseldorf, 1988), 160.

22. The foll. is based on Mathilde Jamin, 'Zur Rolle der SA im nationalsozialistischen Herrschaftssystem', in Gerhard Hirschfeld and Lothar Kettenacker (eds), *Der 'Führerstaat': Mythos und Realität. Studien zur Struktur und Politik des Dritten Reiches* (Stuttgart, 1981), 329–60 (337, 342).
23. Michalka, *Das Dritte Reich*, i. 41–3, including the foll. quote.
24. Klaus-Jürgen Müller, *Armee und Drittes Reich, 1933–1939* (Paderborn, 1987), doc. 57, 192–5 (195).
25. Thamer, *Verführung*, 327.
26. Michalka, *Das Dritte Reich*, i. doc. 40, 54, on the foll., doc. 41; Kershaw, *'Hitler Myth'*, 83–95, 77.
27. Otto Groehler, 'Das Revirement der Wehrmachtführung 1937/38', in Dieter Eichholtz and Kurt Pätzold (eds), *Der Weg in den Krieg* (Berlin and Cologne, 1989), 113–49 (113).

Chapter 3

1. Michalka, *Das Dritte Reich*, i. 23–4.
2. Günter Wollstein, 'Eine Denkschrift des Staatssekretärs Bernhard Wilhelm von Bülow vom März 1933', *Militärgeschichtliche Mitteilungen*, 13 (1973), 83–94.
3. Michalka, *Das Dritte Reich*, i. doc. 198, 261–5 (261).
4. Josef Henke, *England in Hitlers politischem Kalkül* (Boppard, 1973).
5. The foll. is based largely on Wilhelm Deist, 'The Rearmament of the Wehrmacht', in *Germany and the Second World War* (Oxford, 1990) i. *The Build-up of German Aggression*, 373–540.
6. Müller, *Armee und Drittes Reich*, doc. 140, 303–4.
7. *Documents on German Foreign Policy 1918-1945*, Series C, *The Third Reich: First Phase*, 1933–7 (6 vols., Washington, US Government Printing Office; London, Her Majesty's Stationary Office, 1957–83) i. doc. 16; Repgen and Booms, *Akten der Reichskanzlei*, i. doc. 17, 51.
8. Quoted in Volkmann, 'The National Socialist Economy in Preparation for War', in *Germany and the Second World War* (Oxford, 1990) i. 233.
9. Hans Jürgen Schröder, 'Südosteuropa als "Informal Empire" Deutschlands', *Jahrbuch für die Geschichte Osteuropas*, 23 (1975), 70–96.
10. The foll. figures are based largely on Volkmann, 'The National Socialist Economy', 251–8.
11. Dietmar Petzina, *Autarkiepolitik im Dritten Reich: Der nationalsozialistische Vierjahresplan* (Stuttgart, 1968), 34 (15 Mar. 1936).
12. Wilhelm Treue (ed.), 'Hitlers Denkschrift zum Vierjahresplan 1936', *Vierteljahrshefte für Zeitgeschichte*, 3 (1955), 184–210.
13. Volkmann, 'The National Socialist Economy', 356–7.

Chapter 4

1. Goebbels, *Tagebücher*, I. ii. 410 (22 Apr. 1933).
2. Domarus, *Hitler*, 1877.
3. *Der Parteitag der Freiheit* (Munich, 1935), 287 (16 Sept. 1935); Rudolph Binion, *Hitler Among the Germans* (DeKalb, Ill., 1984), p. xix (13 Sept. 1936).
4. Gottfried Benn, 'Züchtungen I' (1933), in *Gesammelte Werke* (Wiesbaden, 1968), iii. 776–7; Josef Becker, *Hitlers Machtergreifung*, 283–4 (3 May 1933).

5. Lothar Kettenacker, 'Sozial-psychologische Aspekte der Führerherrschaft', in Hirschfeld and Kettenacker, *'Führerstaat'*, 98–132 (114); Ansgar Diller, *Rundfunkpolitik im Dritten Reich* (Munich, 1980), 159; Reinhold Merker, *Die Bildenden Künste im Nationalsozialismus* (Cologne, 1983), 262 (Hoyer), 261 (Erler).

6. *Adolf Hitler: Bilder aus dem Leben des Führers,* publ. Cigaretten-Bilderdienst (Altona-Bahrenfeld, 1936), 5 (Göring), 7 (Goebbels).

7. Albert Speer, *Inside the Third Reich* (New York, 1970), 65.

8. Jutta Lambrecht, 'Nicht jede Musik paßt für jeden ... Anmerkungen zur Musik', in Bazon Brock and Achim Preiß (eds), *Kunst auf Befehl* (Munich, 1990), 154.

9. Kater, *Nazi Party*, 200; additional figures in Karl Dietrich Bracher, *The German Dictatorship: Origins, Structures and Consequences of National Socialism* (New York and Washington, 1970).

10. Kershaw, *The 'Hitler Myth'*, 100–1.

11. Peter Hüttenberger, *Die Gauleiter* (Stuttgart, 1969); Dietrich Orlow, *The History of the Nazi Party* (2 vols., Pittsburgh, 1969, 1973) ii. 55 ff.; on Bürckel, cf. Hans Fenske, 'Joseph Bürckel', in Dieter Rebentisch and Karl Teppe (eds), *Verwaltung contra Menschenführung im Staat Hitlers: Studien zum politisch- administrativen System* (Göttingen, 1986), 153–172.

12. Franz W. Seidler, *Fritz Todt: Baumeister des Dritten Reichs* (Munich, 1986) and 'Fritz Todt: From Motorway Builder to Minister of State', in Ronald Smelser and Rainer Zitelmann (eds), *The Nazi Elite* (New York, 1993), 245–56, with other short biographies, esp. Corni on Darré, Dülffer on Speer, Fröhlich on Goebbels, Kube on Göring; Karl Heinz Ludwig, *Technik und Ingenieure im Dritten Reich* (Düsseldorf, 1974).

13. Timothy Mason, *Arbeiterklasse und Volksgemeinschaft: Dokumente und Materialien zur deutschen Arbeiterpolitik 1936–1939* (Opladen, 1975), doc. 152, 908–33 (916), and *Social Policy in the Third Reich: The Working Class and the National Community* (Providence, RI, 1993).

14. Ronald Smelser, *Robert Ley: Hitler's Labor Front Leader* (Hamburg, 1988), 155, 161.

15. *Das Deutsche Führerlexikon 1934/35* (Berlin, 1934), 26; the foll. quote according to Horst Gies, 'Die Rolle des Reichsnährstands im nationalsozialistischen Herrschaftssystem', in Hirschfeld and Kettenacker, *'Führerstaat'*, 293, 278 (figs. for 1944).

16. Alfred Kube, *Pour le mérite und Hakenkreuz* (2nd edn., Munich, 1987); Stefan Martens, *Hermann Göring: "erster Paladin des Führers" und "zweiter Mann im Reich"* (Paderborn, 1985).

17. Bernd Wegner, *Hitlers politische Soldaten: Die Waffen-SS 1933–1945* (3rd edn. Paderborn, 1988), fig. 81, quote 111.

18. Goebbels, *Tagebücher,* I. iv. 39 (10 Feb. 1940).

19. Jost Dülffer, Jochen Thies, and Josef Henke (eds), *Hitlers Städte: Baupolitik im Dritten Reich. Eine Dokumentation* (Cologne and Vienna, 1978), quotes 30, 297.

20. Michaelis and Schraepler, *Ursachen und Folgen*, xi. 138–9 (2 Nov. 1938).

21. Jay W. Baird, *To Die for Germany* (Bloomington, Ind., 1990); Volker Ackermann, *Nationale Totenfeiern in Deutschland von Wilhelm I. bis Franz Josef Strauss: eine Studie zur politischen Semiotik* (Stuttgart, 1990); Sabine Behrenbeck, *Der Kult um die toten Helden im Nationalsozialismus: Nationalsozialistische Mythen, Riten und Symbole* (Vierow, 1995).

22. Peter Stachura, 'Das Dritte Reich und Jugenderziehung: Die Rolle der Hitler Jugend 1933–1939', in Manfred Heinemann (ed.), *Erziehung und Schulung im Dritten Reich* (Stuttgart, 1976), i. 90–112 (99).

23. Michalka, *Das Dritte Reich,* i. 261–2.

Chapter 5

1. Michaelis and Schraepler, *Ursachen und Folgen*, xix. 71–86 (85: 4 Oct. 1942).
2. Ibid., xiii. 19–21 (21–30 Jan. 1939). Cf. also Andreas Hillgruber, 'Der Ostkrieg und die Judenvernichtung', in Gerd Ueberschär and Wolfram Wette (eds), *"Unternehmen Barbarossa"* (Paderborn, 1984), 219–36.
3. *Documents on German Foreign Policy 1918–1945*, Ser. D, 1937–1941 (14 vols., Washington, US Government Printing Office; London, HMSO, 1949–1976) viii. *The War Years,* 4 Sept. 1938–18 May 1940, doc. 157.
4. Walther Hubatsch (ed.), *Hitlers Weisungen für die Kriegführung 1939–1945* (Koblenz, 1962), 32–3 (memo. of 9 Oct. 1939).
5. Dülffer, Thies, and Henke, *Hitlers Städte,* 36 (facsimile); on the foll., Bernd Martin, *Friedensinitiativen und Machtpolitik im Zweiten Weltkrieg 1939–1942* (Düsseldorf, 1974), 234–336.
6. Michalka, *Das Dritte Reich,* ii. doc. 23, 49–50.
7. Franz Halder, *Kriegstagebuch,* ed. Hans-Adolf Jacobsen (3 vols., Stuttgart, 1962–4), ii. 49 (31 July 1940).
8. Ibid., iii. 38 (3 July 1941).
9. *Akten zur deutschen auswärtigen Politik 1918–1945*, Ser. D, 1937–1941, (13 vols., Baden-Baden, Frankfurt on Main, Bonn and Göttingen, 1950–1970) xiii. App. II, 829–34 (829). Cf. also Andreas Hillgruber, *Der Zweite Weltkrieg. Kriegsziele und Strategie der großen Mächte* (5th edn., Stuttgart and Berlin, 1989), 70–7.
10. Speer, *Inside the Third Reich,* 440; Domarus, *Hitler,* 2236–9 (2237).
11. Wolfgang Michalka, 'Das Dritte Reich', in M. Vogt (ed.), *Deutsche Geschichte* (2nd edn., Stuttgart, 1991), 646–727 (670, facsimile).
12. According to Hermann Weber, 'Die Ambivalenz der kommunistischen Widerstandsstrategie bis zur "Brüssler" Parteikonferenz', in Jürgen Schmädeke and Peter Steinbach (eds), *Der Widerstand gegen den Nationalsozialismus: Die deutsche Gesellschaft und der Widerstand gegen Hitler* (Munich and Zurich, 1985), 73–85 (78, 84).
13. Herman Graml, *Anti-Semitism in the Third Reich* (Oxford, 1992), 103. Concerning the faith Jews had in law, cf. Dirk Blasius, 'Zwischen Rechtsvertrauen und Rechtszerstörung', in Dirk Blasius and Dan Diner (eds), *Zerbrochene Geschichte* (Frankfurt on Main, 1991), 121–37.
14. Avraham Barkai, ' "Schicksalsjahr 1938". Kontinuität und Verschärfung der wirtschaftlichen Auspünderung der deutschen Juden', in Ursula Büttner (ed.), *Das Unrechtsregime. Internationale Forschung über den Nationalsozialismus: Festschrift für Werner Jochmann zum 65. Geburtstag* (2 vols., Hamburg, 1986) ii. 45–68 (47).
15. Lothar Gruchmann, *Justiz im Dritten Reich 1930–1940: Anpassung und Unterwerfung in der Ära Gürtner* (2nd edn., Munich, 1990), summarized in Gruchmann, 'Rechtssystem und nationalsozialistische Judenpolitik', in Martin Broszat and Horst Müller (eds), *Das Dritte Reich. Herrschaftsstruktur und Geschichte: Vorträge aus dem Institut für Zeitgeschichte* (Munich, 1983), 83–103.
16. Manfred Messerschmidt and Franz Wüllner, *Die Wehrmachtjustiz im Dienste des Nationalsozialismus: Zerstörung einer Legende* (Baden-Baden, 1987), 84, 307.
17. Martin Broszat, 'The Concentration Camps', in Martin Broszat, Hans Buchheim, Hans-Adolf Jacobsen, and Hermann Krausnick, *Anatomy of the SS State* (London, 1968), 397–497.

18. Hermann Krausnick and Hans-Heinrich Wilhelm, *Die Truppe des Weltan-schauungskrieges: Die Einsatzgruppen der Sicherheitspolizei und des SD 1938–1942* (Stuttgart, 1981), 13 ff.; Krausnick's part also as *Hitlers Einsatz-gruppen: Die Truppen des Weltanschauungskrieges 1938–1942* (Frankfurt on Main, 1985).

19. Hans Umbreit, *Deutsche Militärverwaltungen 1938/39* (Stuttgart, 1967); for an overview, cf. Umbreit, 'Besatzungsverwaltungen', in Wolfgang Michalka (ed.), *Der Zweite Weltkrieg: Analysen, Grundprobleme, Forschungsbilanz* (Munich, 1989), 710–28, and 'Auf dem Weg zur Kontinentalherrschaft', in Horst Boog *et al.*, *Organisation und Mobilisierung des deutschen Machtbereichs, Kriegsver-waltung, Wirtschaft und personelle Resourcen 1939–1941, in Das Deutsche Reich und der Zweite Weltkrieg*, ed. Militärgeschichtliches Forschungsamt (10 vols. projected, Stuttgart, 1979–1990), v.1, 3–345.

20. Dietrich Wolfanger, *Die nationalsozialistische Politik in Lothringen 1940–1945* (diss. Univ. of Saarbrücken, 1977), 45 (25 Sept. 1940, memo by Stuckart). On the foll., cf. Werner Jochmann (ed.), *Adolf Hitler, Monologe: Aufzeichnungen Heinrich Heims* (Hamburg, 1980), 51 (1–2 Aug. 1941).

21. Wegner, *Hitlers politische Soldaten*, 210, 290–1; Hans Buchheim, 'Command and Compliance', in Broszat *et al.* (eds), *Anatomy of the SS State*, 303–90; Ruth Bettina Birn, *Die Höheren SS- und Polizeiführer: Himmlers Stellvertreter im Reich und in den besetzten Gebieten* (Düsseldorf, 1986).

22. Jost Dülffer, *Weimar, Hitler und die Marine* (Düsseldorf, 1973), 547 (22 Jan. 1938); on the foll., Hans Umbreit, 'Auf dem Weg zur Kontinentalherrschaft' (cf. n. 19 above), 265; Dietrich Eichholtz, *Geschichte der deutschen Kriegswirtschaft 1939–1945* (2 vols., East Berlin, 1969, 1985) ii. 459 (25 July 1944).

23. Götz Aly and Susanne Heim, *Vordenker der Vernichtung: Auschwitz und die deutschen Pläne für eine europäische Ordnung* (Hamburg, 1991), 153, 45, 160.

24. Cf. Norbert Müller, (ed.), *Die zeitweilig besetzten Gebiete der Sowjetunion (1941–1944), in Europa unter dem Hakenkreuz: Die Okkupationspolitik des deutschen Faschismus (1938–1945)* (8 vols. and supplements, Berlin, 1990–1991 and Berlin and Heidelberg, 1992–1994) v. doc. 19, 160–4. Cf. also Czesław Madajczyk, *Die Okkupationspolitik Nazideutschlands in Polen 1939–1945* (Berlin and Cologne, 1988) 86 ff.; Eichholtz, *Geschichte der deut-schen Kriegswirtschaft*, ii. 439; Rolf Dieter Müller, *Hitlers Ostkrieg und die deutsche Siedlungspolitik* (Frankfurt on Main, 1991); Michalka, *Das Dritte Reich*, ii. 199–200, 228 ff. (Himmler, 3 Aug. 1944).

25. Ulrich Herbert, *Fremdarbeiter: Politik und Praxis des "Ausländer-Einsatzes" in der Kriegswirtschaft des Dritten Reiches* (Berlin and Bonn, 1985); the foll. figures according to Herbert (ed.), *Europa und der 'Reichseinsatz': Ausländische Zivilarbeiter, Kriegsgefangene und KZ-Häftlinge in Deutschland 1938–1945* (Essen, 1991). On labour requirements in 1939, cf. Dülffer, *Hitler, Weimar und die Marine*, 508.

26. Werner Röhl (ed.), *Polen (1939–1945), in Europa unter dem Hakenkreuz*, ii. doc. 43, 152; doc. 45, 153–4; Czesław Łuczak, 'Polnische Arbeiter im national-sozialistischen Deutschland während des Zweiten Weltkriegs' (90–105) and Yves Duvand, 'Vichy und der "Reichseinsatz"' (184–199), in Herbert (ed.), *Europa und der 'Reichseinsatz'*.

27. Michalka, *Das Dritte Reich*, ii. doc. 28, 174; Christian Streit, *Keine Kamraden: Die Wehrmacht und die sowjetischen Kriegsgefangenen 1941–1945* (Bonn, 1991).

28. Herbert (ed.), *Europa und der 'Reichseinsatz'*, 8; for a higher estimate, Eichholtz, *Geschichte*, ii. 246–7. Eichholtz also gives a figure of 8.1 M foreign workers in

the area of Rosenberg's Ministry for the Occupied Eastern Territories as of mid–1943.

29. Wolfgang Jacobmeyer, *Vom Zwangsarbeiter zum heimatlosen Ausländer* (Göttingen, 1985).

30. Broszat, 'Concentration Camps', 465–6.

31. Albert Speer, *The Slave State: Heinrich Himmler's Master Plan for SS Supremacy* (London, 1981).

32. Hermann Krausnick, 'Denkschrift Himmlers', *Vierteljahrshefte für Zeitgeschichte,* 5 (1957), 194–8 (197); foll. quote in Röhl, (ed.), *Polen in Europa unter dem Hakenkreuz,* ii. doc. 26, 134 (SD-Einsatzkommando 16, 20 Oct. 1939).

33. The best summary is in Eberhard Jäckel and Jürgen Rohwer (eds), *Der Mord an den Juden im Zweiten Weltkrieg: Entschlußbildung und Verwirklichung* (Stuttgart, 1985). Cf. also Uwe Dietrich Adam, *Judenpolitik im Dritten Reich* (2nd edn., Königstein, 1979), including (233) the quote from *Mein Kampf;* Raoul Hilberg, *The Destruction of the European Jews* (rev. edn., 3 vols., New York and London, 1985).

34. Graml, *Anti-Semitism in the Third Reich,* 204.

35. Wolfgang Benz (ed.), *Dimensionen des Völkermords: Die Zahl der jüdischen Opfer des Nationalsozialismus* (Munich, 1991), 36–60.

36. Krausnick and Wilhelm, *Die Truppe des Weltanschauungskrieges,* 26–7, 29; Günther Schubert, *Das Unternehmen 'Bromberger Blutsonntag': Tod einer Legende* (Cologne, 1989).

37. Peter Longerich (ed.), *Die Ermordung der europäischen Juden: Eine umfassende Dokumentation des Holocaust, 1941–1945* (Munich, 1989), doc. 4, 47; Goebbels, *Tagebücher,* I. iii. 612, 628.

38. Madajczyk, *Die Okkupationspolitik Nazideutschlands,* 220; Christoph Kleßmann (ed.), *September 1939* (Göttingen, 1989); in Röhl (ed.), *Polen,* in *Europa unter dem Hakenkreuz,* ii. doc. 54, 165–6 (Frank, 2 Mar. 1940); Longerich, *Die Ermordung der europäischen Juden,* doc. 5, 47 ff. (Heydrich, 29 Sept. 1939); cf. Eberhard Jäckel, *Hitler in History* (Hanover, NH, 1984). On Niško, cf. Christopher Browning, *Fateful Months: Essays on the Emergence of the Final Solution* (New York, 1985).

39. Röhl (ed.), *Polen,* in *Europa unter dem Hakenkreuz,* ii. doc. 83, 195; Halder, *Kriegstagebuch,* ii. 335–6; for Hitler's speech cf. also Michalka, *Das Dritte Reich,* ii. 51.

40. Krausnick and Wilhelm, *Die Truppe des Weltanschauungskrieges;* Jäckel and Rohwer, *Der Mord an den Juden;* Longerich, *Die Ermordung der europäischen Juden,* doc. 30, 116–18 (116, Heydrich, 2 July 1941); cf. Peter Longerich, 'Vom Massenmord zu "Endlösung"', in Bernd Wegner (ed.), *Zwei Wege nach Moskau* (Munich, 1991), 251–74 (266, *Einsatzkommando 5,* 17 Sept. 1941).

41. Longerich, *Die Ermordung der europäischen Juden,* doc. 33a, 121.

42. Graml, *Anti-Semitism,* 213–14, doc. 3a (4 Oct. 1943).

43. Jäckel and Rohwer, *Der Mord an den Juden,* esp Hilberg, 'Die Aktion Reinhardt', 125–44, and other articles on individual extermination camps. On the number of dead, cf. Benz, *Dimensionen,* 17.

44. Longerich, *Die Ermordung der europäischen Juden,* doc. 14, 78; doc. 18, 83–92 (Wannsee Conference), cf. doc. 19.

45. Benz, *Dimensionen,* 17; Franticek Piper, 'Estimating the Number of Deportees to and Victims of the Auschwitz-Birkenau Camp', in *Yad Vashem Studies,* 21 (1991), 49–103; Danuta Czech, *Kalendarium der Ereignisse im Konzentrationslager Auschwitz-Birkenau 1939–1945* (Reinbek, 1989), each on the politically motivated over-estimation of the number of victims in Poland.

46. The figures for Jewish victims in individual countries in this Chapter according to Benz, *Dimensionen* (authors: Ino Arndt, Heinz Boberach, Frank Golczewski, Hagen Fleischer, Gerhard Grimm, Gerhard Hirschfeld, Hans Jürgen Hoppe, Oskar Mendelsohn, Liliana Picciotto Fargion, Gerd Robel, Eva Schmidt-Hartmann, Lásazló Varga, Hermann Weiss, and Krista Zach).

47. On the following, esp. *Das Deutsche Reich und der Zweite Weltkrieg,* iv. Horst Boog *et al., Der Angriff auf die Sowjetunion;* v.1, Bernhard R. Kröner *et al., Organisation und Mobilisierung des deutschen Machtbereichs, Kriegsverwaltung, Wirtschaft und personelle Resources 1939–1941;* vi. Horst Boog *et al., Der globale Krieg: Die Ausweitung zum Weltkrieg und der Wechsel der Initiative 1941–1943* (Stuttgart, 1979–1990); Alexander Dallin, *German Rule in Russia, 1941–1945: A Study of Occupation Policies* (London, 1957); Eichholtz, *Geschichte der deutschen Kriegswirtschaft,* 2 vols.; Tim Mulligan, *The Politics of Illusion and Empire, 1942–1943* (New York, 1988); Theo Schulte, *The German Army and Nazi Policies in Occupied Russia* (Oxford, 1989); Gerd Ueberschär and Wolfram Wette (eds), *'Unternehmen Barbarossa'* (Paderborn, 1984); Müller, *Sowjetunion,* in *Europa unter dem Hakenkreuz,* v. doc. 48 (2 Dec. 1941).

48. Detlef Brandes, *Die Tschechen unter deutschem Protektorat 1939–1945* (2 vols., Munich, 1969–1975).

49. Gerd Schreiber, *Die italienischen Militärinternierten im deutschen Machtbereich* (Munich, 1989); Lutz Klinkhammer, *Zwischen Bündnis und Besatzung: Das nationalsozialistische Deutschland und die Republik von Saló 1943–1945* (Tübingen, 1993).

50. Dieter Rebentisch, *Führerstaat und Verwaltung.*

51. Fabian von Schlabrendorff, *Offiziere gegen Hitler* (Zurich, 1959), 138.

52. Martin Broszat, Klaus-Dietmar Henke, and Hans Woller (eds), *Von Stalingrad zur Währungsreform: Zur Sozialgeschichte des Umbruchs in Deutschland* (Munich, 1989).

53. Goebbels, *Tagebücher,* I. iv. 696.

Chapter 6

1. Jäckel, *Hitler in History,* 64.

2. Rainer Zitelmann, *Hitler: Selbstverständnis eines Revolutionärs* (3rd edn., (Stuttgart, 1991), chs. 3 and 4.

3. Wilfried Bade, *Die SA erobert Berlin: Ein Tatsachenbericht* (Munich, 1934), 184 (information from Sabine Behrenbach).

4. Jost Dülffer, 'NS-Herrschaftssystem und Stadtgestaltung', *German Studies Review,* 12 (1989), 69–89 (89: 14 June 1938).

5. Dülffer, Thies, and Henke, *Hitlers Städte,* 307 (10 Feb. 1939).

6. Marie-Luise Recker, *Nationalsozialistische Sozialpolitik im Zweiten Weltkrieg* (Munich, 1985); Smelser, *Robert Ley,* 261–92.

7. Günther Schulz, 'Kontinuität und Brüche in der Wohnungspolitik von der Weimarer Zeit bis zur Bundesrepublik', in Hans-Jürgen Teuteberg (ed.), *Stadtentwicklung, Industrialisierung, sozialer Wandel* (Berlin, 1986), pp. 162–170.

8. Werner Durth, *Deutsche Architekten* (Brunswick, 1986).

9. Michael Prinz, 'Die soziale Funktion moderner Elemente in der Gesellschaftspolitik des Nationalsozialismus', in Michael Prinz and Rainer Zitelmann (eds), *Nationalsozialismus und Modernisierung* (Darmstadt, 1991), 297–328.

10. Dörte Winkler, *Frauenarbeit im Dritten Reich* (Hamburg, 1977); Jill Stephenson, *Women in Nazi Society* (London, 1975); Ute Frevert, *Frauen – Geschichte* (Frankfurt on Main, 1986), 200–43.

11. Michael Kater, 'Medizin und Mediziner im Dritten Reich: Eine Bestandsaufnahme', *Historische Zeitschrift*, 244 (1987), 299–352 (pp. 317–18, 311).

12. Jürgen Reulecke, *Geschichte der Urbanisierung in Deutschland* (Frankfurt on Main, 1985), 154 ff.; Peter Marschalck, *Bevölkerungsgeschichte Deutschlands im 19. und 20. Jahrhundert* (Frankfurt on Main, 1984), 72 ff.; Reinhold Sieder, *Sozialgeschichte der Familie* (Frankfurt on Main, 1987), 228 ff.

13. Rolf Messerschmidt, 'Nationalsozialistische Raumforschung und Raumordnung aus der Perspektive der "Stunde Null" ' in Prinz and Zitelmann, *Nationalsozialismus und Modernisierung*, 117–38; cf. also Aly and Heim, *Vordenker der Vernichtung*.

14. Hans-Werner Schmuhl, *Rassenhygiene, Nationalsozialismus, Euthanasie: Von der Verhütung zur Vernichtung 'lebensunwerten Lebens', 1890–1945* (Göttingen, 1987), 141, 131; Norbert Frei (ed.), *Medizin und Gesundheitspolitik in der NS-Zeit* (Munich, 1991), esp. Dirk Blasius, 'Die "Maskarade des Bösen": Psychiatrische Forschung in der NS-Zeit', 265–86.

15. Michael Kater, *Medizin und Mediziner*, 307.

Suggestions for Further Reading

Published Documents in English Translation

Documents on German Foreign Policy, ser. C. 1933–1937, *The Third Reich: First Phase* (6 vols., Washington and London, 1957–83); ser. D. 1937–1941 (14 vols., incl. index vol., Washington and London, 1949–76).
Hitler's Mein Kampf (London, 1969).
The Testament of Adolf Hitler: The Hitler–Bormann Documents, February–April 1945 (London, 1961).
The Trial of the Major War Criminals before the International Military Tribunal: Proceedings, vols. I–XXII (Nuremberg, 1947–9); *Documents in Evidence*, vols. XXIV–XLII (Nuremberg, 1947–9).
Baynes, N., *The Speeches of Adolf Hitler 1922–1939* (2 vols., London, 1942).
Maser, W. (ed.), *Hitler's Letters and Notes* (New York, 1974).
Noakes, J./Pridham, G. (eds), *Nazism 1919–1945: A Documentary Reader*, vol. I: *The Rise to Power 1919–1934* (Exeter, 1983); vol. II: *State, Economy and Society 1933–1939* (Exeter, 1984); vol. III: *Foreign Policy, War and Racial Extermination* (Exeter, 1988).
Taylor, F. (ed.), *The Goebbels Diaries 1939–1941* (London, 1982).
Trevor-Roper, H. (ed.), *Hitler's Table Talk 1941–1944* (London, 1973).
Trevor-Roper, H. (ed.), *Hitler's War Directives 1939–1945* (London, 1964).

Historiography

Hiden, J. and Farquharson, J., *Explaining Hitler's Germany. Historians and the Third Reich* (2nd edn, London, 1989).
Hildebrand, K., *The Third Reich* (London, 1984).
Kershaw, I., *The Nazi Dictatorship: Problems and Perspectives of Interpretation* (3rd edn, London, 1993).

General Works

Das Deutsche Reich und der Zweite Weltkrieg, ed. Militärgeschichtliches Forschungsamt (6 vols. publ. of 10 projected. Stuttgart, 1979–90). In English:

Germany and the Second World War (vols. I and ii at present translated, Oxford, 1990–2).

Bessel, R. (ed.), *Life in the Third Reich* (Oxford, 1987).

Bracher, K.D., *The German Dictatorship: Origins, Structures and Consequences of National Socialism* (London, 1971).

Broszat, M., *Hitler's State: The Foundation and Development of the Internal Structure of the Third Reich* (London, 1981).

____, *Hitler and the Collapse of Weimar Germany* (New York, 1987).

Frei, N., *National Socialist Rule 1933–1945: The Führer State* (Oxford, 1993).

Jäckel, E., *Hitler in History* (Hanover, NH, 1984).

____, *Hitler's World View* (Cambridge, Mass., 1981).

Kolb, E., *The Weimar Republic* (London, 1988).

Rich, N., *Hitler's War Aims* (2 vols., London, 1973–4).

Biographies

Breitman, R., *The Architect of Genocide: Himmler and the Final Solution* (London, 1991).

Bullock, A., *Hitler and Stalin: Parallel Lives* (London, 1991).

____, *Hitler: A Study in Tyranny* (London, 1952; rev. edn 1962).

Carr, W., *Hitler: A Study in Personality and Politics* (London, 1978).

Fest, J.C., *Hitler* (New York, 1974).

Kershaw, I., *Hitler* (London, 1991).

Overy, R., *Goering: The 'Iron Man'* (London, 1984).

Reuth, R., *Goebbels* (London, 1993).

Séreny, G., *Albert Speer: His Battle with Truth* (London, 1995).

Smelser, R., *Robert Ley: Hitler's Labour Front Leader* (Leamington Spa, 1988).

Foreign Policy and the Conduct of the War

Bartov, O., *Hitler's Army: Soldiers, Nazis and War in the Third Reich* (Oxford, 1991).

Berghahn, V.R. and Kitchen, M. (eds), *Germany in the Age of Total War* (London, 1981).

Carr, W., *Arms, Autarky and Aggression: A Study in German Foreign Policy 1933–1939* (London, 1972; rev. edn. 1979).

Carr, W., *Poland to Pearl Harbor: The Making of the Second World War* (London, 1985).

Hildebrand, K., *The Foreign Policy of the Third Reich* (London, 1973).

Overy, R., *Why the Allies Won* (London, 1995).

Watt, D.C., *How War Came: The Immediate Origins of the Second World War, 1938–39* (London, 1989).

Weinberg, G., *The Foreign Policy of Hitler's Germany vol. I: Diplomatic Revolution in Europe 1933–1936* (Chicago, 1970); vol. II: *Starting World War II* (Chicago, 1980).

____, *A World at Arms: A Global History of World War II* (Cambridge, 1994).

The German Economy and Working Conditions in the Third Reich

Farquharson, J.E., *The Plough and the Swastika: The NSDAP and Agriculture in Germany 1928–45* (London, 1976).

Harrison, M., 'Resource Mobilization for World War II: the USA, UK, USSR and Germany 1938–1945', *Economic History Review* 41 (1988).

Hayes, P., *Industry and Ideology: I G Farben in the Nazi Era* (Cambridge, 1987).

James, H., *The German Slump: Politics and Economics 1924–1936* (Oxford, 1986).

Mason, T., 'The Primacy of Politics – Politics and Economics in National Socialist Germany', in H.A. Turner (ed.), *Nazism and the Third Reich* (New York, 1972).

Mason, T., 'Women in Germany 1925–1940: Family, Welfare and Work', in *History Workshop Journal* 1–2 (1976).

Mason, T., *Social Policy in the Third Reich: The Working Class and the National Community* (Providence, RI, 1993).

Mosse, G.L., *The Nationalization of the Masses: Political Symbolism and Mass Movements in Germany from the Napoleonic Wars through the Third Reich* (Ithaca, NY, 1994).

Milward, A.S., *The German Economy at War* (London, 1965).

Overy, R., *War and Economy in the Third Reich* (Oxford, 1994).

Speer, A., *Inside the Third Reich* (London, 1970).

Turner, H.A., *German Big Business and the Rise of Hitler* (New York, 1985).

Walker, M and Renneberg, M. (eds), *Science, Technology and National Socialism* (Cambridge, 1993).

The Führer State and Developments in Germany

Baldwin, P., 'Social Interpretations of Nazism: Renewing a Tradition', *Journal of Contemporary History* 25 (1990), pp. 5–37.

Balfour, M., *Withstanding Hitler in Germany 1933–1945* (London, 1988).

Beck, E., *Under the Bombs: The German Home Front 1942–1945* (Lexington, Kentucky, 1986).

Childers, T., *The Nazi Voter* (Chapel Hill, NC, 1968).

Hoffmann, P., *The German Resistance to Hitler* (Cambridge, Mass., 1988).

Kater, M.H., *The Nazi Party: A Social Profile of Members and Leaders, 1919–1945* (Oxford, 1983).

Kershaw, I., *The Hitler Myth: Image and Reality in the Third Reich* (Oxford, 1987).

____, *Popular Opinion and Political Dissent in the Third Reich: Bavaria 1933–1945* (Oxford, 1983).

Koonz, C., *Mothers in the Fatherland* (London, 1987).

Mason, T., *Social Policy in the Third Reich* (New York, 1993).

Merkl, P., *The Making of a Stormtrooper* (Princeton, 1980).

Müller, K.-J., *Army, Politics and Society in Germany 1933–1945* (Manchester, 1987).

Orlow, D., *The History of the Nazi Party* (2 vols., Pittsburgh, 1969–73).

Peukert, D.J.K., *Inside Nazi Germany: Conformity, Opposition and Racism in Everyday Life* (London, 1987).

Schoenbaum, D., *Hitler's Social Revolution: Class and Status in Nazi Germany 1933–1945* (London, 1967).

Smelser, R. and Zitelmann, R. (eds), *The Nazi Elite* (London, 1993).
Stephenson, J., *Women in Nazi Society* (London, 1975).

Occupation and Annihilation Policy

Baird, J.W., *To Die for Germany* (Bloomington, Ind., 1990).
Bartov, O. *The Eastern Front, 1941–45: German Troops and the Barbarisation of Warfare* (London, 1985).
_____, *Hitler's Army: Soldiers, Nazis, and War in the Third Reich* (Oxford, 1992).
Broszat, M., Buchheim, H., Jacobsen, H.-A. and Krausnick, H., *Anatomy of the SS State* (London, 1968).
Browning, C., *Fateful Months: Essays on the Emergence of the Final Solution* (New York, 1985).
_____, *Ordinary Men: Reserve Police Battalion 101 and the Final Solution in Poland* (New York, 1992).
Burleigh, M and Wippermann, W., *The Racial State: Germany 1933–1945* (Oxford, 1991).
Burrin, P., *Hitler and the Jews: The Genesis of the Holocaust* (London, 1994).
Cesarani, D. (ed.), *The Final Solution: Origins and Implementation* (London, 1994).
Dallin, A., *German Rule in Russia, 1941–1945: A Study of Occupation Policies* (London, 1957).
Dawidowicz, L.S., *The War Against the Jews* (New York, 1975).
Friedländer, S., 'From Anti-Semitism to Extermination: A Historiographical Study of Nazi Policies Towards the Jews', *Yad Vashem Studies* 16 (1984).
Graml, H., *Anti-Semitism in the Third Reich* (Oxford, 1992).
Hilberg, R., *The Destruction of the European Jews* (3 vols., New York, 1985).
_____, *Perpetrators, Victims, Bystanders: The Jewish Catastrophe 1933–1945* (New York, 1992).
Lumans, V.O., *Himmler's Auxiliaries: The Volksdeutsche Mittelstelle and the German National Minorities of Europe, 1933–1945* (Chapel Hill, NC, 1993).
Mayer, A., *Why Did the Heavens Not Darken? The 'Final Solution' in History* (New York, 1988).
Schulte, T., *The German Army and Nazi Policies in Occupied Russia* (Oxford, 1989).

Index